THE
GENTEEL
POPULISTS

THE GENTEEL POPULISTS

SIMON LAZARUS

HOLT, RINEHART AND WINSTON
New York   Chicago   San Francisco

Copyright © 1974 by Simon Lazarus
All rights reserved, including the right to reproduce this book or portions
thereof in any form.
Published simultaneously in Canada by Holt, Rinehart and Winston of
Canada, Limited.

Library of Congress Cataloging in Publication Data
Lazarus, Simon.
The genteel populists.

Includes bibliographical references.
1. Liberalism—United States. 2. Social reformers
—United States. 3. United States—Politics and
government—20th century. 4. Business and politics—
United States. I. Title.
JA84.U5L32   322.4′4′0973   76–182767
ISBN 0–03–007511–4

First Edition

Printed in the United States of America

Contents

ABBREVIATIONS

AAA	Agricultural Adjustment Act
ABA	American Bar Association
ABC	American Broadcasting Company
ACLU	American Civil Liberties Union
ADA	Americans for Democratic Action
AEC	Atomic Energy Commission
AFL-CIO	American Federation of Labor–Congress of Industrial Organizations
AID	Agency for International Development
AMA	American Medical Association
AMAA	Agricultural Marketing Agreement Act
APHA	American Public Health Association
CAB	Civil Aeronautics Board
CEQ	Council on Environmental Quality
COPE	Committee on Political Education (of the AFL-CIO)
CPA	Consumer Protection Agency (proposed)
CU	Consumers Union
EPA	Environmental Protection Agency
FCA	Federal Corporation Agency (proposed)
FCC	Federal Communications Commission
FDA	Food and Drug Administration
FPC	Federal Power Commission
FRB	Federal Reserve Board
FTC	Federal Trade Commission
HEW	Department of Health, Education, and Welfare
IRS	Internal Revenue Service
ITT	International Telephone and Telegraph Corporation
NAS	National Academy of Sciences
NFBF	National Farm Bureau Federation
NLRB	National Labor Relations Board
NWRO	National Welfare Rights Organization
OEO	Office of Economic Opportunity
OPA	Office of Price Administration (a World War II agency)
SDS	Students for a Democratic Society
SEC	Securities and Exchange Commission
UAW	United Automobile Workers
UMWA	United Mine Workers of America
UPI	United Press International
USDA	United States Department of Agriculture

To my parents—
who taught me to believe
in democracy.

Acknowledgments

This book could not have been written without the help of many friends. Chief among these are Leonard Chazen and Leonard Ross; their careful criticisms of the manuscript were literally invaluable to me. Joseph Onek also offered extensive comments, as did my wife, Rosalind Avnet Lazarus.

My editor, Steven M. L. Aronson, invested many hours and much sensitivity in a final edit that greatly sharpened the final text.

A number of others offered useful criticism: Geoffrey Cowan, Jan Deutsch, George Gilder, Lewis Kaden, Doris Kearns, Duncan Kennedy, James Kurth, Lance Liebman, Victor Navasky, and Richard Stewart.

Still others contributed insights that have found their way into the book: Ed Berlin, Leonard Bickwit, Ken Bode, Stephen Breyer, Stephen Cohen, Lanny Davis, William Dobrovir, Clarice Feldman, Gary Gerlach, Mark Green, William Greider, Charles Halpern, Peter Hart, Philip Hart and the staff of the Senate Antitrust and Monopoly Subcommittee, Harry Huge, Theodore Jacobs, Louis Jaffe, Sanford Jaffe, Nicholas Johnson, Victor Kramer, Jeremy Larner, Simon Lazarus, Jr., Philip Moore, Bess Myerson, Irv Nathan, Michael Pertschuk, Robert Pitofsky, Paul Porter, Joseph Rauh, Marc Roberts, Reuben Robertson, Mitchell Rogovin, David Rosenbloom, Joseph Sax, Philip Schrag, Eli Segal, Michael Sohn, John Steinbruner, Henry Stern, Bruce Terris, Robert Thorpe, Lawrence Tribe, Marna Tucker, Harrison Wellford, and Tracy Western.

Two teachers influenced my thinking about the issues covered in this book. One is Gabriel Kolko, whose daring reinterpretations of twentieth-century economic reform I was privileged to hear first hand during my junior year at Harvard. The second is Alexander M. Bickel, whose skeptical wit furnishes all his students at the Yale Law School with an enduring sense of the constraints and costs of social reform.

The project could not have been completed without the dedication of Jennifer Delgado, Muriel Goodridge, and Maria McMahon, who typed the manuscript.

Preface:
The Dupont Circle Conspiracy

Lunching under a tree in Washington, D.C.,'s Dupont Circle, Philip Moore reflected on the two-year term he was completing as director of the Project on Corporate Responsibility. As soon as he had raised enough money to assure that the project could continue its various crusades for still another year, Moore was to resign to accept a teaching position at Georgetown University Law School. He had to wind up his fund-raising work before the end of summer, as the foundations make their commitments at their third-quarterly meetings in mid-September. Although now, in August, 1972, the project was starting its third year, new sources of funds had yet turned up. The big foundations—Ford, Rockefeller, and Carnegie, which had invested heavily in many of Moore's friends' "public interest" litigation and research enterprises—considered the project too risky. For two years, the Internal Revenue Service (IRS) had declined to act on the project's application for tax-exempt status, and the foundations had no stomach for a fight with the government over that. So Moore was at this late moment turning back to the familiar handful of small but aggressively liberal donors—the Stern Family Fund, which had just promised $20,000 for the coming year, the Norman Fund, which was offering an additional $7,500, and a few others to whom he would once again have to look to supply the $150,000 or so he needed to keep the project going.

Moore started the project in 1970 with three other young lawyers of similarly reformist inclinations. With moral support from Ralph Nader, they launched the project's first, and greatest, crusade, the "Campaign to Make General Motors Responsible," better known as Campaign GM. The unique idea was to make the shareholder proxy context a nationally televised pageant to dramatize corporate indifference to the public interest.

xi

As Moore observed: "It was a fantastically efficient device for public education." The David-versus-Goliath dimensions of the young lawyers' insurgency against a multibillion dollar corporation caught the fancy of the media. The very fact that Moore and his colleagues lost overwhelmingly to management at the 1970 annual meeting got their point across to the television audience: shareholder democracy is a myth; hence, the existing legal system is helpless to constrain corporate power. If GM wishes to spend millions of dollars to lobby to death state and federal support for mass transit, there is simply no way to stop it, no constituency or official to whom GM's managerial elite is accountable.

But after two years of broadcasting that message, Philip Moore was tired. "It's the hustling," he said, "hustling all the time—the foundations, the universities, the churches, the press. But every time a group of citizens somewhere writes to ask what they can do about this or that corporation that's hurting them in some way—and this happens more and more—I feel I've accomplished something. But it's hard to know where all this is going," he concluded. "And the same can be said for everyone else around here," he added.

By "everyone else around here," Moore meant the dozen or so other little centers, institutes, and groups peppered about Dupont Circle, self-consciously shabby beside the boutiques and glassy office buildings. Staffed by intense lawyers two or three years out of the prestigious law schools, they masked their ambitious hopes for reform behind indistinguishable and barely pronounceable nameplates. Two blocks south at 1156 19th Street is the headquarters of Nader's own conglomerate, the Center for the Study of Responsive Law, and catty-corner to it, the Corporate Accountability Research Group. One block to the west at 20th and P are Public Citizen, Inc., the Public Interest Research Group, and the Nader Congress Project, and at 20th and Q, the Center for Law and Social Policy shares a rambling townhouse with the Natural Resources Defense Council. Further south in a two-story box-like building in the parking lot at 20th and L are the Stern Community Law Firm and the office of William A. Dobrovir, a sole practitioner of public interest law who is financed completely by his clients, just as in traditional law firms; one of his sometime clients, Common Cause, Inc., is just across the street, in a large office building. The Media Access Project and the Citizens Communication Center flank Arnold & Porter's offices at 19th and N. And around to the east near 17th Street are the Center for Political Reform, Marion Wright Edelman's Washington Research Project, the public interest law firm of Berlin, Roisman, and Kessler, the Environmental Defense Fund, and the American Bar Association's (ABA) "pro bono publico project" in the ABA's relatively plush offices across from the Mayflower Hotel on Connecticut Avenue just south of L.

Like Moore, this entire cadre of activists has "hustled" day and night over the past three years. The results have been prodigious. By every indicium, from editorials to opinion polls to the plot lines of daytime television soap operas, wide public sympathy has been generated for their hope of taming the corporate tiger. Both political rhetoric and public law acknowledge their aims. While this corps of young reformers cannot justly claim credit for the nomination of George McGovern—as Republican orators and even the press sometimes alleged—they were responsible for the reforms that restructured the nomination system of the Democratic Party and thereby made McGovern's victory over traditional powers in the party possible. They were further responsible for inventing and popularizing the only ideological theme available to the Democrats in 1972, the populist, redistributionist rhetoric, just as audible in the speeches of McGovern's major rivals for the nomination as in his own. They had a major hand in bringing the Watergate scandal to light and in maximizing its potential as a lever of reform. Their agitation over the preceding few years had sensitized public opinion to official corruption and lawlessness. The campaign finance disclosure law, which new populist forces imposed on a recalcitrant White House, succeeded beyond its authors' dreams in baring the seamy underside of high politics. The new populist technique of private lawsuits, by William Dobrovir on Nader's behalf, by Mitchell Rogovin and Ken Guido for Common Cause, and by Joseph Califano for the

Democratic Party, helped to put conspirators on the spot under oath and thereby to crack the cover-up.

But despite this remarkable success, Moore and his colleagues were anxious about the fate of their enterprises of reform. "One thing I'm sure of, though," Moore said, "is that we've made people aware that they are powerless and now they all want to do something about it. The real problem is solutions and I really don't know what they are. You ought to talk to some of the GM employees I've talked to; you'd be astonished, they sound like the 1908 Democratic Platform. Have you ever read *that?* It's the most radical anticorporate, pro democracy political document I've ever seen—it even proposed that corporations be required to get their charters from the federal government not the states, which is just what Ralph and all of us want to do now." But Moore added, ominously, "It sometimes makes you wonder, though, if our solutions are much different from theirs or likely to be any better than theirs."

The question worrying Philip Moore is the question that prompted me to write this book. I too had graduated from law school into the ranks of this movement of reformers around Dupont Circle. I first worked for FCC Commissioner Nicholas Johnson, one of the movement's principal heroes. Then I worked with Iowa Governor (now Senator) Harold Hughes' Commission on the Democratic Selection of Presidential Nominees; the Hughes Commission initiated the reform effort within the Democratic Party which transformed its nomination procedures for 1972. I left Washington to work for New York City's Department of Consumer Affairs, where I helped Commissioner Bess Myerson create an aggressive local outpost for the consumer movement.

While churning out press releases, speeches, legislation, and briefs, I became troubled about the high goals we proclaimed and about the means we were fashioning to reach them. But it was impossible to explore questions and give in to doubts about reform while working to bring about reform, so I took a year off.

Is it true, I wanted to know, that the great liberal economic reforms of the Progressive era and the New Deal had been subverted? Had these earlier reformers, then, failed to redress the balance of social power in favor of the public, against the privileged and the special interests? And if they had failed, had they failed because they chose the wrong means, or because the end itself was a mirage, a noble futility? What *are* the realistic limits of democratic control in an industrial society? What theories and what techniques offer the best hope of reaching or expanding those limits?

This book is the result of the work that I completed during that year. It is not a profile of the protagonists of the movement, nor even a comprehensive chronicle of its programs and achievements, even though all these matters are dealt with. But I have focused on the *ideology* that animates the activities of the crusaders of Dupont Circle and elsewhere, an ideology inherited, as Philip Moore noted, from the early American reformers. I set out to gain a sense of the place of the present movement in history, to compare its hopes and achievements with those of its predecessors.

As Phil Moore's anxiety indicates, the new populism of the early 1970s has vented a philosophical crisis of American liberalism. This is a time of testing, a moment when the American reform tradition stands suddenly unsure of both its popular constituency and its moral relevance.

Any doubts that such a crisis was at hand were put to rest, of course, by the 1972 campaign. Liberals, especially those attracted to the populist themes in George McGovern's rhetoric, were bewildered when Nixon's lead held firm, despite the rash of spectacular scandals at the highest levels of his administration. Observers could not understand how the people could reelect a president so brazen in pandering to ITT, the dairy co-ops, the grain traders, and all the magnates and lobbies who contributed to Maurice Stans' $10 million secret fund. Don't the people care enough about democracy, McGovern admirers wondered, to protect even their own pocketbooks? "We are going to have a tough time keeping up morale after this," mused Mark Green, director of Ralph Nader's Corporate Accountability Research Group, a few days before the election. "We have been counting all along on a massive citizen-action response," Green said; "if this is all McGovern can get from the people, when and where is that citizen-action response going to come from?"

Green's discomfiture was understandable. For a considerable period, the new populists had warned that, despite America's affluence and technical might, the integrity of its status as a democracy is in doubt. They had made their case widely understood and, or so they had thought, widely accepted. But the 1972 campaign brought them up short. Whether they could ever engineer the changes necessary to restore the democratic ideal they cherish was no longer clear.

The new populist leaders tend to believe that the answer to this question lies largely outside themselves. They operate as if the main practical issue is whether the nation will respond to them and whether effective support can be mobilized to implement their aims. The question, as they see it, is whether their proven ability to generate favorable ratings in opinion surveys can be converted into power. In general, they have been optimistic. In a democracy, they have assumed, there ought ultimately to be a relatively direct connection between popularity and power. Ultimately, public favor for populist views would oblige legislators and bureaucrats to follow the reformers' ideological lead, or face rebuff at the hands of the electorate.

I disagree. I believe that the fate of the reformers is primarily in their own hands, or more precisely, in their own heads. The future of the populist ideal of democracy will depend largely on the populists' ability to reexamine the ideal itself, to redefine some basic assumptions that underlie their efforts at reform as well as the efforts of their predecessors.

Certain critical aspects of our liberal credo are superficial and foolish, even pernicious. The fact is that, as some intelligent conservatives warned, the great liberal reform programs often did not work at all and that sometimes they caused harm. For decades liberals ignored this. Indeed, their hold on public office was sustained in great measure by the public's belief in the old liberal myths. But in many cases the public no longer set store by those myths. If reformers continue to parrot them uncritically, to shape their programs around the obsolete premises that pervade their propaganda, then they will not only lose their power and bring discredit upon their ideals, but invite contempt for the idea of democracy itself.

The irony is that failure, if it comes, may be no more apparent to us than it was to the Progressives and the New Dealers. Populist reform depends necessarily on the techniques of pageantry, as the case of Campaign GM exemplifies. How else can the people be roused to support the defenders of their needs against the secret depredations of the special interests? But public relations is a very dangerous game. Reformers have often used it merely to elicit applause from the public rather than to stir the public to press for change. The hope now, of course, is that the pageantry will lead to something more substantial—some new "system" that will "institutionalize" the democratic aims of the movement. Then the people will finally have real power. Then they will meet the special interests on their own terms.

In the past, however, reformers often have not been able to bring all this about—and certainly not for long. Instead of institutionalizing reform, each new step merely pitted the same antagonists against each other in a new arena. In the new setting the reformers find themselves once again involved in a public relations struggle, though often—when the arena is bureaucracy—these tactics prove less effective than they did in the legislature where the battle originated. The public bout goes on. But the underlying realities never seem to change; the terms of the struggle remain the same—the "interests" have power, the "public" and its representatives do not.

This, in brief, is what the new populist movement must cope with. The efforts of Philip Moore and his colleagues will *not* lead to any apocalyptic transformation of the infrastructures of power. They must face up to this and dispense with grand schemes for reform that are as vulnerable to subversion as the artifacts of the Progressives and the New Dealers were. The real hope lies in more modest, even more conservative, measures. The proper goal is not to redistribute power and thus create a populist utopia in America; it is merely to reinforce the inherently limited sources of support for the populist ideal, and thereby to keep alive and extend the pageant of reform itself.

THE
GENTEEL
POPULISTS

1

The New Populist Revival:
An Overview of the Issues

The 1970s—I count the decade as having begun the day Robert Kennedy died—have been a confusing time. On the face of it, perhaps, they have seemed simply a regressive time, years when most voters fell truculently into step behind leaders who promised to protect their schools and neighborhoods from racial change, to punish their children for ideological or moral deviance, and to reduce their obligations to the poor. "This country is going so far to the right that you won't recognize it," John Mitchell gloated soon after becoming Richard Nixon's first attorney general. His forecast has been confirmed by trends since 1969 regarding race, poverty, dissent, crime, and most other issues that interested liberal reformers of the postwar era. But this period has had a different side. As any corporate public-relations executive would acknowledge—and as Mitchell himself came painfully to understand in 1973—public opinion has swung dramatically to the left on the issues that preoccupied the nation from the turn of the century to the outbreak of World War II. These concerns had languished for decades off the political stage altogether, the hobgoblins of

1

parochial sects and radical pamphleteers alone. Then, in response to the Vietnam War, to the traumas of the 1968 presidential campaign, and to the agitation of Ralph Nader and his followers and imitators, they suddenly reappeared.

The New Old Radical Orthodoxy

The new issues sport many labels, some new, some old—campaign finance, consumerism, military-industrial complex, minimum income tax, national health insurance, auto emissions control, percentage depletion, conglomerate mergers, ombudsman, import quotas, effluent charges, public interest law—but they express a common theme, which is old. The theme is suspicion of corporate power, or more precisely, suspicion of corporate subversion of government power. Despite the network of regulatory institutions established earlier in the century to control business in the public interest, people sense that special interests have freed themselves from effective governmental or market controls. They suspect, further, that corporate power is operating far afield from the immediate markets in which resources are gathered and products distributed, that corporate influence sets critical national budgetary priorities, rewrites tax policies, and generally plays a vast but largely unseen role in determining how the nation's resources will be deployed. "Five percent of the American people control 90 percent of our productive national wealth," protested the 1972 Democratic Party Platform in the course of "deplor[ing] the increasing concentration of economic power in fewer and fewer hands."

The complaint, however, is not nearly so much against business as it is against government, and in particular with the executive branch of the federal government. After all, no one really expects business to serve the public interest when its own interests are not coincident. No one, not even conservative politicians, really denies anymore that strong safeguards must be established and enforced wherever necessary.

In all the many recent congressional debates about environmental and consumer protection, only the faintest echoes were heard of the old laissez-faire rhetoric favored by prewar conservatives. There is dispute over methods, and even deceit about promises of strict enforcement, but there are no longer any differences of opinion about the need for regulatory constraint —as a matter of principle. As a nation we faced this question during the Progressive era and again during the New Deal years, and we thought that we had settled it once and for all. Until very recently, that is. For three decades, we thought that, because the need for control had been acknowledged in principle, the battle for public control of corporate power had been won. Nobody thought very much about the tiresome problem of how to implement this principle; everyone assumed that public control would follow automatically from the creation in the federal government of institutions broadly empowered to regulate and oversee big business. We took comfort from the very existence of the Federal Trade Commission, the Securities and Exchange Commission, the Civil Aeronautics Board, the Department of the Interior, the Federal Reserve Board, the Department of Agriculture, the Antitrust Division of the Department of Justice, and the myriad other bases of federal regulatory power.

When such reform institutions were created, we assumed that they would work out as set up and intended. In this belief we were sustained by our most eminent social analysts. As recently as 1962, Arthur M. Schlesinger, Jr., assured his liberal audience that, because of the success of economic and political reforms,

> The capitalist state . . . far from being the helpless instrument of the possessing class, has become the means by which other groups in society have redressed the balance of social power against those whom Hamilton called the "rich and well-born. . . ."
> [The state] is the means by which the non-business classes may protect themselves from the business community, if not actually launch a counterattack against long-established bastions of business power.[1]

A mere ten years later, Schlesinger's encomium sounds downright antique, more like the sermon of a high-school civics teacher than the judgment of a discerning historian. His optimism has been replaced by a new orthodoxy, a cynical vision of government as the captive of corporate power. In the words of its most prominent exponent, Ralph Nader:

> Much of what passes as governmental power is derivative of corporate power whose advocacy or sufferance defines much of the direction and deployment of government activity. . . . So much of government resources is allocated and so much government authority is utilized to transfer public wealth into corporate coffers that Washington can be fairly described as a bustling bazaar of accounts receivable for industry-commerce.[2]

This charge—that government's legal control over business has been neutralized by business's political control over government—has shocked liberals, schooled as they have been to revere the reforms of the recent past. "White papers, blackbooks, indictments: Do they add up to anything generalizable?" John Leonard of *The New York Times Book Review* asked in disgust while reviewing some "Nader's Raiders' " reports, "It seems to me they add up to an accusation that the New Deal has failed." He concluded dismally, "On the evidence of these books, agencies established to protect the consumer from corporate venality . . . do no such thing. [They] take as their client not the consumer, but the very industry they are supposed to regulate."[3]

Similar doubts have widely disturbed the electorate. In 1966, Louis Harris reported that 58 percent of Americans felt "a great deal of confidence" in the nation's "major companies." Just six years later, in 1972, only 29 percent of Harris's respondents were willing to admit to such trust—a remarkable drop of 50 percent, which Harris attributed to "the impact of consumerism." Equally marked has been the rise in public esteem for the leaders who have inspired this new skepticism about corporate power. By 1971 Ralph Nader ranked among the nation's ten most admired men. In the spring of 1973 Bess Myerson retired after four vigorous years as New York City's consumer affairs commissioner to discover that she had become the city's most popular candidate to succeed John Lindsay as mayor.

The rise of populist feeling has forced tangible responses from Congress and even from a frankly conservative national administration. Ralph Nader has shepherded so many bills through to enactment that he already rivals no less a reform figure than Woodrow Wilson as an architect of regulatory legislation. For his part, Richard Nixon in his first term as president deferred, at least in his rhetoric, to the public side of most current issues that pit industry against some "public interest." In some instances he went surprisingly farther; he established a new, legally powerful, and administratively vigorous Environmental Protection Agency (EPA); his Justice Department launched a flurry of lawsuits under Section 7 of the Clayton Antitrust Act against some prominent conglomerates, which preceding Democratic administrations had declined to prosecute; he appointed a consumer-minded FTC chairman who succeeded, at least for a time, in transforming that relic of previous reform crusades into a stern overseer of the nation's advertising practices (although rumors in early 1973 made the FTC's 1972 revival seem possibly to have been merely a Prague spring); he set up a new Atomic Energy Commission (AEC) regime, which publicly conceded that its predecessor deferred excessively to industry views, and pledged to emphasize the public interest from now on; he established a tough SEC regime that shocked Wall Street with its radical new policy of prosecuting venerable law firms for acquiescing in the alleged misdeeds of their clients; he created a wage-price control program, which had been dismissed initially as the radical suggestion of economist John Kenneth Galbraith—prior to its adoption in August, 1971—and which was based openly on Galbraith's radical allegation that the power of big business and big labor cannot be contained by market pressures alone.

None of this suggests that President Nixon was even a leader —or even an enthusiastic participant—in the widening struggle to restrain special interests. On the contrary, even before he exposed the reactionary arrogance of his second term, he had demonstrated beyond purview that the raising of a $60 million campaign war chest was far more important to him than the support of Ralph Nader or John Gardner. Indeed, he often openly fought for entrenched privilege, as when he rejected his own task force's recommendation to eliminate oil import quotas or when his assistants forced Consumer Affairs Advisor Virginia Knauer to recant her support for consumer class-action legislation. But to a remarkable extent the cautious Nixon of 1969–72 felt obliged by the growing power of anticorporate sentiment to avoid direct clashes with the new populist advocates. He even joined some new populist causes when the thought of leaving them to the opposition appeared politically unwise.

A case in point is Nixon's management of his wage-and-price control apparatus. Within a year after the inception of the New Economic Policy (NEP), the president's Price Commission was steering the traditional bureaucratic course, quickly settling into the familiar discreet *modus vivendi* with industry, arranging decisions in private, and studiously ignoring the requirement of the Economic Stabilization Act that:

> To the maximum extent possible, the President or his delegate shall conduct formal hearings . . . on a change in . . . prices . . . which have or may have a significantly large impact on the national economy, and such hearings shall be open to the public. . . .

On May 17, 1972, after the big four automakers had indicated that they would seek price increases for the 1973 model year despite the record profits they had gained in 1972 from tax subsidies and import surcharges, Ralph Nader wrote to

Price Commission Chairman Jackson Grayson to demand that hearings be held. In June, Grayson wrote back, refusing. His contention was that most of the information on which the commission would base its determination was "confidential," and that to expose it to public scrutiny in a hearing would destroy "the trust and cooperation of the business community without which we could not conduct our analysis and have sufficient data on which to base resulting decisions." Nader replied with a lawsuit.

Nader and his litigation chief, Alan Morrison, were confident that they could win in court. But they were never given a chance to find out. The day before the argument was scheduled, the White House switched sides and turned against the industry. With loud public fanfare, Cost of Living Council Executive Director Donald Rumsfeld announced the president's disinclination to let the industry get away with its planned price hikes. Finally, at 12:30 P.M. on the following Friday, an hour and a half before the argument was scheduled to begin, a messenger from the Justice Department hand delivered to Morrison formal notification that public hearings would, after all, be held, late in September, and that price increases would, in the meantime, be stayed.

In short, once the administration had been smoked out in the open by Nader's threat to force public hearings, Nixon virtually out-Nadered Nader. Now that Ralph Nader and the press would be present at the battle, the issue was suddenly too big and the trend of opinion in the country too clear for the president to side publicly with the industry against the consumer.

Thus, by the 1972 elections Nader and his followers had made a substantial start toward making the integrity of the federal regulatory establishment into a major national issue. At the same time the new populism had registered even greater success in attacking the processes and institutions that select the president—the conventions, the electoral college, the major parties, and the mechanisms for campaign finance. All these components of the federal electoral system now face wide popular distrust. Partisans of direct democratic reform have had forces in the field for only three years. Their success has been remarkable and widespread. They nearly enacted a constitutional amendment that would have abolished the electoral college and, incidentally, sharply increased opportunities for independent candidates to reach the White House without the aid of a major party nomination. The amendment passed the House, and was only defeated in the Senate by a determined filibuster. The reformers have also gained unprecedented disclosure requirements and greatly tightened restrictions on private contributions to political campaigns; they have persuaded six states to establish new presidential primary systems (a greater than one-third increase over 1968, when there were only sixteen); they have passed the Democratic Party's eighteen-point code that forced every state in the nation to fashion a genuinely open delegate selection system. Traditional party cadres often found the new system so unfamiliar and bewildering that they failed to control, and in many instances even to attend, the 1972 Democratic National Convention. Finally, in 1973, the Watergate affair showed that means had been found for exposing violations of new legal norms of integrity in government, and that the political penalty for violating them could be prohibitive.

Populism as an Ideal of Democracy
Taken together, these attacks on the electoral and administrative systems of the federal government comprise a massive critique of the integrity of the mechanisms of national power. They call into question the very institutions in which reform-minded sectors of the populace recently vested their greatest faith—the presidency and the federal executive branch. The new crusades revive a reform ideology that has lain all but dormant since the New Deal. Not since before World War I, when the nation managed its first response to industrialism, has this spirit appeared in so pure a form. William Jennings Bryan

would have felt perfectly at home with the 1972 Democratic Platform, with a good number of the feature reports in daily newspapers, and even with some of the judicial opinions issued by the federal courts. Once again, the notion is abroad that uncontrolled aggregations of power and remote elites have shut the people out of the process of governing and have fashioned policies inimical to the public interest. The demand is being pressed for pervasive and direct democracy in governmental and economic affairs.

Some may protest that, if this is the new populism, it is hardly different from the "old liberalism" that certain "new populists" are ostentatiously fond of denouncing. After Jack Newfield, who likes to use "liberal" as an epithet, outlined his "Populist Manifesto" in late 1971 in *New York* magazine, old liberal Joseph L. Rauh, Jr., wrote to the editor to congratulate Newfield on catching up with the things that Americans for Democratic Action had been saying ever since Rauh, Hubert Humphrey, Arthur Schlesinger, Jr., John Kenneth Galbraith, and James Loeb had founded ADA in 1948. Rauh had a point, of course. Nevertheless, though Newfield and his generation may exaggerate the differences between themselves and their elders, Rauh is wrong to imply that major differences do not exist. While Rauh himself has emerged as a leader of the new brand of liberalism he is not typical, and he has had to pay a price for his new role. He has had to shatter his once-intimate relations with old liberals like Humphrey—who, Rauh told a Yale Law School seminar as recently as 1965, was "the finest man in American public life." In 1972 Rauh literally did not speak to Humphrey. By then, Humphrey's ally George Meany had apparently forgotten that Rauh was one of the nation's most prominent labor litigators; he had become an apostate. AFL-CIO leaders reported that Rauh's association with George McGovern was one of the private reasons Meany refused to endorse the 1972 Democratic ticket.

Meany's instincts are not wrong, though it may be fairly contended that his reactions, like Jack Newfield's, are extreme.

The emphasis of the new populists on the distribution of power and the integrity of democracy is indeed new in our time. It clashes sharply with the relatively jaded consensus of the 1950s and 1960s, which conceded the autonomous power of "interest groups," like George Meany's unions or even ITT, but believed that their power yielded benign results, extending democracy, not subverting it.

The philosophical contrast between the populism now embraced by Joseph Rauh and Jack Newfield and the political creed practiced by George Meany is most clearly apparent in recent academic political theory. During the 1950s and 1960s political scientists uniformly favored Meany's version of democracy. Their faith in the virtues of political competition among social interests was called "pluralism." Like the populists, whom they ridiculed, the pluralists were themselves heirs of a revered American tradition. They traced their ancestry to Number 10 of *The Federalist,* probably the nation's only significant contribution to Western political philosophy. Inspired by James Madison, author of *Federalist* Number 10, and one of the Constitution's fathers, pluralist thinkers have disdained and sometimes even feared populist literalism about the requisites of democratic government.

For their part, heirs of the contrasting populist tradition deeply distrust the pluralist ideal. They draw more inspiration from Rousseau's concept of the general will than from Madison's equilibrium of muted factional strife. From their Rousseauian perspective, the American political economy cannot be summed up as a competition *among* many interest "groups." Instead, populists see an endless succession of quasi-conspiracies by a relatively few, extremely powerful "special interests" *against* the will and interests of "the people," the majority, the masses, the public, or some similar concept. The populist tradition abjures the notion that private interests, no matter how powerful, should be left free to work their will. It emphasizes a contrasting ideal, that "the people"—a term which pluralist theorists no less than George Meany dismiss as a vacuous abstraction—should subject special interests to firm public control.

Since industrialism placed unprecedented power in the private hands of great corporations (and subsequently in labor unions, agricultural, trade, and professional associations), the populist ideal of democracy has followed two separate programmatic paths. First, it has produced the idea of "big government," of regulation—the notion that government, as representative of the people, should expand its power to offset and control the power of private interests, especially business. Second, the populist ideal has found expression in the idea of "direct democracy." Its proponents have sought measures addressed to opening government itself to more direct popular participation and control. Both themes—"big government" and "direct democracy"—are opposite sides of the same ideological coin; both seek to enhance the capacity of the public, through the mechanisms of democratic government, to control the special interests that dominate the nation's economic and social structure.

These two themes were each voiced by the original Populist Party of the early 1890s. They shaped the objectives of the Progressive movement as it emerged a decade later. And twenty years after the 1912 election—in that year public support for populist ideology was so unanimous that all three major party candidates ran on platforms that virtually copied the Populist Platform of 1892—the Populist ideal returned to structure much of the New Deal. However, the reform philosophy of the 1930s left half the Populist tradition behind. Although New Deal leaders were out to subordinate corporate power to the public interest, they showed unquestioning confidence that government could get the job done—that it could "take control" of the economy and the nation. They assumed that their grand reform enterprise would represent the public interest, and saw no need for direct democratic measures to assure popular control of government.

The current generation of populists resemble their turn-of-the-century forebears more nearly than they resemble the New Dealers. The new populism is ambivalent about government. Its adherents want to use government for public ends, but they fear its ultimate subordination to private designs. Both in their hope and in their distrust, they are working close to the core of the Populist tradition, to the simple ideal that the people should be master of the interests. Their special kinship with the Progressive-Populist generation is reflected in their common instinct that the integrity of democracy is not self-regulating.

The New Dealers agreed that the integrity of the market was not self-regulating. But they trusted "big government" to keep faith and conscientiously regulate business in the public interest. It never occurred to them to notice any need for external checks on the regulatory operations of government; indeed, the elaborate system of jurisprudence constructed by New Deal graduates like Justices Frankfurter and Jackson—which amounted to a form of statism—stood for decades as a shield *against* citizen participation in the federal bureaucracy.

On this basic issue, the new populists and the old Progressives (as well as the original members of the old Populist Party) differ from the old New Dealers. Because the Progressives and the new populists distrust government, they both designed measures *to permit private citizens to intervene directly in governmental affairs and put a halt to official wrongdoing.* The remedy of the Progressives was intervention by the entire —presumably, concerned and virtuous—citizenry, through special *elections*—initiative, referendum, and recall. The new populists' remedy concedes the failure of this old hope for mass intervention; the new hope contemplates action by a concerned and virtuous elite, through citizens' lawsuits in the courts.

Populism as a Style of Politics

In addition to its ideological tradition, American populism has spawned a distinct political *style*. The populist style can be seen in politicians who scorn the speech, dress, education, income, or other attributes of prestige and class associated with most members of the national political elite. It is heard in mass political appeals that encourage radical distrust of established institutions and elites, that aim at the lower economic strata and urge their constituencies to consider themselves uniquely oppressed, powerless, yet nevertheless qualified to equate their interests with the public interest. To some people, this side of populism connotes mass hysteria, demagogic excess, and the pillorying of blameless elites and defenseless minorities. It is also true that this style of politics has been used as much by right-wing politicians such as Senator Joe McCarthy and Governor George Wallace as by reformers such as Robert LaFollette and Ralph Nader. Tom Watson, the turn-of-the-century Georgia leader who, failing to form a coalition of poor blacks and poor whites in the 1890s, became a rabid racist demagogue in the next decade, could in this view be considered a genuine "populist" at both stages of his career.

During the postwar years, antipopulist liberals allowed themselves to be persuaded by the late Columbia University historian Richard Hofstadter that populism consisted of *nothing* but the political style of demagogues like Watson and Wallace. "Populism" itself was an epithet and any politician or propagandist caught indulging in populistic rhetoric was assumed to be a combination of bigot and crank. Even now, the hangover from this antipopulist period has not vanished. Many prominent liberals now watch the spread of populist enthusiasm with genuine fear. Joseph Kraft, for example, felt called upon to shake a cautionary finger when he reviewed Jack Newfield's and Jeff Greenfield's eloquent and influential book, *A Populist Manifesto*. "[M]any . . . things of value in American life—especially high culture and civil liberties," Kraft scolded, "would . . . go up against the egalitarian wall" in a populist revival such as they advocated.[4]

But fears such as Kraft's are groundless, not to say laughable, insofar as they relate to the brand of populism preached by

Newfield and Greenfield. Newfield and Greenfield may occasionally traffic in ill-considered attacks on "concentrated wealth" and "elitism" *per se*—as when they denounce the Ford Foundation, without which the new populist movement would have to make do with perhaps one-fourth of the meager resources it now commands. But no one need fear that these residents of Manhattan's West Side are about to lead the masses in an attack on the outposts of established East Coast liberalism. Like the new populist lawyers fighting for reform from Dupont Circle in Washington, Newfield and Greenfield are attracted to populism as an ideology, as an abstract ideal of democracy. They are not about to join George Wallace in promoting an alliance of right-wing and left-wing populists built on the populist style of demagogic politics. But, even if they were to try, there is no reason to fear that Wallace and his followers would be foolish enough to perceive any grounds for accommodation.

As Richard Nixon has never doubted, there is little substantive basis—and less practical likelihood—for uniting the populist style of George Wallace with the populist ideal expounded by George McGovern and Ralph Nader. Logically the two components of the populist tradition are quite distinct. And from a historical standpoint, though the populist ideal and the populist style are often linked in practical political endeavors, they have maintained a separate life. Their histories have been distinct ever since the collapse of the Populist Party converted Tom Watson from a radical to a racist, even as legions of relatively genteel Americans were becoming Progressive reformers and champions of the populist ideal. The capacity of the populist ideal to attract as its most ardent proponents upperclass, professional, and well-educated individuals did not disappear with the decline of the Progressive era. The same tendency was present, though perhaps not so predominant, during the New Deal. And it is especially apparent in the composition of new populist leadership today.

The Pattern of Populist Failure

Joseph Kraft was not wrong to sense a broadly based resurgence of populist sentiment in the Newfield-Greenfield manifesto. By April, 1972, even *Time* magazine had been so swept along by the tide, that it featured a three-page broadside against the "cozy relationship" between big business and Richard Nixon's White House. Kraft was, however, off-base altogether in warning that the rhetoric affected by *Time* and Newfield and Greenfield might, if not carefully watched, trigger an unruly mass uprising. Far closer to the mark would be the opposite criticism—that the new populists' bark might turn out to be worse than their bite. As a more astute social commentator, Mr. Dooley, had observed of the Progressives' trustbusting proclamations seventy years earlier: "th' noise ye hear is not th' first gun iv a rivolution. It's on'y th' people iv the United States batin' a carpet." Undoubtedly, the most important question about the current movement is whether it too will finally be judged merely to have been "batin' a carpet."

To ask this question may seem snide. In fact, it is a compliment. For in politics, even to have raised the question of whether a movement will have a lasting impact is to have been important. To achieve even short-term success, cadres of activists have to be mobilized, resources have to be tapped to support them, and most important, a new consciousness has to be disseminated. If these formidable obstacles are overcome, even failure, in the ultimate, historical sense, can be an impressive achievement.

Still, the aim of any rational political movement should be not merely to generate ephemeral popularity, but to institutionalize its objectives in a manner that will promote and defend them after the original wave of public enthusiasm has run its course. And it remains true, as Robert Dahl has shrewdly observed, that "A large part of politics consists of purely expressive actions with little or no consequence for social, eco-

nomic, or political change. . . ."[5] Noting the peculiar incidence
of such "purely expressive" pageants on the present scene,
Dahl wonders pessimistically whether "we are in for a period
of putting rococo decorations on existing structures," rather
than producing meaningful change. Dahl is, in this passage,
referring to the revolutionary fantasies of the campus left of
the late 1960s, but he may just as well have been talking about
crusaders for the public interest in Washington and elsewhere.
For, programs to tame the corporate tiger and to dethrone the
bosses invite—and deserve—substantial skepticism. The same
ideal has been aimed at, and missed, before. After all, if the
new populists are right in denouncing the artifacts of previous
reform generations, how can we be so sure that private power
will not similarly overwhelm their new reforms as well?

The problem is not merely what Bess Myerson has called,
in a 1970 warning to the national convention of Consumer
Assembly, the "danger of fake reform." In all periods reformers have worried about this specter—the possibility that years
of propagandizing could come to naught, as conservative forces
usurp the symbols of reform and manage to palm off a "weak"
measure that satiates the public's desire for change. Happily,
however, the new movement is blessed with leaders who combine the highest integrity, intelligence, and public credibility.
The hope is that they will be able to keep the public from confusing loophole-riddled proposals with the real thing. Still, the
fear is that even "strong" measures—that is, measures considered adequate by new populist leaders themselves—will not
withstand the mysterious corrosion that time seems to hold in
store for even the most robust agencies of democratic reform.

The past teaches that, even when populist sentiment is strong
enough to force through reform legislation by overwhelming
margins, there is no guarantee that the social changes contemplated by the law will take place. Take the case cited by Mr.
Dooley, the early history of the enforcement of the Sherman
Act, the nation's first antitrust law. The act passed both houses
of Congress during the spring of 1890, with exactly one dis-

senting vote (in the Senate) in an atmosphere that, five years earlier, had prompted a special Select Committee to warn that *"no general question of Governmental policy occupies at this time so prominent a place in the thoughts of the people* [as] controlling the steady growth and extending influence of corporate power. . . ."[6] The bill that Congress approved in response to this tide of public demand, though broad and somewhat vague, was not weak. It banned "all" agreements in restraint of trade and "any" attempt to monopolize. These terms were stiff enough to lead present-day Antitrust Subcommittee Chairman Philip A. Hart to claim that the Sherman Act could not pass the gauntlet of the archconservatives now sitting on James Eastland's Senate Judiciary Committee.

But though the act did manage to sail through the Congress of 1890, it mysteriously failed to pass muster with the Justice Department. President Benjamin Harrison's attorney general waited exactly one year before sending instructions to enforce the statute to his district attorneys in the field. During the next twelve years (and three administrations), only eighteen antitrust prosecutions were initiated (two of which were directed against labor unions) and none of them by the home office in Washington.[7] After the department lost its case in the Supreme Court against the Sugar Trust in 1896, because of its own (possibly deliberate) technically sloppy pleading, President Cleveland's conservative Attorney General Richard Olney seized upon the occasion to suspend antitrust enforcement altogether. While the government stood aside, the captains of industry entered upon the most massive wave of mergers in the nation's history, linking most or all of the leading enterprises in the nation's major markets, and giving the American economy the highly concentrated profile it has retained ever since. Such still-familiar giants as United States Steel, International Paper, General Electric, International Salt, United Fruit, American Tobacco, American Can, Nabisco, and U.S. Rubber were formed during this period.

Not until the popular outcry against the trusts became deafening, during the second decade of the life of the Sherman Act, did President Theodore Roosevelt interest himself in enforcing the law. And even his prosecutions and those of his two Progressive successors, Taft and Wilson, were far more ceremonial than substantive. They did not begin, or attempt to begin, to undo the results of the great turn-of-the-century merger wave.

Some regulatory legislation has been structured expressly to shield a new agency from industry domination. But even then the agency may not be safe from an immediate industry coup. For example, while legislation to create a Federal Reserve Board (FRB) was before Congress in 1913, President Woodrow Wilson haughtily dismissed pleas by leading bankers to explicitly reserve certain seats for bankers. "Will one of you gentlemen," Wilson demanded in a famous confrontation, "tell me in what civilized country of the earth there are important government boards of control on which private interests are represented?" Yet, for some reason, after the bill was signed into law he decided to change course. Ignoring the Progressive legislators who had fought with him for the Federal Reserve Act, Wilson appointed leading bankers to the board in numbers sufficient to assure industry control of the agency.[8] Since that time, the Federal Reserve System has functioned, for the most part, as a self-regulating system for the dominant bankers, the major New York banks, in particular.

The pattern repeats itself endlessly. Muckraking by Ralph Nader's legions has supplied present-day newspaper readers with an apparently unlimited supply of similar cases of bureaucracy gone bad, many with consequences more devastating than the still-birth of the Sherman Act or of the concept of an independent Federal Reserve Board. These revelations have had their effect on public opinion. Already, some important new laws to curb pollution and protect consumers have been put on the books. The question concerning the newly awakened public is how to exploit this new opportunity for change. As the public becomes convinced that old reforms have not worked, what plan or set of new institutions can be offered for them to champion, a scheme that will work where past schemes have failed?

Liberalism and the Captive Bureaucracy

Much depends on the outcome of this revived search for a democratic response to concentrated patterns of power. Today we hear a great deal about the bankruptcy of American liberalism, of a paralysis of liberal nerve and creative drive. Some blame the Vietnam War. Others blame this malaise on the slackening of economic anxiety among the increasingly affluent working class, along with their deepening disenchantment with civil rights and civil liberties. However, the crisis of the captive regulatory bureaucracy poses a greater threat to the American liberal tradition than either foreign policy or the conservatism of the majority. The very concept of the captive regulatory agency mocks the liberals' most cherished assumptions.

It was, after all, the liberals who promised the American people that big government and regulation would bring progress, that, in New Dealer James Landis's heady terms, it would square "the rise of industrialism" with "the rise of democracy." "To the far-sighted," pontificated Harold Ickes in 1932,

> it has long been obvious that the only way out is for the government to take control and develop a better system for the people . . . if it is our purpose to make industrialism serve humanity instead of laying ourselves as victims on the cruel altar of industrialism. . . .[9]

Today, such optimistic forecasts seem less prophetic than the forecasts of conservatives like Attorney General Olney who in 1894 wrote a famous letter to the president of the Burlington Railroad, urging him not to fear the fledgling Interstate Commerce Commission (ICC):

> The Commission is or can be made of great use to the railroads. It satisfies the public clamor for supervision

of the railroads, at the same time that the supervision
is almost entirely nominal. Furthermore, the older such
a commission gets to be, the more inclined it will be to
take the business and railroad view of things. . . . The
better course is not to abolish the Commission but to
utilize it. . . .

By 1960, when New Dealer Landis was called upon to report
to President-elect John F. Kennedy on the status of the New
Deal regulatory agencies, it seemed that Olney had been right
all along: "The Interstate Commerce Commission," Landis sadly
observed, "has been characterized as railroad-minded, the
FCC [Federal Communications Commission] as dominated by
the networks, while the actions of the Federal Power Commission speak for themselves."

The problems for liberals is that, if political conservatives
like Olney were right in favoring regulation from bad motives,
then it must be admitted that ideological conservatives like
Friedrich Hayek, Milton Friedman, and even William F.
Buckley may have been correct in condemning regulation
from good motives. If affirmative government has merely
relabeled or reinforced existing patterns of power, then liberalism may not only be in danger of losing its constituency, as
analysts like Kevin Phillips have alleged, but of being stripped
of a viable philosophy, as well. The apparent failure of hopes
to achieve reform through regulation reopens the old debate
about the proper role of government in the economy—though
on somewhat different terms than it was originally conducted.
Liberals have long assumed that they won this once-great
debate. And it is true that few people can be found anymore
who deem it morally objectionable that government *should*
intervene to "redress the balance of social power." The problem
is that no one is sure any longer that it *can.*

But now that the public can see that government has not
solved the basic problem of power, it is evident that liberalism
is in trouble. The difficulty is not merely that liberals have
lost an argument with conservatives about which strategy of

government is most effective. It is not merely that they must revise their program for impressing democratic ideals on industrial America. The prospect looms that the goal itself is unattainable and that the entire exercise may be academic and futile.

Perhaps industrialism and populist democracy are simply incompatible. Perhaps reform efforts to refute that grim hypothesis can *never* be more than "rococo decorations on existing structures." After all, haven't the disclosures of Ralph Nader and his compatriots taught us not only that "the New Deal has failed," but that the same resources which confer economic might on great corporations convert easily into the means of political might as well, especially into the forms of power needed to influence bureaucratic appointments and policies? And if that is true, what confidence can we have that the institutions of formal democracy can ever provide the people with the substance of power over the interests that rule the economy?

Thus, at the same time that liberals must fend off "I told you so" assaults from the right, they must face even more fundamental attacks from the left, based on the charge that no reform strategy can expect to reorder power in America. Two recent revisionist histories of the early days of railroad regulations suggest this convergence of conservative and radical critiques. One of the essays was written by Paul McAvoy, an economist at MIT's Sloane School of Management, who was reared in the conservative "Chicago" school of economics presided over by Milton Friedman;[10] the other is the work of the prominent radical historian Gabriel Kolko of the University of Toronto.[11] Despite their diverse backgrounds, both scholars present the same thesis: the struggle for railroad regulation did not, as has always been assumed, pit Populist and Progressive legislators (representing the public) against a united front of railroad monopolists. Rather, the more perceptive elements of the industry itself, which was actually characterized by fierce competition and continually *declining* rates charged to shippers, *favored* regulation as a means of establishing a stable cartel regime that would make competition and low prices illegal. The two scholars demonstrate that, without the force of law behind price-fixing agreements, the cartels could not endure, as members continually "chiseled" through secret price cuts and rebates.

Both analyses, as Kolko took special pains to emphasize, show up liberal legislators as false prophets whose objective function—whether deliberate or otherwise—was to trick the public into accepting "reforms" that served to abet rather than control monopoly. Kolko's contention, made explicit at several points in his argument, is that liberal economic reformers *always* and *inevitably* fall into playing this insidious role.

Although this issue has not been faced widely, hints of Kolko's despairing counsel have entered the more moderate literature of social criticism. In his 1969 book, which has already become a staple of university political science curricula, Chicago Professor Theodore Lowi has pounced on the example of the ICC in particular to proclaim "the end of liberalism."

And on the moderate left, the same phenomenon can be discerned. Charles Reich's vision of America as a vast "corporate state," in which regulatory bureaucrats and corporate managers share control, tells the same Orwellian story about the perversion of reform symbols and mechanisms: rather than reform, the New Deal produced a state dominated by corporate power and "impervious to democratic or popular control." This is "a complete reversal of the original American ideal and plan," Reich says, but he implicitly concludes that the problem is insoluble and that there is no way to restore an effective democracy. The only "answer" to the corporate state that he finds he is able to recommend is a complete Thoreauian retreat from politics.

Like Reich, John Kenneth Galbraith hides his despair— the implication that no reform strategy can solve the problem of power posed by his "new industrial state." Galbraith also directs hopes for change outside of politics. He looks to the miraculous healing action of the humane sentiments of "the scientific and educational estate," a concept which seems to refer to fellow travelers of Reich's "Consciousness III," after they have matriculated to graduate school and, beyond that, to university faculties.

In Galbraith's world, predominance is now passing to the "technostructure," by which he appears to mean a class of scientist managers who people the upper levels of corporate and some public bureaucracies, especially the Pentagon and its clients. In this conception, the traditional struggle between populist reformers and business has become a sham in that both are losing out to the technocrats. Robert Heilbroner has made the point in an especially striking manner:

> [The] comparison . . . is best made to the merchants who huddled around the walls of thirteenth-century castles, wholly subservient to the prevailing order, and oblivious to the thought that some day it might be *their* interests and ideas, and not those of the feudal seigneurs, that would establish the laws of motion of the social universe. In like manner, the technicians, scientists, planners, etc., who constitute the vanguard of the society of the future, have no independently formulated conceptions of society and are happy to lend themselves to the ends specified by their capitalist masters. . . . The change may require several decades, perhaps even generations. . . . But I suggest that the direction of change is already established beyond peradventure of doubt.[12]

Implicit in this vision is a harsh fate for the traditional populist anxiety about preserving democracy: the new technology, as it elevates the knowledgeable technocrat over the dilettantish entrepreneur, must constrict even more radically the role of the wholly ignorant public. Formal democratic constraints become meaningless when the real basis of power is knowledge. Populist reformers who would apply traditional, legalistic strategies to an increasingly technological economy are quixotic seekers after a futile goal. Or, worse, they appear as Luddites trying to halt the triumph of technology (a charge made more credible by the sound of some environmentalist rhetoric). Zbigniew Brzezinski has stated this view effectively:

> The crisis of American liberalism is hence both a crisis of confidence and of historical relevance. It presents the bleak prospect that liberalism, historically the most vital source of innovation in contemporary American democracy, may become the critical expression of a doctrinarian minority—increasingly reactive in spite of its rhetoric— and a haven for philosophic protest against the dehumanizing effects of science, while the active shaping of the future passes into the hands of a socially somewhat conservative but technologically innovative elite.[13]

If one takes seriously such prophecies of a technocratic future, the clamor of Ralph Nader and other contemporary reformers must be the death rattle of the populist ideal, rather than the prelude to a grand new era of reform. And, pending the conveniently far-off day when Robert Heilbroner's technocrats displace their present capitalist masters, the rise of technology is bound to make business even more secure against public comprehension or control.

Doubts and Hopes About Reform
New populist leaders have not pursued the ultimate question raised by such critiques of the liberal regulatory state, whether *any* formal democratic methods can alter the fact of corporate dominion. Nor have they shrunk from supporting reforms that suspiciously resemble the very institutions they have exposed as vulnerable to subversion. Inevitably, therefore, they invite us to doubt the value of their own enterprise.

This failure should not be surprising. Since activists are so busy just being activists, they cannot spend time devising the ideas and proposals they champion. They must make do with whatever new ideas for change happen to have been made available by others blessed with comparative leisure and creative intelligence. In this case, that means, mainly, academic social scientists. But the new populism has not had a large fund of relevant social criticism on which to base a program for change. Social scientific thought has oscillated between the smug axiom articulated by Schlesinger, that the New Deal had successfully "redressed the balance of social power," and the counteraxiom that thinking about the distribution of social power was in any event futile, since an affluent and apathetic populace could never be galvanized to support any new democratic crusade. The result was that the policy-oriented disciplines offered no critiques applicable to the ideological and institutional legacies of the New Deal generation. As Daniel Patrick Moynihan has said with respect to the chance for reform on behalf of the poor that suddenly opened in 1963 and 1964, there were few designs for change available when new populist issues about democracy unexpectedly surfaced on the public agenda in the late 1960s.

But wherever the blame should fall, it seems all too likely that although the 1970s are bound to be a fertile period for new populist reform measures, the net gains for democracy from all this agitation and legislation will prove disappointing, especially to their sponsors. The problem is that the job that must be done, as it has traditionally been understood, is impossible to do. The difficulty lies in the basic ideal that new populist reformers inherited from their predecessors in both the New Deal and Progressive eras—the concept of conferring power on the people, of giving the people direct democratic control over government, and using government *affirmatively* to master centers of social power on behalf of the unorganized public. On the basis of all our experience, this has to be regarded as a frail hope, one almost never realized in practice, regardless of whatever legal restrictions manage to get written into the legislative blueprints.

Failure is certainly the rule when it comes to evaluating the effects of regulation—at least in terms of whether the regula-

tion has served to subject organized interests to the effective
control of the public. Indeed, failure—in these terms—is
substantially more pervasive than has yet been generally acknowledged.

The important point is that the conditions that have caused
past reform schemes to fail cannot be banished by new statutory formulas or formidable administrative sanctions. They
inhere, ironically, in the very structure of our democratic faith
and institutions. These inherent conditions of democratic government sharply curtail the scope of populist reform. In order to
succeed where its predecessors have failed, the new populism
must acknowledge these limits. It must adopt a vision that
is at once strategically more modest and philosophically more
conservative.

2
A Paradox of Democracy: The Captivity of Government

The Democratic Contradiction
and the Elements of Democratic Influence

Recurrent exposés prove, if nothing else, that there will never be a dearth of muck to rake about our capitalist democracy. This fact underscores an enduring and fundamental contradiction of democratic government: precisely because our institutions are formally open to participation by all elements in society, they are vulnerable to domination by the most powerful elements in society. Reformers are continually stymied by this law of democratic politics. It helps to explain why their calculations so frequently go awry. It helps to explain why measures designed to make government more responsive to the interests of the public often end in making it less responsive —why small claims courts in the big cities have often become collection agencies for major creditors of the poor, why primaries have often increased the subservience of political candidates to special interests. Odd as this seems, it is easily explained by a common-sense derivation from the most basic postulate of liberal democracy: every individual and group should be free to persuade, organize, and raise and spend money, in other words to acquire and to use the means of political influence.

These three items—wealth, organization, and persuasion—comprise the elements of influence in democratic politics. If everyone can participate by right in the political process, then, inevitably, those who are best able to amass and deploy the ingredients of influence will participate most effectively. This does not have to mean that some interests will tyrannize over others. It does mean, however, that changing the structure or the forms of governmental authority cannot radically change the *relative* power of the various participants in the underlying political process. Hence, arranging formal institutional changes is not likely to effect radical change.

This is not an inflexible rule. Though the means of influence are the same in all arenas of democratic politics, their relative value does vary somewhat from one forum to another. Persuasion counts for more and money for less before the courts and even before administrative agencies, than before congressional committees. So a new entity may work, at least for a time, to diminish the relative influence of formerly dominant groups. But the variations are rarely as great as reformers anticipate. Money may not be able to purchase a new administrator's decisions as directly as it may purchase some legislator's vote, but it can finance battalions of lawyers, a fact that renders the old interests something less than helpless in litigation before—and against—a new agency.

Even the total transfer of a particular social problem from outside the political process into the domain of government may have little effect. Relevant interests may retain, or even increase, their capacity to have their way at the expense of the public. The wealth and organization that enable members of an industry to form cartels will also prove useful in influencing regulators to approve, or even to enforce, their cartel agreements.

There is indeed only one way to wall off a new reform-oriented entity from the influence of the interests it is supposed to control. That is to take the entity out of the democratic process by allowing it to amass truly autonomous political influence. Needless to say, we are (or should be) cautious about taking such a step. Our federal courts are relatively immune to the pressures of wealth and organization, precisely *because* federal judges need seek neither reelection nor even reappointment. Of course we permit the courts such undemocratic autonomy only because we drastically limit their authority. By themselves, they cannot exercise the basic prerogatives of government—the legitimate use of force or authority over the public purse. And in terms of political influence, they have neither wealth nor organization, but only the capacity to persuade the public and other branches of government to support their decisions.

There are instances where more substantial means of influence and authority have been conferred on autonomous governmental entities and officials. Public authorities, like the Port of New York Authority, which have vast organizational resources and can raise their own revenues, furnish one example, though one which many people would not want to emulate too frequently.

Of greater current interest is the example of campaign finance reform. It is widely acknowledged that the dependence of political candidates on campaign contributions hamstrings policies aimed at curbing special interests. It is just as widely assumed that the only roadblock in the way of solving this problem is political: the politicians and private interests who benefit from the present system fight to preserve it. That is true as far as it goes. But there is an additional and possibly even less tractable problem that is philosophical in nature. The cure —at least the complete cure—for the inequity of our system of financing campaigns might turn out to be worse than the disease.

The problem is this: unfortunately, the only secure way to make a decisive change in the present sordid situation is to give money to some designated new group, individual, or institution to distribute to deserving candidates. But the designee, whoever he is, will then have all the power that the contributors used to have. This may not leave us any better off than we were. In some respects it will surely diminish the democratic principle. If the money goes to national party organizations, or to their candidates directly, then the constituent elements within the loose confederations that we call Democrats and Republicans will lose much of their power. In other words, government financing would render the national political elite more immune than previously to all outside influences—not only the influence of "special" interests, but to efforts from any quarter to replace them or to change their policies. It is by no means clear that democracy will gain if a Larry O'Brien or a Leonard Hall is given the autonomy that Austin Tobin long enjoyed. Commenting on the Democrats' 1971 campaign subsidy bill, Tom Wicker was virtually the only observer thoughtful enough to ask, "Do we really want to make Presidents and the men who compete for the office more powerful and independent than they are now?"[1]

The only honest answer to this probing question is that no one knows. The facts about campaign finance are so shrouded in secrecy that there is no way to measure or compare the costs and benefits of what the new populists now regard as reform. But it is enough to note here that there *are* costs—as well as benefits—and they may be prohibitive.

The False Ideal of the Grand Design

In sum, corporate and other potent special interests threaten the democratic process, but they are also part of it. Unless one is willing to restrict democracy in some significant respect, it is difficult to design a scheme for reform that can effectively diminish the power of normally dominant interests. And it is all but impossible to diminish their power drastically.

This simple fact severely limits the opportunities open to populist reformers. The option of taking a basically undemocratic route to reform is foreclosed completely in all normal circumstances. Even if, for example, reformers wanted to empower a new consumer protection agency to levy an excess profits tax from which to finance its own operations, it seems unlikely that many congressmen would find the idea appealing. (It is interesting in this regard to note that since the New Deal, Congress has been bitterly hostile to efforts by federal agencies to gain a measure of autonomy by advertising and pamphleteering; in general, Congress has strictly limited the agencies' access even to this relatively weak ingredient of independent political influence.) In practical fact, therefore, populist reform measures must take into account the existing distribution of influence. In most cases, such measures will work only if they are drawn cautiously to achieve modest advantages for traditionally disadvantaged interests.

All this is obvious, and would not be worth belaboring, except for the fact that populist reformers have often chosen in many cases not to notice it at all. Instead, their schemes have tended to play right into the hands of the interests they were meant to control.

Populist movements have consistently shown a preference for an approach we might term the "grand design" concept of reform. This concept emphasizes plans to empower government broadly, as proxy for the people, to "take control," to "redress the balance of power," to determine the public interest and enforce it. Generally, this impulse expressed itself through the creation of administrative agencies that had wide jurisdiction, broad discretion, and substantial powers or sanctions with which to enforce their commands. Administrative law expert Kenneth Culp Davis has quipped that statutes creating such agencies have often delegated so much authority with so little direction as to how to use it that they merely say, "Here is the problem. Deal with it." Some years later, however, he conceded that this formula understated the problem. In fact, he said, reform statutes often say, "Here is your power; find a problem and solve it as you wish."[2]

During the Progressive and especially the New Deal periods, reformers buttressed their enthusiasm for such regulatory grand designs with their abiding faith in the executive branch of the federal government as the most progressive institution of government, and a belief in the magical qualities of "expertness"; this last, as Louis Jaffe has observed, "was envisaged as an objective force which if left to itself would inevitably produce reform."[3] Though these notions and the grand design ideal in general no longer enjoy automatic obeisance, they have proved far more tenacious than post–New Deal reformers have liked to admit.

Before the New Deal was even over, official circles had begun to raise questions about the regulatory agencies. President Roosevelt appointed a commission under the direction of Cornell political scientist Robert Cushman to investigate and recommend reforms. The commission report and Cushman's subsequent book concluded that things were not all as they should be, but suggested that they would tend to improve, if the president could assume more direct control over the agencies.[4] Most of the agencies at that time were considered legally "independent," in the sense that their commissioners served for fixed terms and could not be fired by the president. Originally, this formal "independence" had been looked upon as the basis of the agencies' supposedly unique strength; freed from "political" influence, the theory ran, they would be free to follow wherever their expert administrators wanted to lead. But Cushman's cure nevertheless soon took hold and became the dominant new liberal conception of how the regulatory establishment should be restructured.

Only this year, President Nixon's Council on Executive Reorganization (popularly know as the "Ash Council" after its chairman, Litton Industries' President Roy L. Ash) embraced this traditionally liberal conception of regulatory reform. Echoing the line of criticism originated by Cushman and thereafter repeated and refined by Marver Bernstein,[5] James Landis,[6] and most recently, by reformist FTC member Philip Elman,[7] the

Ash Council contended that, if the president were empowered to assume full formal control over the now-independent regulatory agencies (i.e., if he could dismiss their top administrators just as he can dismiss the heads of executive branch departments and agencies), these agencies would lose their parochialism and sympathy for the narrow objectives of client industries.

This faith in presidential control derives from one of the touchstones of liberal thought in this century—the notion that the presidency is the most beneficent locus of governmental power in the nation, and that granting the federal executive branch jurisdiction over any domestic social problem will inherently produce progressive results.

It was the great liberal presidents, "Theodore Roosevelt and Woodrow Wilson and Franklin Roosevelt"—to quote another characteristic paean from Arthur Schlesinger, Jr.—who "put out the revolutionary fires within capitalism lit by the great industrialists of the nineteenth century."[8]

Schlesinger may be right about the historical role of the presidency. But if so, it is probably due more to myths about the office than to facts of its performance.

Long before the 1972 campaign exposed White House minions auctioning off the public weal piecemeal to special interests from the Teamsters to ITT, the facts gave little support for this unquestioning faith in the presidency. Formal presidential control seems to provide no greater security of regulation in the public interest than does formal independence. In the first place, giving the president more legal authority over a particular agency does not necessarily mean that actual control will follow as a matter of course. In particular, such a change does not necessarily mean that the agency will become less responsive to the concerns of the industry or industries with which it is familiar and more responsive to conflicting public concerns expressed through the president. If the industry has substantial influence over relevant parts of Congress, especially over the appropriations subcommittee for the agency, then the president may be helpless to counter industrial influence over the agency. Even if the option is available to him, moreover, he may well decide not to exercise it. It rarely makes political sense for a president to arouse the antagonism of a powerful industry. Only when the public is deeply disturbed by the industry's position, can the president expect any political benefits from such action, and even then the benefits are likely to be somewhat speculative.

But the political detriments that will flow from any decision to oppose an industry and its sympathetic regulators are relatively definite. In short, the president will probably conclude —and quite rightly—that the risks of opposing industry would more than offset the gains. Hence, regulatory agencies that the president controls directly are often as subservient to industry as are independent agencies. For example, USDA has a variety of regulatory functions that involve important issues of protection for both consumer and environmental concerns. But the existence of formal presidential control, through the power to hire and fire the secretary of agriculture, has not significantly interfered with the pronounced tendency of USDA's subagencies to favor agricultural interests in their discharge of these functions. For example, until recently, the Pesticides Regulation Division of Agriculture had primary responsibility for carrying out the provisions of the 1947 Federal Insecticide, Fungicide, and Rodenticide Act. But, after holding extensive hearings, the House Government Operations Committee concluded that

> until mid-1967, the USDA Pesticides Regulation Division failed almost completely to carry out its responsibility to enforce provisions of the Federal Insecticide, Fungicide, and Rodenticide Act intended to protect the public from hazardous and ineffective pesticide products.[9]

To be sure, it can be argued that USDA regulation of pesticides is not strictly analogous to the structure the Ash Council has in mind for the functions that the independent agencies now perform. Unlike the case of USDA's regulatory functions, or those of the Food and Drug Administration (FDA), which is part of HEW (Department of Health, Education, and Welfare), the regulatory agencies, revamped along the lines sketched by the council, would not disappear into large bureaucracies but would remain individual entities and would report directly to the White House, rather than simply to a higher layer of bureaucracy within the same agency. But, depending on the particular administration's priorities, this could mean that the agencies would receive less supervision, rather than more.

Also, and more important, it is a misconception to think that the president is, in general, more responsive to public interests vis-à-vis private interests than is an administrative entity. In fact, the reverse has quite often been the case. Again, recent examples are not hard to locate. In 1969, public opposition to oil import quota policies mounted as inflation spurred popular anxiety about the $5–$8 billion annual cost of the import program to the consumers. A cabinet level task force, headed by George P. Schultz, then secretary of labor and now secretary of the treasury, recommended that quotas be replaced by a tariff system that would reduce prices and assure that the public treasury would benefit from the exclusionary policies alleged to promote the national security. The president ignored the task force report even though he had to cloak his support for oil interests in an elaborate and prolonged ceremony involving the appointment of still another committee to review (and reject) the findings of the Schultz task force.

Another example was furnished in 1970 and 1971 by the EPA and the Council on Environmental Quality (CEQ), agencies that are both under direct White House control. They did not oppose the aircraft industry's side of the SST battle, despite the contrary demands of their environmentalist constituency. Their position was dictated by White House policy.

Similarly, in 1970, the Office of Consumer Affairs in the White House found itself overwhelmed by industry pressures expressed through the White House. Although Mrs. Virginia Knauer, head of the office and the president's special assistant for consumer affairs, had publicly endorsed the concept of class action lawsuits in consumer cases, and had promised to introduce legislation establishing the right to bring consumer class actions into the federal courts, she was soon induced to change her mind. The American Retail Federation and other industry groups opposed to class action legislation later gloated publicly about how they had succeeded in turning the White House against Mrs. Knauer on the class action issue and in having her legislative proposal substantially diluted. Ultimately, she appeared in congressional offices as a lobbyist against strong class action bills proposed by Democratic senators and congressmen.

The one point that can be made in favor of increased presidential control of the independent agencies, from the standpoint of the agencies' responsiveness to public interests, is that when public enthusiasm for consumer, environmental, or similar regulatory objectives suddenly becomes intense (after a long period of public nonconcern), agencies subject to direct presidential control will respond more speedily than will formally independent agencies. But even in such periods—the present era is one of them—the results of formal control cannot be predicted confidently. In this period of increasing public consciousness of consumer and environmental needs, all the federal regulatory agencies have shown at least some disposition to respond to the public mood. But whether the response has been more far-reaching and dramatic, for example, at FDA, which is subject to direct White House control, than at the FTC, which is not, appears doubtful at best.

The Ash Council report on regulatory agencies did not elicit a chorus of acclaim from any quarter. It therefore happily appears that liberals may have lost some of their traditional assurance that transfer of formal control to the White House automatically promotes the public interest. On the other hand, the more general faith that brave new bureaucracies with vast grants of authority can uproot underlying structures of economic and political power infects a variety of contemporary efforts at change. In this important respect, reformers have only been able to move halfway up from the old liberalism, to borrow a phrase from William F. Buckley, Jr.[10] Ralph Nader's rhetoric bristles with criticism of the old liberals' too-exclusive reliance on big government as the answer to corporate power. But Nader's inventory of specific programs and proposals includes some very grand—and dubious—schemes. His Consumer Protection Agency (CPA), which Congress enacted in 1972 after Nader told them it was "the most important consumer legislation ever considered" on Capitol Hill, and his still more ambitious plan to require corporations to obtain federal charters are the main cases in point. These schemes harbor the most egregious defects of the grand design mentality favored by past generations of reformers.

In 1970 Professor Galbraith urged that "The Democratic Party must henceforth use the word socialism; it describes what is needed." He has suggested "a consolidated regulatory body for all regulated industries." Both Galbraith proposals are based on the familiar statist logic of Progressive and New Deal enthusiasts of big government: "it takes a large public bureaucracy to police powerful private bureaucracy."[11] Galbraith thinks that his prescription for making big government bigger still will lift urban and interurban transportation and housing, among other things, from their present squalid state. Unfortunately, there are a few better examples of industries with a track record of controlling their regulators than those for which he dreams of streamlined socialist solutions. What, after all, are the precedents he has in mind—the ICC? the CAB? the FHA? the Port of New York Authority?

The Appeal of the Grand Design

The grand design ideal exerts a persistent appeal because it fulfills certain specific needs that liberals at most times have manifested. The first and most important of these is an *ideological* need. Belief in ambitious reform schemes serves to validate the populist faith that American democracy can work as high-school civics lessons insist that it should—that "the people" can really run the show, that they actually can maintain active and affirmative direction of the nation's affairs, including positive control over wayward agglomerations of private power. This populist, "affirmative" concept of democracy has been consistently posited by Americans in general and by liberals in particular. But when industrialism spawned vast and powerful private organizations, the possibility loomed that democracy in this positive sense was no longer a reality. In fact, these powerful private interests might well become the secret motive force affirmatively guiding government policy. This was a real and a widespread fear. "The masters of the government of the United States," cried Woodrow Wilson at the height of Progressive anxiety about corporate power in 1912, "are the combined capitalists and manufacturers. . . . The government of the United States at present is a foster child of the special interests."[12]

Such thoughts greatly disturb most civic-minded Americans. But belief in big government's ability to reorder power along democratic lines suppresses this disquieting possibility and helps to keep the old faith; it inspires confidence that the people can still stand up to the interests.

Second, belief in grand designs for reform also serves a *psychological* function. It provides an appealing rationale for the ambition reform-minded people generally have to exercise broad power to dictate the public interest. Liberals use "the public interest" the way conservatives use "national security"— to rationalize their desire for unchecked power. In reminiscing about the bright young men of the New Deal, Professor Louis Jaffe has remarked,

> When I served the New Deal as a young man I was prepared to support the theory that the so-called independent agencies could save the world. It was somehow thought . . . that well-intentioned young men appointed to [run the agencies] could and would do whatever they thought to be right. We were misled by the fact that we were in power and were appointing our men and that we were

being given fresh and powerful mandates by Congress. In such circumstances an agency can get off to a good head start before the political facts of life catch up with it. But how naive we were in believing that any organization of government—yes, even the courts—can be free to do what seems right to do![13]

Despite Jaffe's gentle mockery, the problem is not without its serious aspect. The blend of ambition and naive optimism so characteristic of reformers of all periods has had much to do with the substantive approaches they choose to follow, and the results are not always beneficial.

Finally, there is a strong *political* incentive encouraging liberals to turn to big government plans for reform. Grand designs are eminently suitable for embodiment in legislation. Because of the characteristic vagueness of their terminology, such laws defer explosive political questions and thereby save legislators the embarrassment of trying to resolve the conflicts themselves. Legislative grand designs, furthermore, are relatively easy to sell to the public. Liberal leaders have always been good at engineering campaigns to put such legislation across and get it enacted—far better, indeed, than they have proved to be at molding permanent constituencies or representative organizations to see that the aims of their laws are faithfully executed. Their eagerness to promote grand designs through legislation has often been buttressed by the semiconscious fear that the popularity of their aims will prove ephemeral, and that it must therefore be tapped quickly for some dramatic use, or else they will have nothing to show for their efforts.

For all these reasons, movements to assert democratic control over powerful private interests have often yielded such grandiose blueprints for change as the Sherman Act of 1890, the Federal Trade Commission Act (created in 1914 to protect consumers from "all acts of unfair competition," but which until 1969 showed little interest in protecting consumers at all), the National Industrial Recovery Act (NRA) (F.D.R.'s first answer to the Great Depression, which turned out in practice to be a cumbersome and ultimately ineffectual effort by industry to organize a corporate state), and the notion of federal chartering of national corporations (which was backed originally by the right wing of the Progressive movement and has resurfaced recently as a major objective of the new populists of the 1970s).

Hamiltonian Ends for Hamiltonian Means: the NEP.

To put it as Marx would have, liberals assume too easily that manipulation of government—society's superstructure—can force changes in the underlying structures of social and economic power. Shrewd conservative political leaders have at last grasped this point. Accordingly, they have embraced the old liberal nostrums—though liberals have by no means abandoned them. These conservative politicians have come to recognize how innocuous liberal strategies for change really are, and, at the same time, what advantages these strategies enjoy in persuading enlightened (generally liberal) opinion, and sometimes even the more cynical (and often more sensible) public that change is actually taking place, even when the status quo is, if anything, being reinforced.

The most important example of this awakening on the right is President Nixon's New Economic Policy (NEP). At first the president and his advisers themselves scorned this policy as dangerously radical. In the beginning its support centered in the left wing of the Democratic Party; its primary champion was Professor Galbraith. And indeed this grand design for wage-price control is, by all traditional ideological criteria, a radical, or left-liberal, idea. It presumes a chronic and massive failure of the private market; it requires pervasive supervision and sanction by the government. The NEP is, in short, an exceptionally pure version of the kind of scheme to which liberals have traditionally turned to control private power centers that seemed to threaten the public interest. And, after the president rendered it respectable, honest liberals did not disown it. As TRB in the *New Republic* recognized, "Phase II . . . is largely based on [the Galbraithian thesis that] power is now concentrated so narrowly in big corporations, and the big unions [though pure new populist expressions generally downplay the power of the unions] that a recession doesn't drive down prices. They are 'administered.'" TRB thought that the only answer to the malignant power of business and labor was to have the government step in and move toward a "managed economy." This is what he thinks the president gave us with Phase II and Phase IV—by stealing an idea from the Democrats.[14]

Indeed, the program confers on government experts a legal power to dictate to industry and labor unmatched in its breadth since the National Industrial Recovery Act was enacted. But, as became apparent almost immediately after the president's dramatic announcement of the Phase I freeze on August 15, 1971, the government was not really able to exercise this vast power as an independent political force. The power of the relevant interest groups was so great that, first, they had to be accorded direct representation in the decision-making bodies (such as President Wilson had denied the bankers when the FRB, which had similar powers over banking, was structured). Then the Pay Board was conceded formal autonomy and freedom from White House supervision. At length most of organized labor resigned from the board, abandoning altogether the pretense that the board's determinations reflected anything more or less than a kind of bargaining between political sovereignties.

In their first year the board and the Price Commission did make consistently conscientious decisions regarding the thousands of individual labor and business situations that came before them where no substantial political force was involved. The rise in consumer prices had slowed to an annual rate of 3 percent from the 4.5 percent rate that helped spur President Nixon to adopt the program in August, 1971. Even though many experts disputed the administration's claim that this change was produced by the wage-price control machinery, and even though wholesale prices were still climbing at a much faster and more ominous rate of 4.4 percent, these results certainly entitle the NEP to claim that it was something more than futile or fraudulent. But the virtues, such as they may have been, of the new regulatory apparatus were not much in evidence on occasions when it had to collide with major centers of private power, such as the auto industry. Until Nader threw a special spotlight on the issue and threatened to hand the Democrats a campaign issue for the fall, the Price Commission, hoping that the deed could be completed as discreetly as possible, was ready to look the other way while Detroit hiked its prices by as much as it wished.

The reason the brave New Economic Policy turned out to be something of a paper tiger is no mystery, of course. Despite the government's arrogation of legal power to itself, business and labor groups retained all the formidable components of political power they had held before the announcement. At first the power of the unions was especially in evidence— because the control of wage levels in unionized industries was especially vital to the success of the program. The administration, and even more obviously the Democrats in Congress, showed their considerable respect for the impressive resources of organized labor—the ability to lobby, to fund, and otherwise to promote political campaigns, and, most importantly, the capacity to strike, and thereby to sabotage hopes for economic recovery and, very possibly, the president's chances for reelection as well.

In the end—despite intense public support for the objective of the NEP—inflation control—the new bureaucratic structure served mainly to confirm preexisting patterns of power. That the controls managed to moderate excessive wage and price rises by big business and big labor can be attributed mainly to the high pitch of public concern. Indeed, the actual function of the program was not in fact to redistribute power at all, for the controllers could not in any meaningful political sense actually *dictate* to the major interests; its function was a ritualistic one, aimed at helping to keep public attention riveted on major wage and price determinations, so as to focus the influence of public opinion and maintain it at its maximum potential for as long as possible. The chief advantage of NEP over the formally more moderate guidelines of Presidents Kennedy and Johnson lay not in the fiction that NEP gave more *power* to the president, but in the fact that NEP had superior virtues as a public-relations pageant; the legal trappings that go with power—when dramatically used—provided many more occasions for newsworthy drama and, in effect, routinized the symbolism of presidential and public concern that President Kennedy was able to generate only with such histrionic displays as his "steel crisis" scene. After the NEP's procedures for attracting public attention atrophied, the administration could get its way with industry only by adopting the same sort of White House histrionics as had proved necessary under the "jawboning" regimes of the Democrats in the 1960s.

It should be added that NEP, though grand in concept, was in part an alternative to simpler approaches that would have been more effective. Upward pressure on prices could have been fought by taking action to eliminate strategic concentrations of market power, as for example, by dropping recently erected bars to the importation of steel or automobiles, or by initiating antitrust action in these industries. Such measures, however, were apparently unthinkable; the power of the interests affected was too great. Thus, the choice of wage-price controls as the government's strategy for combating inflation was partly a government-contrived diversionary tactic, a way of keeping the public from noticing that government was (and is) *promoting* high prices through various forms of action and inaction at the behest of the same interests formally regulated by the NEP.

The experience with NEP should remind us that grand regulatory designs are not dangerous for the reasons that political conservatives have generally alleged; unconfined delegations of legal power to bureaucrats rarely enable government to intimidate and abuse the economic interests concerned; in fact, quite the opposite is true. The interests do not lose their access to the resources of persuasion, money, and organization which they had before the new law was passed.

Even if the informal structures and compromises that shape the administration of all regulatory programs were as visible as in the case of NEP, probably not very much would change in the operation of existing programs. This is so because public opinion, even when invited into the regulatory process, usually proves to be an extremely weak participant. But at least economic reformers would see more clearly than they do now how limited is the capacity of democratic government to function as more than the sum of the pressures upon it.

Most members of the literate and politically aware public have been taught the cliché that the modern state has "applied Hamiltonian methods to the achievement of Jeffersonian ends." Sadder but wiser, we now know that state regulatory activity, however reformist in inspiration, inevitably tends to become Hamiltonian in object and effect as well as in techniques.

3

A Second Paradox of Democracy: The Powerlessness of the People

The New Left of the 1960s gained notoriety late in its short life by inventing advanced guerrilla theater tactics to protest the Vietnam War. At its birth, however, the movement was more conventional. Its leaders expressed their aims through linear formulas whose level of abstraction could rival a political-science monograph. Witness the 1961 *Port Huron Statement,* founding document of what would later be recognized as the New Left:

> In a participatory democracy, the political life would be based on several root principles:
>
> That decision-making of basic social consequence be carried on by public groupings; that politics be seen positively as the art of collectively creating an acceptable pattern of social relations; that politics has the function of bringing people out of isolation and into community. . . .
>
> That the economy itself is of such social importance that its major resources and means of production should be open to democratic participation and subject to democratic social regulation.

In the long run, the goal embedded in this turgid rhetoric has probably had a wider influence than the movement's exhibitionist experiments on camera. The goal was to expand the formal frontiers of American democracy, to devise new legal forms that would enable the people to participate directly in major social decisions.

This ideal of participation for all attracted many contemporaries of Tom Hayden and Rennie Davis who went to law school at the same time that the radicals were taking to the streets. These moderates could not accept the New Left's commitment to a world without neckties. But they did join in condemning misuse of bureaucratic and corporate power. They endorsed the demand that the people should participate directly in all important political decisions.

In thus seeking to strengthen public control over government, the moderate successors to the New Left moved into the mainstream of the American populist tradition. The same participatory objective has consistently marked populist reform movements. This emphasis on direct democratic controls is a mirror image of the basic populist assumption that, because government is in form and in law the representative of the public, it ought to (and therefore, in fact, can) control powerful special interests. This same point of view is responsible for the obverse assumption—sometimes equally careless of the realities of social power in a democracy—that, because government makes decisions in the name of the people, the people should (and therefore, in fact, can and will) actively participate in the governmental process to promote their own interests.

The First Hope: Participatory Democracy
In our time, the first and most dramatic expression of this traditional populist interest in direct democratic checks on government was the concept of "participatory democracy" which originated in the *Port Huron Statement* itself. Interest in this idea sprang from disillusion with bureaucracy as an instrument

of reform; so many national and even metropolitan administrative agencies had turned out to be remote and unresponsive. Participatory democrats emphasized that all people directly affected by a decision or social issue should be able to participate directly in its resolution as stated in the charter of Students for a Democratic Society, "That the individual share in those social decisions determining the quality and direction of his life. . . ."

In the specific case of ghetto demands for inclusion in urban government agencies run by (often traditionally hostile) whites, "participatory democracy" served as a rallying cry for the affirmation of traditional symbolic ethnic politics (and the application of the principle to nonwhites). In cases where black control was sought, the concept represented a kind of Calhounian solution to the problem of oppression by the social majority.

But as a general answer to the remoteness and unresponsiveness of bureaucratic systems, especially at the national level, participatory democracy was irrelevant. It was applicable, even in theory, only to very small-scale decision making, like the model of the New England town meeting. This fact did not immediately dull the enthusiasm of many reformers for the participatory concept, or for its watered-down cousin—decentralization. SDS leader Tom Hayden and Mark Pilisuk argued in 1965 that many major national decisions could and should be determined in part by constituent participation in small local meetings; ". . . the voice of the unemployed urban worker may have to be heard," they contended, ". . . on decisions about where a particular major corporation will be relocated and where the major resource allocations of the country will be invested."[1] More moderate activists conceded the possibility that direct participation would only be useful in local government decision making, but urged therefore that the jurisdiction of governments should be reduced: "The general guide should be," Richard Goodwin gravely counseled from the *New Yorker* as late as 1969, "to transfer power to the smallest unit consistent with the scale of the problem."[2]

Understandably, few operative results followed such suggestions. It has become clear, by now, that participatory democracy was not a corrective, even in principle, for the undemocratic features of most large-scale bureaucratic decision making.

The Second Hope: Participation by Group Representatives

Participatory democracy therefore gave way to less radical-seeming but more practical alternatives. One was the concept of participation by groups affected by decisions, through representatives. The Project of Corporate Responsibility urged that this concept be applied to the internal government of big corporations. In 1971, the second round of Campaign GM proposed to shareholders that "each of GM's three [other] most important constituencies—consumers, dealers, and employees—[have] the right to select a director from among their number to represent them."[3] Other reformers have invoked the representative concept of participation in bringing public-interest challenges to the actions of regulatory bureaucracies. These groups have secured from the federal courts one of the most fundamental advances yet engineered by the new populist movement, the concept that representative citizens have a right, in law, to participate in the federal administrative process. In a landmark ruling in 1966 by Chief Justice Burger, then a member of the U.S. Court of Appeals for the District of Columbia Circuit, the FCC was ordered to permit representatives of the black community in Jackson, Mississippi, to appear as parties and challenge the renewal of the television broadcasting license of station WLBT. Burger held that "Experience demonstrates consumers are generally among the best vindicators of the public interest," and ruled that "responsible and representative groups [were henceforth] eligible to intervene before the Commission,"[4] and, by implication, before all other federal agencies.

In practice, of course, the exercise of the important right granted by Justice Burger has meant that only those "groups" that happened to be organized in the first place ended up participating. As often as not, the impetus to organize comes from the would-be representatives rather than from the group in whose name they speak. There is relatively little actual grass-roots group participation in the representative enterprise. This is especially true when the problem is a nationwide matter such as food labeling regulations at USDA, rather than a community problem such as the renewal of WLBT's broadcast license at the FCC.

Nevertheless, this new accent on participation in the law has given federal regulators the first public-oriented challenge they have ever had to face. Even though group representation in court and administrative litigation is not actually participatory in any strict sense, the effects of the new development have been important.

Public-interest litigation as a surrogate for participatory government has worked because the courts and the law are there as checks. They can prevent individuals or organizations who have no direct ties to their mass constituency from abusing their purported representative status merely in order to gain a platform. But the idea cannot work where there is no such impartial observer to whom would-be representatives can be made accountable in any meaningful way. They cannot in fact be controlled by the very groups that they purport to represent. If the public constituency could organize sufficiently to hold accountable its new self-appointed representatives, then presumably it could have organized earlier. But if it had, there would be no need for the new representatives; the constituency would have been able—all along—to look out for its interests itself.

Outside the public-interest litigation area, new populist enthusiasts have frequently been reluctant to come to terms with this fact. For example, Campaign GM's proposal that consumers vote for a representative director would surely produce an overwhelming show of indifference; if consumers rarely read informational labels or send in to a company material necessary to put the company's warranty into effect, how can it be imagined that they could become meaningfully involved in the process of selecting representative directors?

Since meaningful political choice by consumers and other such disparate constituencies is impossible, the only people who can select public representative directors are the same people who select the regular directors—corporate managers themselves. And such house rebels are not likely to be too vigilant in their scrutiny of management behavior. It is therefore not surprising that, since the Project on Corporate Responsibility first proposed the idea of constituency representation on corporate boards, at least seventy major corporations have placed an "independent" woman or a black on their board.

In what one hopes is a less serious vein, the *New Yorker* offered, in the spring of 1972, a proposal that similarly underscores how intractable is the problem of making representative organizations directly accountable to their constituencies. The idea was the establishment of a special five-dollar per taxpayer assessment to go to a "Citizens' Lobby," which would be "completely independent of the government and which would act for citizens precisely as, say, the oil lobby acts for the petroleum industry." According to the author of this notion, accountability would be assured by attaching to tax forms a questionnaire. The questionnaire would "[touch] on various issues of the day. . . . For example, 'Do you think we should get out of the war in Southeast Asia? Should the federal government take vigorous action against all those who pollute our air and water?' " Unfortunately, the proposal does not show how "citizens" could select the staff to run the Citizens' Lobby, nor does the *New Yorker* explain who would decide what the questions on the tax forms should be.[5] If the IRS—which tried in the fall of 1970 to cripple public-interest law firms by withdrawing their tax exempt status—drew up the questions, they would obviously not be the ones the *New Yorker* would like to see asked.

The Third Hope: Direct Election

In many situations where democratic objections to the exercise of power by remote elites have been raised, it is patently clear that direct participation of any sort is not feasible. In some of these cases, expanded use of popular elections has been offered as a substitute. This has been especially true with respect to the presidential selection process; angered by their inability to control party officials unsympathetic to their antiadministration, antiwar views in 1968, peace democrats inspired and, in a variety of instances, sought and often achieved a kaleidoscope of guarantees of public participation, restrictions on party elites, and a nearly adopted constitutional amendment to replace the electoral college with a direct popular vote.

Apart from moves to democratize the presidential election machinery, the desire to expand the range of electoral decision has been applied to a variety of metropolitan bureaucracies. Those involved in administering new federal programs to aid the poor became the targets of often successful demands to substitute neighborhood election for centralized administrative appointment as the means of selecting managers.

Both in the case of primaries for major political offices, and in the case of direct election of urban bureaucratic supervisors, advocates of greater use of elections have run up against the stubborn fact that people often do not vote. Take for example the efforts of the Johnson Administration to bring direct democracy to the urban poor. The philosophical heart of the "war on poverty" was the requirement of Section 202(a)(3) of the Economic Opportunity Act of 1964 that Community Action Programs be conducted with "maximum feasible participation" of the poor people served by the program. This provision was seized upon, as Leonard Chazen has recounted, as "a mandate for federal assistance in the effort to create political organizations of the poor."[6] Then four years after passage of the Economic Opportunity Act, the more ambitious Model Cities legislation also deferred to participationist ideology. It required that funding proposals submitted by individual cities be contingent on a showing of "widespread citizen participation in the program."

As it turned out, the hopes (and fears) invested in these reforms proved baseless. Giving people the right to participate did not assure that they would participate. Community elections held under the Community Action and Model Cities programs drew astonishingly small turnouts, even in comparison with traditional primaries and other elections of little public interest. A recent study by Lewis Kaden and Michael Schwartz of the impact of these programs in New York City showed that, in the 1970 elections to Community Action Boards, in neighborhoods whose population in 1965 was 2,199,613 and the number of eligible voters was estimated at 1.2 million, a mere 29,728 individuals voted. During the following year Model Cities elections were held in the city's three areas under the jurisdiction of the Model Cities program—Central Harlem, Bedford-Stuyvesant, and the South Bronx; the turnout was 5,976. Understandably, Kaden and Schwartz conclude that "these results indicate little participation except by those closely associated with the programs' delegate agencies, their immediate friends and families. . . . [Elections] are substantially fruitless methods of providing participation [in government programs to aid poor urban communities]."

As a result of voter indifference, those shifts in power that do occur when direct election regimes are imposed, do not necessarily produce a system more representative of the views (or the interests) of those affected. Indeed, the systems often produce decisions that are *less* representative; they systematically confer disproportionate power on relatively interested and well-organized groups who can "turn out the vote," or they simply produce arbitrary results, which vary wildly from one election to the next, and award victory to candidates with unrepresentative views. Here again, in an effort to extend formal democracy, reformers have come up against the underlying sociological foundations of power.

Mass Politics: The Illusory Adventure

If this inclination to overestimate the public's appetite for governmental participation has discredited some new populist reforms after their enactment, its most detrimental impact has been on strategies for establishing reform. Because reforms that promise to curb special interests are in the interest of the public, it is assumed that the public—and often only the public —can be persuaded to support them. Therefore, the projected strategy for achieving reform inevitably assumes the shape of past efforts: a national campaign to stir intense—if momentary —public interest, culminating in enactment of major legislative changes. "You can't have a mass movement," Fred Harris said when he started his abortive presidential campaign, "without the masses." A corollary of this notion, and evidently Senator Harris's premise in jumping into the race, is that populism will pay off at the polls. By standing up for the interests of the general public against the interests of the wealthy and powerful, a political candidate will gain the support of the public he is pledging himself to aid. Newfield and Greenfield explicitly touted their populist program as a presidential campaign strategy. It was, they believed, a way to build a "new majority" on the debris of the old New Deal coalition. Senator McGovern followed their advice. But populism, it turned out, had surprising shortcomings as a campaign strategy. The surprise consisted not so much in McGovern losing the election, as in what happened to his populism while the campaign was still in progress.

Efforts to play up trustbusting and strict regulation of business never became more than a leitmotif for the campaign; polls indicated that these themes never swung many voters to McGovern's side. The one populist theme that did become a major part of the McGovern program was, of course, his tax-welfare proposals for the redistribution of income. In great measure, the political failure of this program has to be read as a final judgment on income redistribution as a campaign theme in national politics.

As presented during the primaries, the Demogrant plan would have assured that any family of four with an income of $12,000 or less per year would literally pay no federal taxes. This was surely a radical idea, but its radical features lay in the fact that it was designed to provide substantial economic benefits to the middle class and especially to the lower middle class, not merely to the poor; after all, President Nixon's own Family Assistance Plan was designed to redistribute at least some income to the poor. But even though it was designed to fatten the pocketbook of middle America, the Demogrant plan turned out to be an albatross. After the primaries the Democrats' economists were sent back to the drawing boards. Their new plan amounted merely to a patching up of some of the standard tax loopholes and a guaranteed annual income for the poor; it was President Nixon's plan in principle, but greater in amount.

There seems to be one conclusion to draw from the fate of the original Demogrant plan: the prospective winners were not interested enough in the benefits the plan offered to offset the antagonism of the prospective losers. The latter were fewer in number by far, but the fuss they put up pulled more weight. This—superficially undemocratic—result obtained, even though the forum of decision was a plebiscite, where each person's vote counts equally.[7]

Obviously, the problem of building or using mass support for populist measures against special interests becomes far more difficult when the forum is an administrative agency or the Congress rather than a direct election. An index of just how difficult collective public action in such contexts can be is provided by the extraordinary situation at the Civil Aeronautics Board. Much of the impetus for creating this agency came from the big four airlines (American, TWA, United, and Eastern), who sought through regulation to do what the railroads, the telephone company, and others had done before them—to stabilize their market shares through the creation of a government-sponsored cartel. According to Michael Levine, writing in 1965, this objective has been so thoroughly fulfilled that, since the Civil Aeronautics Act was passed in 1938, "Not one carrier has been certificated to perform domestic trunk service which was not operating on May 14, 1938. . . ."[8] The impact on consumers of this government-promoted monopoly can be gauged by the disparity between the CAB-regulated price of a ticket between Washington, D.C., and New York, on the one hand, and on the other the price of a ticket between Los Angeles and San Francisco, where rates are unregulated and fixed by free competition, since the route is *intra*state and beyond the jurisdiction of the board. Flying from Los Angeles to San Francisco costs about 60 percent of the price of a trip from Washington to New York—even though the distance between the latter two points is only about 60 percent as great!

These facts have been well-known for years. Yet consumers of airline services have never made any move to abolish the official cartel managed by the CAB, or even to try to participate in CAB proceedings to obtain more consumer-oriented rulings on specific issues. Ralph Nader's Aviation Consumer Action Project, which was founded in 1971, is the first institutionalized effort to assert the consumer interest at the board, but it is not in any sense a mass organization. The absence of consumer organizations to counter the influence of the airlines is perhaps especially remarkable when one considers the professional and social status of consumers of airline services. They are not by any means the atomized, guileless poor who declined to participate in community action elections. They are, in large measure, officials of corporations, men who are relatively well-off, and relatively well-versed in the value of organization for the pursuit of a collective good. Of course, it may be argued that it is not the officials but their employers who pick up the tab for this use of airline services. But if that is true, then the public injured by the airlines' government-sponsored cartel consists mainly of corporate America itself! Yet the fact remains that, with the exception of the gadfly activities of Nader's cadre and a few consumer advocates in Congress, nothing has been done.

In any event, whether or not Nader succeeds in making fundamental changes in airline regulations, it should be as clear to his CAB gadflies as it now is to Senators Harris and McGovern that the notion of relying on a mass movement has serious defects.

Consistent with new populist rhetoric, it is true in many (though by no means all) cases that current struggles to master corporate power pit the interests of the general public against the interests of more or less narrow elites such as corporations or industries and their satellite constituencies. But just because the welfare of the masses is at stake, it does not follow that the masses must, or can, or should play an exclusive or even a leading role in the process of securing the protection of their welfare. Part of the difficulty is that mass concern is easily appeased and swiftly dissipated. Although Senator Harris has said, "I just don't believe that President Nixon's television proclamations could convince the American people that he had a serious new program to attack water pollution," the polls indicated otherwise; the people were apparently convinced by the president's pageantry. But a more illuminating way to view the matter is to note that most new populist issues are generally not the first or second most important political issues to most people; they usually rank no better than third or fourth.

The lever of power on which mass political techniques ultimately rely, namely the power to withhold or grant votes in an election, is inherently an ineffective way to promote third- or fourth-ranking public concerns, even if they are widely held. Social choice through elections is necessarily crude, at least in comparison with the individuated choices that can be made through the market. In the marketplace, individuals can use their power (*i.e.,* their money) *when* they want to, toward the acquisition of each specific item they want, in amounts that are *precisely ranked* according to their importance to the acquirer (set off against the expense that others must incur to supply the items). But elections are much more cumbersome. An election allows individuals to choose one candidate but not, normally, specific policies, and it requires that the choice be made at a particular time. In this situation, candidates (including incumbents) correctly believe that their constituents will vote according to their stand on only a very limited number of issues ranked uppermost in the constituents' minds at the time the election is held.

To be sure, candidates may partially counter this prognosis by calculating that third- or fourth-ranked issues may swing *some* votes, and that in a close election every note is worth trying for; or they may calculate that an opponent can easily neutralize their favorable standing on the primary issues by copying their stand, and that therefore it will pay to take a favorable stand on a relatively less important issue.

But, in general, voters and politicians do not behave this way. In elections, the big issues count and the middle issues tend to be forgotten. Strategies that ultimately depend on elections to vindicate mass interests with respect to such middle-range issues are generally doomed to rude disappointment. This is especially true if, as is the case with many new populist concerns, the special interest involved is capable of withholding or granting campaign support, in the form of field workers, money, or other resources. Such aid is often worth more votes than standing up for the public interest, even where such a stand is favored by the overwhelming majority of the candidate's constituents.

One could object that the problem is not inherent in the structure of democratic political choice, but is merely a function of transitory popular consciousness. Once new populist propaganda educates the public to achieve a more sophisticated understanding of the causes of society's ills, this argument goes, the system will prove responsive to new populist concerns. Although the public now defines "prosperity" and "inflation" as its uppermost concerns, reeducation will produce acceptance of the new populist contention that the structure as well as the level of economic activity is important, and that the people cannot enjoy the fruits of abundance unless they direct their political representatives to take appropriate steps to democratize control over the power of various producer interests to fix prices, restrict output, freeze development, and inflict external costs like pollution and physical injury on the public.

There is something to this argument. New populism has produced astonishing changes in public perception of the role of structure in the nation's political economy. Public suspicion of industries and bureaucracies in general, and certain industries, like automobiles and medicine, in particular, has risen dramatically; and the rhetoric and the substance of politics has shifted as a result. Moreover, the effects of such a change of consciousness need not be completely ephemeral. Even if in ten years the population has lost its relatively intense concern about corporate power as an issue, people will still *remember* the kind of rhetoric associated with the present period if a reform politician invokes it at some point in the future; and a whole new process of education, such as Nader and his imitators have engineered, will not be necessary, at least for some decades. That fact alone will make the process of checking the power of special interests through government action much easier than it was in 1955 or 1965.

From Mass Crusade to Grand Design
Still, even though sustained propaganda campaigns can greatly increase public receptivity to populist causes, this process of consciousness-raising cannot alter the features of democratic government that make it ultimately an unreliable curb on special interests. For, although such issues as safe auto design and inflated health costs have become substantial public concerns in our time, they are nevertheless too narrow to become, at least for more than a moment, the nation's *most* important concerns; it is not likely that a presidential election will turn on issues such as these—though for some voters, they could well play a decisive role. But in order to put the career of many

congressmen or the fate of an administration at stake, it would be necessary to dislodge "prosperity" or "peace" or "crime" or whatever the issue of the voters' first concern happens to be.

To do this, it would be necessary to *aggregate* specific, narrower issues like auto safety or health costs. "Prosperity," for example, is itself just such an aggregate term, in which many specific questions are subsumed. Broad generalities like prosperity are necessarily selected as major campaign themes. Not only are they inclusive and vague enough to appeal to many different voters with distinct problems and concerns, they are also an imperative simply because the people are not capable of keeping more refined and complex definitions of issues in their heads.

But a pledge to restore prosperity is innocuous; it commits a candidate to no particular attack on any particular problem. For the same reason, any new populist substitute for prosperity or crime or peace as the main issue of the day would also provide candidates with a chance to make a substantially innocuous commitment. To find a new populist equivalent of these major themes of the day, the key would have to become a similar aggregate, like "corporate power." But if reformers become involved in a campaign aimed at convincing the public that they should be gravely concerned with "corporate power" as a general phenomenon, they will be driven to devising a program that can be billed as a general response to this general problem. Rather than address their efforts to specific remedies for specific situations where corporate power can be said to be causing social harm, they will struggle to enact broad laws replete with glittering generalities, but lacking in concrete commitments. They will in short find themselves fighting for a new and especially vacuous grand design.

The Roots of Powerlessness
Thus, participationist formulas and bureaucratic grand designs both aim to increase the ability of the public to control

special interests. But in a sense both prescriptions presume the nonexistence of the condition they are supposed to cure; they depend for success on the assumption that the "public" can be activated in the political process. It is difficult for many well-intentioned Americans to accept this pattern of nonparticipation as permanent and ineradicable. Yet, on the basis of experience alone, it seems safe to say that to a greater or lesser extent, the inability of large public constituencies to mobilize their potential resources for effective political participation seems an inherent condition of democracy.

In particular, large public constituencies do not readily promote their interests through the formation of the kind of disciplined, well-financed organizations that are necessary to ensure that legislative designs will become working regulatory institutions. We know little about why this is so, because social scientists—in common with activists—traditionally have been unwilling to accept the public's political anemia as a fact, and then to examine it clinically. But one recent exception, Princeton economist Mancur Olson, argues that the absence of strong public organizations to offset business and labor reflects a kind of natural law of political economy.[9] Olson points out that, strictly speaking, it is not in the self-interest of individual members of a group to pay the costs in time, labor, and money necessary to form organizations capable of political activity on behalf of the group. Others can do the donkey work of organizing and the lazy individual member can still benefit from their efforts.

In a narrow, economist's sense, he will thus be "better off" than if he had contributed. Since every individual knows that all others in the group share this disincentive to contribute, his own doubts about the worth of *his* making any sacrifices are magnified. How can one know, after all, whether others will contribute enough to make the joint enterprise a success?

It is obvious that the difficulty of exchanging mutually credible reassurances increases rapidly with the size of the group in question. Therefore, Olson concludes, it is *logically* as well as physically implausible to expect large groups to organize to protect their common interests. And, as a matter of history, he contends, the only instances of large groups that have organized, such as labor, professional, and agricultural interests, have involved some measure of *coercion* (usually government-sponsored), or the use of gimmicks promising *individualized* as well as joint benefits.

Olson may have somewhat overstated his case in view of the plethora of potent and disciplined associations involving many members in atomized industries and professional groups. Nevertheless, the theory is provocative. At the very least, it seems safe to say that efforts at large-scale political organization overcome Olson's "law" only when a constituency shares either a strong professional or occupational interest or a very strong ideological or religious faith. Interests, including economic interests, outside these categories, are also outside organized politics. They exist almost exclusively as temporary public enthusiasms, sometimes capable of defeating candidates, or of eliciting legislation and rhetoric from officials. But rarely do they match the American Medical Association (AMA) or the United Steelworkers of America or the American Farm Bureau Federation in bending government to serve their interests affirmatively, rather than just talk about them. Indeed, the failure of many large public constituencies even to avail themselves of the chance to make the minimal personal sacrifice of casting an informed vote on behalf of group concerns could be seen to be the extreme, but logical, extension of Olson's theory. At least it should serve as one more strong reminder that reform schemes that demand far greater levels of group organization and participation than mere elections must be regarded with very great skepticism.

For want of such skepticism, populist reform strategies have often foundered. The fact is that for most political purposes, most of the time, the "majority," the "public," the "people," is a shadowy and ephemeral presence. Walter Lippman may have overstated the point when he wrote *The Phantom Public* in 1925, but the public is surely more elusive than conventional democratic theory assumes it to be.

The Myth of Conspiracy

We should pay attention to one final disability created by the preference of new populist reformers to think in terms of mass political strategies. Concentrating on such approaches reinforces a perverse habit of thought common to reformers of all eras, which causes them to underestimate the strength and endurance of their opposition. Reformers tend to identify their antagonists as a small, malevolent elite, conspiring against the masses. The aficionados of contemporary populism are no exception. They are not prone to admit, even to themselves, that the interested parties in many issues of concern to the new populists are more nearly opposed alliances of classes and other interests. And they are far less likely to concede that their own interest might in some situations be class based.

For example, environmentalist reform is now cast as a drama of the public versus a few huge corporations; the fact is, however, that environmental protection may threaten labor groups and slum residents as much as narrowly based corporate interests, and it may benefit identifiable, often relatively wealthy, classes or neighborhoods (where the liberal environmental leaders themselves happen to live). Indeed, the phrase "corporate power" not infrequently appears in new populist rhetoric as a kind of code word for all forces aligned against new populist positions, many of which are not in fact large corporations, or even businesses.

By thus imagining that the problem is simply a set of disinterested reformers or bureaucrats representing the general public versus a narrow corporate cabal, reformers now and in the past have been able to view the conflict simply as a matter of *power*, rather than as a conflict of *values*. More important, reformers have hidden from themselves and others just how formidable (how "powerful") antireform forces really are and how impervious to all but formal, superficial change the status quo may be. The fact is that, myths about corporate power notwithstanding, a few huge corporations are often *less* capable of defending their interests than organizations of numerous small units, such as labor unions, professional associations, atomistic industries, or governmental subdivisions reflecting regional or class concerns. Candidate McGovern rarely missed a chance to take a swipe at the Nixon Administration's deal with ITT. But he almost never mentioned another, equally corrupt bargain struck by Nixon with powerful special interests—the White House's decision to give dairy farmers a price increase in exchange for campaign contributions. The reason for McGovern's caution was clear enough. Farmers have votes. ITT does not.

The often-surprising strength of organizations comprising many small units rests in part on their access to certain positive assets one or two large corporations cannot as easily command—community contacts, armies of campaign workers, and election votes. In part, however, the power of widely dispersed groups, especially their power to *resist* unwanted regulatory initiatives, lies in the simple fact that they are fragmented. It is vastly more difficult to monitor and discipline retail food stores than it is to monitor and discipline General Foods or Procter & Gamble. Indeed, big business is sometimes *easier* to regulate than small business. For an ironic illustration, there is, again, Richard Nixon's NEP.

The theory of NEP is that big business and big labor have outgrown market constraints, so that government must step in and control them. Accordingly, Phase II established strict controls (in principle) over prices charged by the nation's 1,300 largest corporations, leaving the rest of the nation's businesses to looser scrutiny. Liberals like TRB assume, as they have been instructed to assume by Professor Galbraith, that the reason for controlling the giant companies is that their power makes them directly responsible for inflation. TRB notes that these companies, with sales of more than $100 million annually, account for 90 percent of the manufacturing assets of the nation; therefore, control them and you successfully control the economy.

But over 50 percent of the economy involves *services,* most of which are highly atomized industries. A great deal of the recent inflation has in fact stemmed from these service industries, some of it due to traditional supply and demand imbalances, as in the case of repairs for television sets and autos, and some of it due to the power of relevant interest groups to use government to promote their quest for less competition and more income, as in the cases of health-care delivery and municipal services.

But despite the fact that much inflation originates in sectors of the economy where big business does not hold sway, it still makes sense to aim price controls at the largest corporations. In the first place, it is possible, from an administrative and political standpoint, to maintain some measure of compliance with regulatory standards in concentrated industries. For hairdressers and doctors, government employees and clothiers, controls could never be enforced. In the second place, the people *believe* that big business and big labor have caused inflation (and in some important instances, like steel and automobiles, of course, they are right); therefore, insofar as general "inflationary psychology" is the target of government policy, curbing wage-and-price increases in concentrated sectors should help to *convince* the public that the controls are working and this may ultimately make them work in fact.

But if this is true, it is neither because inflation is exclusively or even mainly caused by excessive corporate power, if that means the power of giant companies, nor because government controls are able to "redress the balance" by "checking" public power with private power. It is, rather, that purporting to control big business pricing practices is an essential part of the stagecraft, the pageantry, of stabilizing the consumer price index. And stagecraft is at the heart of any program to "manage" the economy through wage-price controls—as indeed, stagecraft is at the heart of virtually all populist designs to master the few on behalf of the many.

4
The Pageant of Reform

It is no criticism of the president's management of his NEP to say that his principal concern has been with stagecraft. On the contrary, Nixon's deft maneuvering showed that he understands what it takes to make populist programs work. Persuasion is the sole means of influence populist leaders can command. Their access to money and organization, the two components of "power," is usually limited and precarious. To prevail over opponents who wield real power, populist leaders must gain the approval of the public. To reach them, it is essential to dramatize the message by stagecraft or pageantry.

John Kenneth Galbraith, in one of his many satiric attacks on big business, quipped recently that the economy requires "organized bamboozlement" to function.[1] Ironically, however, the political forces with which Galbraith is frequently allied are far more dependent than are most businesses on public-relations tactics which, while they may not constitute "bamboozlement," certainly emphasize theatrics as much as simple reason. Tactics differ but the basic strategy is the same. If the populist leader is a housewife trying to block highway construction near her home, she must get attention by engaging in acts of civil disobedience at the construction site. If the leader is a clever but impecunious consumer advocate, he dispatches three clean-cut students to return a prickly critique of the FTC, hoping that the agency chairman will respond with a public fury that will nicely serve to dramatize and confirm the students' charges to a nationwide television audience. If he is a young lawyer concerned about the power of large corporations, he orchestrates a campaign to obtain shareholder approval for resolutions binding General Motors to policies more responsive to consumer, environmental, and minority interests —a campaign which, precisely because it is destined to fail, will show how frail are traditional legal controls over GM's management group. And even if he is the president of the United States, it is necessary to keep public opinion at a high pitch by well-designed regulatory rituals and carefully staged confrontations.

Politics Without Power

It may seem bizarre that the president of the United States, the most powerful man in the world, must resort to flimflammery to counter a Roger Blough or a George Meany. But it is precisely because the president is a democratic official that he is vulnerable to the organizational and financial resources available to such men and to the interests they represent or ally themselves with. Lesser officials in the federal and other governments within the United States must, in general, be far more wary of the power of special interests than the president. Holding office, at any level of government, does not change the fact that populist reform is in essence an exercise in *politics without power*. It is a politics of public persuasion, as distinguished from administration or even bargaining.

To put the point another way, the formal distinction between enacting a program into law, on the one hand, and "enforcing" or "implementing" or "administering" a law once it has been enacted, on the other, corresponds little with the realities of regulation. Populist legislative campaigns emphasize the need to pass "strong" regulatory laws—grand designs that provide their administrators with broad discretionary authority and harsh sanctions. But these paper legal powers often confer almost no usable political or administrative power. An official who takes charge of a regulatory program with the aim of achieving its populist goals will soon find that, from his standpoint, the administrative process is not very different from the legislative process. Passing the law has not dramatically affected the terms of struggle or the relative power of the combatants. Typically, the regulator has little organized support outside his agency. Often he cannot even count on the fidelity of his own subordinates. Unless the interests affected by the program wish to cooperate, agency officials find themselves quite unable to decide what rules to promulgate in order to implement the law, let alone to execute their decisions. If the agency wants the program to succeed at all, it will soon find itself dependent in large measure on the same strategic use of stagecraft that put the law on the books in the first place.

In particular, reformist officials face three distinct obstacles in implementing populist programs. The first of these obstacles is the raw political power that a regulated interest may be able to exercise. If the president wants to force his agriculture secretary to grant milk producers a price increase in exchange for campaign contributions, there is little the secretary can do —unless he was clever enough to dramatize the price issue before the crisis developed—thus putting his own and the president's integrity publicly on the line. In doing so he might tie the president's hands.

But even if a reformist regulator does not have to worry about the danger of political subversion, he still faces two additional administrative roadblocks. In the first place, he will immediately find that he cannot make crucial decisions without extensive and sophisticated information about the state of affairs in the industry. Most of the time, the industry will turn out to be the only repository of such information. Industry leaders will rarely be inclined to give this information up. Of course, in anticipation of this difficulty, Congress may well have provided the agency with broad investigatory and subpoena powers. But by itself such legal authority is rarely very useful. Even without simply suppressing documents—which is illegal, but impossible to prevent—the industry's lawyers can frustrate the regulators' search for information almost interminably—especially since the agency almost always begins by not knowing exactly what it wants. The industry can give over too little information, and thus force the agency to keep coming back for more. Or it can achieve almost the same effect by handing over too much data for the regulators to cope with. When, for example, AT&T says it is entitled to a price increase, a state regulatory commission can be made to pay dearly if it insists on a full hearing and investigation before granting the increase; the massive public utility can paralyze the agency simply by turning over rooms full of undigested and perhaps irrelevant data for the agency's tiny staff to examine and evaluate.

For the agency, the trick is to force the industry to turn over just the right amount of information (in a form that is intelligible and pertinent) in order to make a rational decision. Only through the adroit orchestrating of public pressures—through hearings, demands, denunciations—can the goal be attained.

Finally, once the decision about how to implement a regulatory statute in a substantive manner is made, the agency faces a third obstacle: enforcement. Detecting violations of the agency's new rules may be just as difficult as, or even more difficult than, compiling the information necessary to promulgate the rules. Policing is usually a gigantic task that would overwhelm the agency's enforcement staff if it were taken seriously—which it usually is not. Compelling obedience or punishing disobedience when a willful violator is discovered is often a cumbersome and ultimately a futile proceeding.

In part, these chronic administrative difficulties are reflections of the political weakness of populist reform programs. Reformers can get laws passed, but they cannot sustain the pitch of public enthusiasm—or public sophistication—necessary to get the programs funded at a level adequate to make enforcement feasible. The regulated interests are shrewd and strong enough to maintain control over the legislative committees that have oversight and appropriations authority.

But in many cases the costs of meaningful enforcement would be so exorbitant that even the reformers themselves might think twice before appropriating them; this is especially true where there are many small units and low-visibility activities and transactions to police. This frequent defect in regulatory programs is one more symptom of the grand design mentality: traditionally, reformers' eyes have been bigger than their stomachs. They have fought for laws that pay expansive rhetorical homage to their goals. But they have neither had the political resources, nor been willing to appropriate the funds necessary to achieve their goals.

Unfortunately, some recently enacted new populist programs are showing signs of these infirmities. For example, in the spring of 1972, difficulties were revealed in EPA's efforts to control automobile emissions in an incident involving the Ford Motor Company. During the 50,000-mile durability tests on prototype 1973 model Pintos required by EPA, Ford engineers had tinkered 101 times with the cars' pollution control equipment, thus violating agency rules designed to make the test runs simulate normal maintenance and driving patterns. Sensing a threat to the integrity of its programs, EPA moved with remarkable vigor to punish Ford by levying a $7 million fine. But, despite this tough attitude, two *Wall Street Journal* investigative reporters, Charles Camp and Walter Mossberg, discovered that government and industry officials felt that the episode cast doubt on the agency's ability "to enforce the mounds of anti-pollution regulations it has heaped on the industry in recent years." The agency had, in fact, only ten employees to monitor the entire testing and car certification programs of all domestic and foreign auto makers. Not that a bigger staff would have solved the problem. Agency officials admitted that they would not be able to discover whether company engineers had tampered with test cars even if they examined each engine—since tampering could involve something as simple as a "quick turn of a screw." "As it stands now," the two reporters concluded, "the auto makers themselves, at great cost in time and money, are ultimately the chief enforcers of the standards they are supposed to meet, and federal regulators hopelessly outgunned can do little more than monitor the industry's self-regulation."[2]

It is a rare regulatory program that could not be described in similar terms. Where the interests supposed to be "controlled" by the program won't cooperate, the regulators are little better off—they have little more "power"—than the legislators who put the law on the statute books in the first place.

Stagecraft and Consumer Protection in New York City

A case study from my own short experience as a municipal regulator may help to illustrate the fragility of populist programs, and their dependence on stagecraft to succeed. When I joined Commissioner Bess Myerson's staff in New York City's new Department of Consumer Affairs in early 1969, the idea of "unit pricing" was a key objective within the consumer movement. Unit pricing was supposed to help shoppers cope with the difficulties of rational choice, by forcing retailers to display the "price per measure"—per pound or per foot or per serving—of their products. With unit prices displayed, consumers would be less likely to be fooled by deceptive titles (giant, large, family, economy, medium) or packages of noncomparable size (⅞ pound, 73¼ ounces, 34 inches per roll, ⅔ yard per roll, etc.). Senator Philip Hart had tried to impose unit pricing on a nationwide basis as part of the Fair Packaging and Labeling ("Truth in Packaging") Act of 1966, but he had been stopped by strong opposition from food manufacturers and retailers.

In April, 1969 Commissioner Myerson and her staff considered whether they should try to bring unit pricing to New York City. They confronted two basic difficulties. The first was a question of authority. The relevant law did not make clear whether the Department of Consumer Affairs could simply promulgate a regulation (after going through the required process of notification to affected parties through publication in the City Record) *decreeing* that unit pricing would be required in the city's 8,000 grocery stores, or whether it was obliged merely to go to the City Council and request that such a requirement be enacted as legislation. The second difficulty was to know whether unit pricing was in fact a sound idea after all.

Though they believed that unit pricing would bring benefits to consumers by helping them save money through rational choosing, the agency's staff did not know how much it would cost to put a unit-pricing system into practice. Here they were helpless. All data necessary for devising reliable estimates of the prospective costs of unit pricing were under the control of the supermarket industry. Before the consumer officials could responsibly decide to launch a unit-pricing program on their own, or suggest to the legislature that it enact such a requirement, they needed to obtain the necessary information from the industry itself.

Thus, it seemed that the department was left with no alternative but to go to the City Council and recommend that hearings be held to see whether a unit-pricing law was worth the costs retailers would run up (and pass on to their customers). But this did not seem to be a very promising course. Unit pricing was something no one on the council or in the press or the public had ever heard of. There would be no pressure to pass it, and strong industry pressure against it. Moreover, because of their opposition, it was clear that they would not divulge information in council hearings that would make unit-pricing seem easy or cheap, whatever the real estimates. Industry representatives maintained to the department that they did not have any way of making hard forecasts about unit-pricing costs, and they uniformly refused to provide the department with what information they did have.

Faced with the near certainty that a request to the legislature would get nowhere, Commissioner Myerson decided to go forward on her own, despite the fact that at this early stage the Department of Consumer Affairs did not have enough information to be confident that unit pricing was a sound measure and might not have the authority to promulgate a unit-pricing regulation. Her strategy was to force the industry to yield the information necessary for a sound decision on the merits, by generating public support for unit pricing, and by bluffing that she was prepared to promulgate a unit-pricing regulation in any event, unless they disclosed sufficient data to evaluate their case against it. If the department eventually lost a lawsuit over its authority to promulgate the regulation, she would turn to the City Council and ask for legislation. But she hoped that combat with the industry would focus enough attention on the issue and create enough public support to make it possible to pass the statute by the time legislative action became necessary.

Her strategy worked. Successful hearings packaged by the department's special counsel, Harriet Rabb, convinced the industry that the agency was serious about unit pricing and that it could attract a following among the press and the public. They then relented on the matter of access to data, selecting several typical stores in which Mrs. Rabb's staff could analyze the current costs of price-marking and stocking functions.

This research produced a report that concluded the current cost of price-marking and stocking functions was between .75 percent and 1.5 percent of gross sales, and that unit pricing could not add significantly to the cost of performing these operations—even assuming that none of the increased costs were offset by decreased advertising or other expenditures. With some fanfare, the department released this report at a press conference at which Commissioner Myerson announced that a regulation had been "promulgated" as of that day requiring unit-price posting on selected grocery products sold at retail prices within the city.

Before the regulation could legally take hold, however, a sixty-day delay was required. Pleas for further delays by the industry were accepted, during which time there was some public squabbling as well as intensive but, as it turned out, insincere private negotiating; at length, the industry challenged the department in court and after the usual delays won a decision invalidating the unit-pricing regulation as unauthorized by any statutory authority. However, by that time, passage of a unit-pricing statute by the City Council could be counted on. Also, the battle between Commissioner Myerson and the retail food industry had become a major news story in the city. When she said through a departmental press release, on receiving the industry's legal complaint, that "the masters of the food industry did not tell the truth to me, and they do not want to sell the truth to the consumer," newspaper and television editorialists rallied behind her, and there was every evidence that the public was behind her too. Even the judge who ruled that the regulation was unauthorized, commended the purpose of the program and suggested that the council give the department the authority to reinstate it. The council enthusiastically did so. Finally convinced that its low standing in the public's esteem would only assure an eventual, similar defeat in the state legislature, the industry did not challenge the new city law as unauthorized by New York State's tight restrictions on the city's municipal powers of home rule (even though they might have won such a suit, or at least delayed unit pricing for another year or so).

Populism in Authority:
The Weakness of Government Reformers

The stagecraft that New York City's Consumer Affairs staff used to put across its unit-pricing project was, of course, subdued compared with the tactics to which other governmental reformers have had to resort to combat powerful industry lobbies. Even during the halcyon days of the New Deal, when business was supposedly on the run in Washington, federal FDA Commissioner Rexford Tugwell kept a "chamber of horrors" within the agency's offices, displaying for the press and the public vermin-infested food, death certificates of victims of patent medicines, and photographs of women blinded or otherwise disfigured by cosmetics. (This propaganda campaign led ultimately to the passing of the Food, Drug, and Cosmetic Act of 1938, but only after almost 100 people had been killed by an untested drug that the FDA had previously lacked authority to keep off the market.)

The requirement in Senator Muskie's Clean Air Act of 1970 that auto emissions be cut by 90 percent by 1975, provides a more recent example of the tactic used by Bess Myerson to force information out of a recalcitrant industry. Administrators of the federal auto safety program often use similar "deadlines" in trying to speed installation of passenger protection features in new model cars. The point of this tactic is to force the industry to make the best case it can possibly make against the proposed regulation. Once the regulator has seen the industry's cost estimates, the basis for them, and whatever other arguments the industry can muster, he can identify the real issues at stake. If he finds that the industry's arguments do not stand up to the analysis of his own experts, then he can proceed to implement the new regulation with the confidence that it represents sound policy. Obviously, however, the industry will respond to this kind of pressure in a positive manner only if it feels the weight of public opinion behind the regulator's demands. For this condition to be met, the program itself must have substantial inherent appeal, and the regulator must be adept at marshaling this appeal—like Bess Myerson at New York City's Department of Consumer Affairs, or William Ruckelshaus of the federal EPA, or Ralph Nader on behalf of the National Highway Traffic Safety Administration.

Government does offer some advantages in this enterprise—legitimacy, more and better typewriters, mimeograph machines, and talented publicists. But the prerogatives of public office are mainly useful only insofar as they furnish a better platform for a public-relations campaign. Even the ability to exercise legal powers is often, as in the unit-pricing case, an advantage primarily because it provides occasions for news events. Litigation is especially helpful in this regard because it produces repeated dramatic confrontations between reformers and corporate chieftains, and this is a particularly useful way to build public excitement over a cause.

But the fact that the reformers are public officials brings distinct disadvantages as well—the weaknesses inherent in serving a democratic government. In the unit-pricing case, if industry agents had been more skillful in exploiting these weaknesses, the reform would almost surely have been quashed before it ever got started. The main struggle occurred during the campaign year of 1969 and some efforts were made by the Lindsay campaign finance apparatus to stop the department's crusade. Their effort failed, partly because no major contributors appeared to be seriously exercised about the issue, but most importantly because antagonists did not know how to locate the proper pressure point within the city government; they relied mainly on Deputy Mayor Robert Sweet, who no longer had any influence with Mayor John Lindsay. Consumer Affairs officials could therefore ignore his efforts to stop them.

This was happenstance. The retail food industry had had a great deal of experience in handling federal and state agencies. But they were taken by surprise when a serious regulatory threat emerged from the city bureaucracy and the City Council. Such Washington professionals as Bryce Harlow, who is chief lobbyist for both Procter & Gamble and Republican presidents, would never have made such tactical mistakes.

But, of course, the same expertise could easily be duplicated at the local level in New York. The industry's organizational and financial resources could swiftly be deployed so that in a relatively short period, its agents would be in a position to stop any new initiatives and perhaps even to thwart implementation of the unit-pricing program that had already gotten past them.

Indeed, the only feature of the unit-pricing program that saves it from the charge of being a mini-grand design—of being a reform that could not long survive the headlines announcing its adoption, and the fading of public enthusiasm that made its adoption possible—is the fact that once implemented, it did not seriously injure the interests of most of the businesses covered by its terms. As the Department of Consumer Affairs had predicted from the first, large chains were able without too much fuss or cost to reprogram the computers that generated their weekly price lists to print out unit prices as well as total prices; thereafter they could treat the unit-price labels on their shelves as a consumer aid useful for maintaining customer good will. They had no incentive to subvert the unit-pricing program. Therefore, one can be reasonably confident that unit pricing is one reform that will last, in fact as well as in the laws and newspaper articles that commemorate the populist campaign that brought it into existence. But the industry's acquiescence is the main reason for this hopeful conclusion. The pageant that put unit pricing on the law books could not be kept up forever and could not, therefore, make the law an enduring reality in the marketplace.

Populism or Hucksterism?

To emphasize that ambitious regulatory programs cannot be sustained without effective public-relations campaigns is not necessarily to endorse the standard charges commonly made by enemies of the new populism. Corporate presidents allege, for example, that the movement's leaders are simply a genre of political hucksters, an elite whose values are not shared by the American public. Others dismiss the movement as a creation of the press—itself alleged to be an elite with unrepresentative values.

It is true, to be sure, that new populist leaders are uncommonly effective at merchandising their views through the media. Ralph Nader in particular is surely one of the most gifted interpreters of the role of tribune in the nation's history. He is clever at packaging information and well attuned to the press's own definition of what a "story" is. He tirelessly cultivates reporters. He and his colleagues have in effect opened a public-relations bureau for the new populism; their enterprise serves as a repository of trustworthy data, a place where someone can call to check what is "really going on" when USDA issues a new marketing restriction, to get a list of legal authorities and scholarly literature for a feature article on the energy crisis, or to find out how many worker deaths and injuries can be attributed to lax enforcement of job safety legislation.

Nader has managed to use the press as effectively as he has because he has perceived three basic features of the unwritten code governing the behavior of most professional reporters. First, reporters' assumptions about how government *should* work in the United States parallel the fundamentalist democratic faith of the new populism. At the same time, reporters who have been exposed to the seamy underside of Washington are often receptive to the cynicism and dissatisfaction of the new populists. The press does not harbor these views because it is a social or educational elite, as administration spokesmen Spiro Agnew and Daniel Patrick Moynihan have claimed; statistical profiles of the social and educational backgrounds of the Washington press corps have shown that claim to be a red herring. The populism of the working press is a professional bias, derived from a strong belief in civics-text democratic values—a bias that reporters share with the other professionals who spend their time describing and analyzing government.

Until Nader came along, however, reporters rarely expressed

their populist outlook in their stories because of two additional aspects of their unwritten professional code. The first of these requires that they be "objective" in reporting the news. As interpreted by the profession itself, this means that they could not report as news the fact that the FTC was a lethargic pawn of lobbyists and legislators; they could give the American people this piece of information only if some third party provided a "hook" for a "story." Since they depend on others to create stories, they have fallen into the habit of relying on their sources for research. They become stenographers for the people who are putting out the press releases. Their job, as they see it, is to print whatever information is given them by parties legitimately interested in the story. In short, the press cannot put out a populist critique of America itself; they can only repeat what others say in a press release or press conference or interview.

Nader has understood the dependence of the press on outside sources, as well as their need to receive information in the highly stylized forms to which they are accustomed. In particular, he has taken advantage of a third feature of the unwritten professional code of the working press, which helps him package his messages in a manner appealing to reporters. He understands that the press tends to view public affairs as a species of athletic contest.[3] Conflict is what they are looking for and what they like to write about. An accusation invites coverage, and Nader is not reluctant to attack in order to get attention.

But Nader and his followers are not simply building a left-wing McCarthyism. If their aim was to defame individuals, or simply to get their own names or stories in the papers every day, they would be neither as interesting nor as influential as they have been and are. Their goal has been to spread an idea, and a very abstract idea at that. They have tried to restructure the American public's image of who governs the nation's political economy. Through pageants like Campaign GM they have used the media to create a nationwide classroom. Any social science professor who has discovered on reading his students' exams how poorly he communicated similarly abstract concepts must be impressed by Nader's achievement.

In the present atmosphere of widespread suspicion of corporate power and of corporate-government relations, it is hard to remember the complacent public outlook of just a few years back. The early 1960s produced great turbulence and change, but over the question of the corporate role in society, the pall of the 1950s still hovered. As late as 1964, Robert Heilbroner had to concede that "the antibusiness ideology from which many intellectuals and many parts of the labor movement drew their strength [has] largely disappeared. . . ."[4] Who would have imagined then that the automobile industry would soon be subject to comprehensive government controls covering something as basic to the industry as vehicle design? Who would have forecast that the big multinational oil companies would be spending millions on institutional advertising to convince a skeptical public that "We're working to keep your trust," while they sought to dissuade the same electorate from outlawing the internal combustion engine?

But because Nader and his followers have been so successful in spreading their ideas, it is clear that their views are not unrepresentative. The new populism has tapped a vein that was there waiting to be tapped. After all, respect for the populist ideal of democracy is implanted in every elementary political science text used in American high schools and colleges. The new populists have not had to convert Americans to their ideology. Americans already believed in it. The reformers' task has been to demonstrate that the populist ideal is mocked, day in day out, by the actual practice of government and the economy. Their function has been akin to that of religious leaders. In America the populist ideal of democracy is, after all, something like religion. The new populists used the press to reinforce the predisposition of most Americans to honor that ideal, to distrust its enemies, and to favor reforms that would restore its vitality.

Populist Stagecraft and Public Deception:
The Progressives and Antitrust

There is a danger in populist leaders' virtuosity in using the media. But the danger is not that the public will be caught up in a revivalist frenzy to endorse reforms in which they do not "really" believe. The problem is in fact the opposite of this conservative fear. If history is any guide, the danger is that populist stagecraft will eventually be used to calm the public, rather than to arouse it—to spread the message that the campaign for democracy has realized its goals, and that the reforms have succeeded. The public will be persuaded that great changes have been achieved when in fact very little change has been achieved.

Tendencies that have propelled reform leaders to lend themselves to public deception are inherent in the political logic of populist campaigns. Eventually the leaders realize that the promises embodied in regulatory legislation cannot be fulfilled in practice. They simply do not have—and never can attain—the administrative capability or the political power to realize the goals or to enforce them consistently. But this is not an insight that reformers generally want to share with the public. Hence, they begin to perceive a community of interest with the groups they were supposed to regulate. Ultimately the regulators and those regulated cooperate in convincing the public that the problem has been solved, and that the demand for reform can safely be permitted to recede.

This depressing pattern has been evident in the evolution of the two previous periods of populist reform in this century, the Progressive phase during the 1900s and 1910s, and the New Deal during the 1930s. During the Progressive era, the pattern is most starkly apparent in the public posture of Presidents Theodore Roosevelt, William Howard Taft, and

Woodrow Wilson on what was then the burning question of the trusts.

Ritual denunciations of the trusts were a staple of Progressive rhetoric, and myriad pledges were made to undo the results of the extraordinary merger wave of 1898–1901. By the time that orgy of monopolization had run its course, the trusts, some of which constituted literal monopolies controlling upward of 90 percent of the business in their markets, owned over 40 percent of the manufacturing assets in the nation. But fifteen years later, when the era ended with Woodrow Wilson's decision to placate his War Production Board by suspending major antitrust prosecutions, no dent had been made in the overall level of concentration. Even in those industries where showcase lawsuits had been brought, victory in court had produced changes so negligible that they were ridiculed on Wall Street.

The public at that time (in common with many liberals today) tended to lay most of the responsibility for the ineffectuality of the Progressive presidents' antitrust efforts at the door of a supposedly hostile federal judiciary. Yet even in the harshly reactionary atmosphere of the 1890s, Supreme Court majorities interpreted the Sherman Act broadly enough so that it could have become a potent anti-monopoly weapon, had the White House shown any interest in using it. After the Progressive administration of Theodore Roosevelt attempted to reinvigorate the Sherman Act left to atrophy by his predecessors, so the mythology ran, the court reinterred it with the notorious "rule of reason" enunciated in the landmark 1911 cases against Standard Oil and American Tobacco. In these cases, although the court upheld the particular prosecutions before it and ordered dissolution of the trusts, a majority of the justices nevertheless held that the act did not condemn "all" restraints of trade or attempts to monopolize, but only "unreasonable " ones. The charge was immediately leveled—and widely believed—that the court by virtue of this eviscerating interpretation, had rendered the executive branch helpless to enforce the antitrust act. Yet the agitation over the "rule of reason" served mainly to get the Progressive executive branch off the hook. In fact the rule of reason did not come to deserve its reputation as a shield for monopoly until 1920 when the court invoked the doctrine in deciding not to break up the steel trust (on the ground that U.S. Steel had generously shared its monopoly power and profits with smaller firms in the industry).

But long before the Justice Department lost the steel case in the Supreme Court, it had plainly demonstrated, for the benefit of those few who were paying close enough attention to notice, that it had no serious intention of fighting to preserve competitive open spaces in the industrial heart of the economy. Theodore Roosevelt sought to calm public anxiety about the trusts by showering epithets on these "malefactors of great wealth," and by establishing with no little fanfare, a separate antitrust division in the Justice Department. But he staffed his new enforcement arm with only five lawyers—fewer than a good corporate law firm would employ in defense of a single Sherman Act case.[5] The great *Northern Securities* prosecution against the Morgan-sponsored union of the Hill and Harriman railroad interests in the Northwest is the most important single prop for Theodore Roosevelt's reputation as a trustbuster; he himself privately considered it "one of the great achievements of my administration." Yet though the merger was formally dissolved, Harriman and Hill interests continued to manage the dissolved companies as if they were one; according to Cummings and McFarland, chroniclers of the Justice Department's history, Hill later remarked that from his standpoint the principal impact of the lawsuit was that "he now had to sign two certificates instead of one."[6]

Though the outcome may have seemed almost ludicrously anticlimactic to some, it did not disappoint Roosevelt; he lost interest in the case when the Supreme Court upheld his suit. His objectives had been to achieve a triumph exclusively symbolic in character, to demonstrate to the public that, in principle (and solely in principle), the richest and most powerful capitalists had to answer to the law. Beyond that, he had no intention of going. He was not interested in using the antitrust law to redraw the map of economic power in the United States.

Roosevelt's successor, Wililam Howard Taft, was more conscientious about applying laws duly passed by Congress and doubled the rate of antitrust cases filed by his predecessor. But his interest in turning legal victories into opportunities for meaningful structural change did not exceed Roosevelt's. After its great victories over the oil and tobacco trusts, the Taft Administration negotiated decrees that simply converted the nationwide monopolies into regional monopolies; stock in the old trusts (which rose in value when the terms of the decrees were released) was simply exchanged for shares in each of the new ones, so that the same interests continued to dominate the industries. By 1913, the three principal progeny of the *American Tobacco* decree—American, Reynolds, and Phillip Morris—controlled 91 percent of the cigarette retail market, whereas in 1911, before the dissolution had taken place, the trust had controlled 80 percent. As late as the 1930s, the Rockefeller family and their foundations owned between 6 and 24 percent of the nation's six leading oil companies. "[A] few great and powerful offenders against [the antitrust laws] have been dissolved," confessed a demoralized Maryland district judge, halfheartedly upholding a Justice Department suit against the American Can Company in 1918, but "so far as is possible to judge, the consuming public has not yet greatly profited by their dissolution."[7]

Woodrow Wilson, in the 1912 campaign speeches that Louis Brandeis helped him package, attacked both Taft and Roosevelt for their Wall Street connections and for their announced preference for "regulating" the trusts rather than dismembering them. "Mr. Roosevelt's conception of government," he declaimed,

is Mr. Taft's conception . . . that the Presidency of the
United States is the presidency of a board of directors. . . .
[But] if the government is to tell big businessmen how to
run their business, don't you see that big businessmen
have to get closer to the government even than they are
now? Don't you see that they must capture the government, in order not to be restrained too much by it? Must
capture it? They have already captured it. . . . I do not
expect to see monopoly restrain itself.[8]

The only answer, Wilson insisted, and what his New Freedom
promised to do, was to "pull apart, and gently, but firmly and
persistently dissect." Even in private, Wilson wrote that "Real
dissolution in the case of trusts is the only thing we can be
satisfied with . . . to satisfy the conscience of the country.[9]

But to enforce his pledges, Wilson added only a dozen
lawyers to the antitrust division. He shepherded through congress the legislation establishing the FTC, which was supposed
to supplement Justice as an antitrust enforcer; but he appointed
so many hacks and friends of industry to man the new
bureaucracy that the frustrated Brandeis dismissed the commission's initial regime as a "stupid administration."[10] Wilson
also won enactment of the Clayton Act which was supposed
to correct the (allegedly) grave damage done to the Sherman
Act by the judicially declared "rule of reason" from the oil
and tobacco cases; in fact the law made no mention of the rule
of reason; failing either to strengthen or materially to clarify the
Sherman Act, it remained a superfluous piece of legislation
until it was itself strengthened by the Celler-Kefauver Anti-
merger Act of 1950.

Implications of the Progressives' Default

The Progressive antitrust charade seems to illumine the most
serious danger to which populist reform politics is prone. An
entire generation (and to a considerable extent, the generations
that followed it) seems to have been taken in by its most
revered political leaders. The years between 1900 and 1915

are probably the only period in the nation's history when "corporate power" as such was the dominant public concern, much as racial fears are the dominant public concern today. Just as such fears are the true source of a spate of current political issues (crime, welfare, urban renewal, education, property tax, etc.), popular anxiety about corporate power spawned many of the major controversies of that period—tariff reduction, election reform, pure food and drug regulation, as well as the main question, antitrust. Yet, for all this, the people were able to make their leaders respond to their concern with strong rhetoric, but not with strong measures.

Does the Progressives' default count as a significant failure for populist reform, or as a failure for the even larger claim that the American polity is democratic in substance as well as form? Richard Hofstadter, the most influential American historian of our time, argued that it does not; we should be amused but not aroused, he has said, by the vacuity of Progressive promises to curb the growth of corporate power. Hofstadter argued that by talking a great deal and doing almost nothing about monopolistic conditions in the economy, Roosevelt, Taft, and Wilson were really giving the people what they wanted—the *feeling* that something was being done about a "problem" that did not pose any concrete threat to the public welfare, but only to outmoded values and conceptions of social organization. "[When]," Hofstadter argued in a famous passage from his classic *The Age of Reform,*

> men find themselves enmeshed in institutions and practices that seem to be working to considerable effect but that violate their inherited precepts and their moral preferences, what usually happens is that men are driven to find a purely ceremonial solution.[11]

According to this ingenious analysis, democracy was vindicated and the public will executed by the very hypocrisy of the Progressive leadership's commitment to an effective program for the deconcentration of industry.

But this theory will not wash. Granted, it is perfectly clear that ritual is what the Progressives' antitrust program mostly amounted to in practice. But how can it also be clear that that is what the public desired? Even if Roosevelt's and Taft's ties to industrialists and their reservations about antimonopoly policy had been made clear to the electorate, Woodrow Wilson's ties assuredly had not been. For all one knows, his supporters may actually have expected him to meet, or at least to try to meet, the campaign promises thought up for him by Brandeis. If so, they were obviously unable to distinguish between the symbolic and substantive responses of their leader. In short, it does seem true, as Hofstadter (and, before him, New Deal social critic Thurman Arnold) alleged, that the Progressive presidents' much-ballyhooed antitrust crusade was mainly ceremonial in nature. The implications of this judgment may be more insidious than Hofstadter was prepared to believe. The ceremonial nature of the crusade may have been of a different sort than he maintained. It seems at least as sound to conclude that the ceremony was staged to deceive the public, as to conclude that it was staged in response to the public's coded demand for political entertainment.

It is not difficult to find the reasons populist reform campaigns can be accommodated so successfully by conservative leaders adept at stagecraft. But these reasons are not the sociopsychological considerations that Hofstadter ascribed to the middle-class *Geist* of the Progressive Americans. Rather, the difficulties inhere in the logical and political structure of social choice in a representative democracy—the barriers to the formulation, expression, and enforcement of the popular preferences.

Stagecraft and Populist Self-deception: The New Deal That Never Really Happened

Populist propaganda has resulted in *self-deception* on the part of liberal leaders as much as it has in public deception. This phenomenon is illustrated by Hofstadter himself. He was able to look somewhat condescendingly on the Progressives' professed desire to reduce the concentration of American industry as a soft-headed and impractical fantasy, primarily because he believed that the succeeding generation of reformers, the New Dealers, had come up with a more realistic and serviceable response to corporate power. In this view, the New Deal shrewdly accepted bigness in business, but resolved to place it under effective public control through planning and regulation. "Philosophy was for [the Progressives]," Thurman Arnold had cracked in 1935, "more important than opportunism and so they achieved in the end philosophy rather than opportunity." Arnold maintained that "A great cooperative movement in America might have changed the power of the industrial empire. Preaching against it, however, simply resulted in counter-preaching."[12] What Arnold meant by a "great cooperative movement" was the sort of regulatory program that Theodore Roosevelt had professed to favor over comprehensive antitrust enforcement. In order to deal with the great corporations "on terms of equality," Theodore Roosevelt had explained, rather than try to break them up, it "becomes necessary for . . . ordinary individuals to combine in their turn . . . in their collective capacity through that biggest of all combinations called the government. . . ."

This prescription for the dangers of corporate power was called by its founders the New Nationalism. Hofstadter and his generation believed that the predominant sentiment during the Progressive era had been to reject the New Nationalism in favor of the utopian New Freedom of LaFollette, Brandeis, Bryan, and the Wilson of 1912. However, so the theory ran, New Deal leaders in their superior wisdom embraced the New Nationalist recipe for controlling corporate power. Theodore Roosevelt's remarks about the necessity for individuals to "combine" and use government to check the power of business "came close," Hofstadter said, "to foreshadowing the important developments in this sphere since [Theodore] Roosevelt's time. . . ."[13]

To be sure, New Deal protagonists, especially during the early stages, did widely believe, with the first Roosevelt, that the proper democratic response to corporate power was planning and regulation on a grand scale. Consequently, it is easy to find bits of bluster about the government's prerogatives and responsibilities laced throughout the pronouncements of Ickes, Arnold, Landis, Tugwell, and many others, not excluding the president himself. What is arresting in the accounts of Hofstadter and others is their acceptance at face value of this early New Deal faith in big government. Most striking of all is their belief that the New Dealers had actually succeeded in putting Theodore Roosevelt's prescription into practical operation and had succeeded in "redressing the balance of social power."

It should perhaps be noted, by way of partially excusing contemporary liberal enthusiasts of the New Deal, that they have not been alone in clinging to this grandiose image of Franklin Roosevelt's reign as the womb of a new regime of pervasive regulation of industry. For two decades after World War II, conservatives believed in this image and denounced it. More recently, radicals too have accepted the notion that the New Deal created a vast new apparatus of state power and imagined that it was subsequent corruption of this governmental machinery that had yielded the corporate state.

Yet this widely shared image of the 1930s is substantially false. The New Deal which contemporaries think they remember —whether with admiration or antipathy—never really took place. Except for the ill-fated NRA, which, at least in design, really did resemble Charles Reich's corporate state, the New Deal neither conceived nor implemented any comprehensive planning or regulatory schemes aimed at "redressing the balance of social power." The period did witness a proliferation of new regulatory laws and bureaucracies, but these hardly added up to an equivalent of the defunct NRA.

In the 1930s only eleven new agencies were born that had regulatory (as distinct from welfare) functions. Of these only two—the SEC and the Federal Power Commission (the latter of which was actually created during the Hoover Administration)—were imposed by the public on the industry in question.[14] The others were engineered mainly by the industries or by other affected interests themselves, in several important instances mainly or solely for the purpose of immunizing cartel practices from antitrust restraints. Included in this latter category are such well-known creations of the New Deal period as the CAB, the Motor Carriers Act of 1935 (extending ICC rate-fixing and entry-limiting jurisdiction to trucks and buses), and the Federal Maritime Commission. The unhappy consequences of these "reforms"—higher consumer prices, restricted output, arbitrary curtailment of service offerings, frozen technical development, resource misallocation—have been documented by a large and still-increasing body of scholarly and muckraking literature.[15] Somewhat less well-covered is the story of the origin of these regulatory measures. But enough has been published to make it clear that the reforms were mainly the work of industry pressures, and that their "defects," as they have since come to be viewed by appalled liberal observers, were designed-in; their architects wanted to stabilize competitive and/or technologically volatile markets, and they have not been disappointed by the results.[16]

Furthermore, those New Deal regulatory measures that did benefit the disadvantaged groups—the Fair Labor Standards Act, the Wagner Act, and the Agricultural Adjustment Act seem now to be the most important—were not produced by experts riding a tidal wave of public concern. They were tailored to the specifications of very well-organized interest groups. They too were designed to stabilize what would otherwise have been competitive markets, and in retrospect they cannot be said to have unambiguously promoted the public interest, at least if "public interest" is considered strictly coincident with the economic interest of consumers. FDR's regulatory initiatives are best understood as a parceling out to various organized economic interests of government power to better enable them to control the public. This view is more accurate, at least, than the common assumption that the New Deal was a grand design executed by government reformers, backed by public opinion, to enable the public to control private interests.

Though it may be true that the early New Deal years were the most fertile period in the twentieth century for the sprouting of projected grand design blueprints for controlling the economy, such hopes vanished after the ignominious collapse of the NRA in 1935. FDR exiled grand design enthusiasts, both the leftish technocrats like Tugwell and the overt cartel enthusiasts like Bernard Baruch and Hugh Johnson.[17] Indeed, loss of faith in the idea of regulation as a general instrument for controlling corporate power became so pronounced that antitrust resurfaced as the dominant ideological theme. Roosevelt pledged to "reverse the process of the concentration of power."[18] Unlike Wilson, he actually tried for a time to deliver on this commitment. Ironically, his new antitrust chief turned out to be Thurman Arnold. Arnold promptly recanted his own earlier words of ridicule for the antitrust laws and persuaded Congress to quintuple the size of the Antitrust Division. In his five years as assistant attorney general for antitrust, with his staff of more than 200 lawyers in Washington and in new branch offices, Arnold accounted for over half the total number of antitrust cases filed in the then-fifty years since the Sherman Act had become law. The ninety-two cases he filed in 1940 still stand as a record for the division.

In the end, then, the New Freedom was as much evident in the pattern of New Deal reform as was the New Nationalism. If it has any coherent point, the New Deal experience should be read as a *discrediting* of its early faith in grand designs for comprehensive regulation as a trustworthy or systematic response to corporate power.

In sum, current muckrakers are generally mistaken when they allege that New Deal regulatory agencies have been captive since their creation. Their defects were there to begin with, put there deliberately by the interests that designed them.

Historians who have fostered a contrary view have simply been taken in, just as Progressive voters were taken in, by the bombast of the leaders of that era. As John Kenneth Galbraith observed during a period when he was given to emphasizing the self-regulatory virtues of "countervailing power" in the economy, "The truth is that much of the American liberal's modern advocacy of state intervention and planning has been general and verbal." It has been, he said, "a massive deployment of words. . . ."[19]

5

The Concept of the Ideocracy

With their massive deployment of words, the New Dealers brought off one of recent history's most impressive victories for public relations. The press touted the myth that the New Deal was creating a brave new regulatory state. That convinced the public. Historians also believed in the myth, and they convinced later generations, who have taken comfort in this "fact" ever since.

Only a handful of individuals seem to have fully grasped just how little the foundations of social power were changed by the New Deal, despite its complex new edifice of rhetoric and legislation; these men were the new breed of Washington lawyers—Thomas Corcoran, Clark Clifford, Abe Fortas, Lloyd Cutler, and others—who help chart courses for corporate clients in postwar Washington.

Rhetoric versus Reality

In retrospect it is clear that we should not take the propaganda of past campaigns and administrations any more seriously than we would the propaganda of politicians today. Certainly

93

no one who has ever worked as a political speech writer would make much of the difference between Woodrow Wilson's New Freedom and the New Nationalism preached by his rival Theodore Roosevelt in 1912 and echoed by some New Deal braintrusters twenty years later. The truth is simply that the New Freedom was devised to solve a quite pedestrian political problem that Wilson faced after he secured the Democratic nomination. As often happens in a three-way race, he and Roosevelt were aiming for the same constituency. Hence Wilson had to find a dramatic way to differentiate his position without, however, seeming to be either too radical or too conservative, and without making commitments that would offend particular interests and electoral groups. In the nick of time, on August 28, along came Louis Brandeis, the prototypical public-interest lawyer and author of tracts for his time. Brandeis's ideas and rhetoric suited Wilson's needs to perfection. His decentralist, anticorporate emphasis lent itself well to the politician's demand for slogans that were at once dramatic and nonspecific.

We do not know how sincere Woodrow Wilson was when he made his pledges to "dissect" the trusts or how different he really felt his program was from Theodore Roosevelt's. Such questions are important in biographies of statesmen, but they generally have little to do with assessing the impact of states-men on history, especially in policy areas that affect the na-tion's most powerful social interests. Whatever the differences between the New Freedom and the New Nationalism in prin-ciple, it does not seem likely that the legal and political developments of the four years before World War I would have differed significantly if Roosevelt had won the election of 1912. Nor indeed would the institutional legacy of the New Deal have been other than it was if Theodore had been the second Roosevelt, or if Wilson had risen to power a generation later. Private business would have noticed little tangible differ-ences in the two brands of reformist rhetoric.

The regulatory institutions begotten by the New Deal were mainly the work of the affected interests themselves. These interests would have had their way regardless of who occupied the White House or what philosophy of reform was embraced by his advisers. In the case of Progressive reforms, the story was substantially the same. To be sure, the principal bureaucratic innovations of the Progressive era were, to a greater extent than many New Deal reforms, responses to general public alarm about corporate power; but their specific provisions, as distinguished from the general objectives to which they were supposedly addressed, were hammered out largely by and for interested economic groups. For example, the design of the FTC was much fought over. Agents of big business wanted to make the commission strong enough to give consent to questionable mergers and other transactions. Representatives of small business feared such collaboration and fought to reduce the powers of an agency they assumed would fall under the influence of big business.[1] The final terms of the legislation satisfied neither set of interests, but the appointees President Woodrow Wilson picked to run the new commission apparently pleased them both. The banking reform battle was similarly a struggle between the big New York banks, metropolitan banks elsewhere, and the even smaller "country banks." The backdrop of public concern about the "money trust"—whipped up by the famous Pujo Committee investigations of 1911[2]—was largely irrelevant to the actual terms of the struggle.

This is not to imply, as some have suggested, that the New Deal, or its predecessor, progressivism, was a conspiracy against the public coordinated by clever Wall Street agents. Nor is it to overlook the Adamson Act, social security, progressive income taxation, and other welfare measures as landmark advances on behalf of FDR's "forgotten man at the bottom of the economic pyramid." But as far as New Deal and Progressive regulatory policies are concerned, our present-day images of what happened then are influenced mainly by the considerable verbal output of speech writers and legislative draftsmen inside government and by reporters, historians, and other observers outside government. As it turns out, the words produced by these people had remarkably little to do with the actual institutional developments.

The Verbal Superstructure and the Ideocracy

By concentrating too exclusively on the words the government used to describe itself, observers have missed more than the impact of governmental activities at the operational level; they have made the even more fundamental mistake of failing to isolate and examine—as an independent and integral phenomenon—the verbal dimension itself of the governing process. Neither our journalism nor our scholarship accounts for this verbal superstructure that stands between the public and the operational levels of government.

This superstructure consists of the words of the observers themselves as well as the words of high officials. It ranges from news articles and broadcasts, histories and other scholarly accounts, to speeches, interviews, and press releases, and even to statutes, judicial decisions, regulations, and formal bureaucratic memoranda. Various much-used clichés touch on individual aspects of the verbal superstructure—"biased news," "news management," the distinction between "laws on the books" and laws that are "enforced." But our customary modes of analysis fail to notice that these phenomena can usefully be viewed as parts of a single component of the governing process. In particular, we distinguish reportage and scholarship from statutes and court decisions; the former we see as being outside government; the latter we see as the law and therefore as part of government. But we come much closer to the truth when we view all these manifestations as a unity. Together, they form a body of expressions that purports to *describe* and to *prescribe* the behavior of the operational level of government and of the individuals and institutions in the private sphere who are subject to its jurisdiction.

A substantial group of individuals that plays a highly visible and prestigious role in the governing process is concerned professionally, almost exclusively, with manipulating this verbal superstructure. The group includes writers and judges, communications directors and lawyers, administrators and advertising executives, reform legislators and propagandists. These word manipulators, whether they are formally in or outside government, form a distinct subculture within the governing process. To an extent that is not widely understood, from both a functional and sociological standpoint, they have much in common with each other—more than the reporters and scholars have in common with the public, though they are formally part of the public; and more than the speech writers and top-level bureaucrats have in common with the inhabitants of the lower and middle levels of their own bureaucracy. I would like to label this subculture "the ideocracy."

The introduction of this term may perhaps be excused by the fact that no familiar term adequately emphasizes the relative powerlessness of many top-level appointive bureaucrats in relation to the people who work at subordinate levels; nor is there a term that adequately underscores their mutual alienation from each other. There is no term to describe the intimate and active governing role played by formally external observers, especially (but not exclusively) the daily press. And finally, no existing concept treats the process of *depicting* policy as a unique component of democratic government. Without a concept that illuminates these problems, it is difficult to understand the political process that ensues and recurs whenever organized interests are subjected to populist legal controls.

Within the ideocracy, relations are by no means always harmonious. On the contrary, "do-good" public-interest groups, reformist legislators, and bureaucratic leaders generally distrust each other, and are sometimes openly at odds. Reporters and high-level bureaucrats, the most consistent participants, are deeply aware of the adversary features of their relationship. Sometimes this tension produces public antagonism and squabbling, as in the battles between the press and both the Johnson and Nixon administrations. But these public fireworks misrepresent the normal relationship of the press to the government, especially outside the special case of the White House. In general, relations between the press and high officialdom move along well-grooved routines, if not amicably, then at least according to accepted conventions, and for mutually well-understood reasons.

Reporters and top-level bureaucrats try to minimize adversary outbursts because they recognize their even more important mutual interdependence. The reporter can cut the administrator off from his public; the administrator can cut the reporter off from his source of information, or at least keep him from getting to it as quickly as his competitors. Furthermore, high officials and reporters spend a great deal of time together, both during the business day and often socially as well. The peculiar intimacy of this relationship generates a sense of community; both outsider and insider become jointly involved in an enterprise that sets them apart from the public on the one hand, and from the operating levels of government on the other. The official's command over information unquestionably gives him the upper hand in the relationship. But the feeling is nevertheless inescapable on both sides that the reporter is jointly involved in defining policy—that is, in fixing the manner in which policy will be described to subordinate officials—though this is supposed to be the official's job alone; similarly, the official is deeply involved in structuring the reporter's descriptions of policy and government activity in general (usually limited to high-level announcements of policy) for the benefit of the public.

Very few accounts convey the highly stylized process that results from the common labor of newsman and public official. One exception is an unusually candid piece by David Broder of the *Washington Post* in the *Washington Monthly*.[3] Broder described the atmosphere aboard the campaign plane of Robert Kennedy during the 1968 primaries. Broder observed that Kennedy's speech writers Adam Walinsky and Jeff Greenfield would struggle to finish the speech that the candidate was to give at his next stop in time to meet the deadlines of the reporters flying with the candidate. Once the text was typed, duplicated, and distributed, the reporters would read it eagerly to see what "the story" was. Usually no prodding by Kennedy's press-relations staff was necessary to ensure that the press would find "the story"; such things are defined by conventions implicitly understood by both the speech writers and the news writers. Once the plane landed, the stories would be filed, and the candidate would go about the planned wooing of local voters. This might or might not follow the text of the speech already given to the reporters. But for the millions of television viewers and newspaper readers elsewhere in the nation (and history book readers later on), the "event" of the day was produced in the air, on paper.

Of course, a presidential campaign is not a routine government activity. Outside the White House, contact between writers and officials is neither so frequent nor so intense. And word processing is managed in a less artificial manner, especially on the governmental side. Still, the same elements present in Broder's evocation of the Kennedy campaign plane are also present in the *modus operandi* of the FTC or the EPA (or in efforts to create or resist the creation of an FTC or an EPA). Indeed, because such "normal" situations are less pressured and less visible, reporters are less likely to fear official manipulation and official press relationships can become closer and more sustained.

Again, examples are difficult to find. Victor Navasky's recent painstaking account of Robert F. Kennedy's regime in the Justice Department yields one interesting example—the relationship between *New York Times* correspondent Anthony Lewis and most of Kennedy's high command.[4] Lewis was so close to Kennedy and his chief aides that in at least one instance he became an integral part of the policy-making and executing apparatus. He participated in, and in some ways led the successful effort of, the attorney general and his closest advisers to bring to heel Solicitor General Archibald Cox, when he was skittish about urging the Supreme Court to rule that all state legislatures had to be apportioned on a one-man, one-vote basis.

Ideocracy Versus Infrastructure

Such contacts—perhaps rarely as intimate as those linking Lewis to the Kennedy high command at the Justice Department—encourage and are encouraged by recognition of similar skills and training. Indeed, the similarity is such that there is considerable exchange of jobs; reporters become bureaucratic troubleshooters and press officers, while scholarly observers often become high-level administrators. This common professional background makes for a shared commitment to the values fostered by the frequent and sophisticated use of verbal and conceptual talents. While observers and officials may often disagree about the merits of the debate, they do agree on its terms. They share a frame of reference in which political ideals predominate. A component of this framework—and one that is especially widely held and uncontroversial—is the root populist notion that the people should control the special interests. People who work with one or more aspects of the verbal superstructure of American democracy are certain to understand that ideal and are likely to believe in it, whether or not their commitment to it goes much beyond lip service.

This common familiarity with the populist ideal is a critical feature of the promotion and administration of populist regulatory programs. For in this regard the ideocracy that superintends the word-processing activities in and around the highest levels of government is likely to differ from the ideology of the middle- and lower-level civil servants, industry-oriented members of relevant legislative committees, and representatives of the trade press—those who comprise the political infrastructure that determines the actual content of regulation in its routine operation. Members of this infrastructure are not part of the ideocratic culture. They do not share its values. In fact, they probably favor measures that, for example, suppress competition in a naturally competitive industry, or that in other ways promote the industry or other client interest at the expense of the larger public good. Moreover, they are rarely reticent about making their industry-oriented preferences public. In August, 1972, for example, an assistant secretary of agriculture justified a decision to restrict the flow of imported tomatoes into the United States with this rationale: it is true, the USDA official conceded, that the applicable statute contains some sections "which require the Secretary to consider the interests of consumers"; but, he countered with disarming frankness,

> The primary purpose of the act . . . is to protect the purchasing powers of U.S. farmers and the value of agricultural assets. The *whole objective is to raise the price of particular agricultural commodities* including tomatoes to levels prescribed by the act. . . . [Emphasis supplied.][5]

Their distinctive set of values is reflected in a specialized jargon. A rate increase, for example, becomes "rate relief." What might otherwise appear to be a conspiracy in restraint of trade (were it not immunized from antitrust proscription by the regulatory statute) is described as "cooperation" to prevent "destructive" competition, destructive competition being any form of rivalry believed likely to injure profit levels. The ultimate value of regulatory policy is the maintenance of "economically sound conditions" in the industry, which means the survival of all existing units at stable, and high, levels of profitability, regardless of how this affects the public. Part of the function of such specialized terminologies is Orwellian—to hide from participants themselves the public consequences of their policies. Part of the function (especially in the case of often needlessly formidable technical formulas) is defensive—to put a forest of verbiage between themselves and prying representatives of the public.

Political appointees not selected from this infrastructure often find it expedient to go along with its demands and preferences (and when they do, they will strive to hide that fact from reporters and other potential critics). But high officials are generally less likely to believe in what they are doing in such instances; at least they are likely to be sensitive to the contradictory ideals held by outside observers of the agency's activities. They are not likely to want to defend the agency's policies in terms of the values that animate the infrastructure: the economic welfare of regulated interests and the stability of economic and regulatory patterns.

If, on the other hand, such political appointees choose to fight the infrastructure and pursue a reformist course, then reporters and editorial writers will become their closest and their only allies—except in the still unusual cases where do-good public-interest groups become mobilized and sympathetic judges are brought into the picture. The particular strategy these groups use may be clandestine; officials may leak scandals to a friendly reporter, or stimulate the writing of an editorial, in order to create external pressure to which they can then decide to "submit." Or the official may simply generate news stories himself by staging events or by making routine occurrences appear dramatic. Sometimes the impetus for reform may originate with an enterprising newspaper or reporter who seeks to embarrass high officials into joining a fight against the status quo. Or the alliance may involve not a relatively tight group of individuals, but a broad movement that includes numerous political reformers as well as a substantial body of writers and members of the media (as well as legislators, citizen groups, and perhaps even judges). But, whatever the particular form the coalition decides to take, the press is likely, often actively, to be on the side of populist reform.

Some Cases in Point

This ideocracy-infrastructure paradigm is reflected most faithfully in cases of conventional regulatory schemes, where a particular industry or set of industries is formally subject to the extensive legal controls of an administrative agency. This is especially true when the agency is relatively old, when its functionaries have developed intimate relations with regulated interests and their representatives, and when a new populist-oriented appointee or reform movement supported by editorial and reportorial observers appears to challenge the status quo. Cases in point are the situations generated by reformist FCC Commissioners Newton Minow and Nicholas Johnson, or EPA Administrator William S. Ruckelshaus—vis-à-vis the constituent subagencies of EPA appropriated from the traditionally industry-oriented Department of Agriculture.

However, similar political patterns are evident in situations formally different from these regulatory cases. One could point to well-knit infrastructures that, in formal terms, are almost exclusively private. One example is the automobile industry, which is now engaged in warding off an ideocratic coalition seeking environmental, safety, and antitrust controls. A review of Alfred P. Sloane's biography or an interview with James P. Roche underscores how sharp are the philosophical differences dividing these auto executives from environmentalist agitators, reporters, high-level bureaucrats, and editorial writers; to leaders of the auto infrastructure, the stability and profitability of the industry is an end in itself, to be preferred to safety for passengers or environmental quality for the society. In other situations the infrastructure is almost wholly within the formal boundaries of government—as in the case of the Army Corps of Engineers in its current tussles with environmentalists in and out of government. An especially pertinent case is the struggle reporters and reformist officials in the New York Ctiy government have waged to combat police corruption—although it would be possible to view the police department as a (captive) regulatory agency and organized racketeers as a regulated industry.

In any event, it is not material where, in a particular case, the line is drawn between the private sector and the public sector. To take another example from New York City, the Department of Consumer Affairs regulates the prices charged by and assigns routes and customers served by "private" carting companies that collect garbage generated by all commercial establishments;

in apparent contrast, residential trash collection is handled on a socialist basis—the EPA manages the task itself, with its own employees and equipment. But the political relations between top executives in the Consumer Affairs Department and their regulatees do not differ essentially from the relations between top EPA executives and the powerful sanitation union and lower-level civil servants.

Liberating the FCC: ABC and ITT

The trench line between ideocracy and infrastructure can be seen with special clarity in the case of the FCC. This agency has been a particular target of the charge of "capture." It has also been the focus of a continually growing assault by new populist reform efforts. I went to work at the FCC in 1967, when this "movement" (it is hardly large enough to rank as a movement) was just beginning to assume broad enough dimensions to capture the public's attention—largely through the flamboyant tactics of Commissioner Nicholas Johnson, who had hired me as his legal assistant.

During my first days on the job I overheard in a corridor one commission staff official complimenting another on his attractive office in the agency's new quarters. The lucky employee said credit for his good fortune belonged to a leading broadcast lawyer, whom he named, who had intervened on his behalf with the chairman of the agency. I was startled as well as amused by this little revelation. The matter itself was of no consequence whatsoever. What disturbed me was that an official had gone outside the agency, on such a trivial matter, to reach the agency chairman; this implied a disturbing measure of intimacy between the three participants. Indeed, the story suggested a framework within which even such small favors could be exchanged routinely.

Before long it became clear that just such a framework bound most (though not all) agency officials to members of the FCC Bar Association (like the lawyer in the story), to officials of the broadcast trade associations (the National Association of

Broadcasters and the Association of Maximum Service Tele-casters), to the trade press (especially the belligerent but com-prehensive weekly *Broadcasting*), and to relevant congressional committee chairmen and their staffs. The agency chairman, Rosel Hyde, was deeply familiar with these groups, and a veteran of their years of striving to gain immunity from outside political pressures. Hyde had been a commissioner for twenty years before being named chairman at the age of sixty-seven by Lyndon Johnson in 1967. He had actually been on the staff of the commission before it had had a name, as he had served with the Federal Radio Commission, the FCC's predecessor, in the late 1920s.

Mutual services, often of a more significant character than in the case of the staff member's new office, were performed by the members of this political infrastructure. The industry and its agents continued to show pervasive solicitude about the pro-fessional well-being of FCC officials—a solicitude that did not end when the officials left the commission. Of thirty-three com-missioners and thirty-two high-staff officials who held office between 1945 and 1970, twenty-one commissioners and thir-teen staff officials accepted jobs in the communications industry or satellite law firms, consulting firms, or trade associations upon leaving the agency. And, for their part, commission officials tended to show solicitude for the economic and political well-being of the industry.

When I first came to the FCC, the most graphic demonstra-tion of the agency's solicitude for its clients in the industry was in the attempt of the International Telephone & Telegraph Corporation to take over the American Broadcasting Company. This mammoth merger case was also Commissioner Nicholas Johnson's introduction to the traditional mores of the FCC. It turned out to be the first victory in his seven-year campaign to change those mores and put the agency in control of the in-dustry, instead of at its service.

To Johnson the outsider, the agency leadership's protective attitude toward the mammoth merger seemed astonishing. (At this time Chairman Hyde could count on at least three of the seven commissioners to support just about any stand he chose to take in any given case.) First the commission tried to grant ABC's petition to transfer its broadcast licenses quickly and quietly enough to prevent opposition from forming; then the agency simply tried to bulldoze the case past opponents, including the U.S. Department of Justice. As Commissioner Johnson recounted in his dissent to the commission's initial approval of the merger:

> From the time the merger application was first filed, the outcome of this case has been a foregone conclusion. At one point no hearing at all was to be held. Then, as a compromise to Commissioner Bartley's insistence on "a full evidentiary hearing," the Commission proposed an unprecedented, bobtailed "oral" hearing. It was anticipated the Commission would merely meet informally *en banc* with the principals of ABC and ITT and hear their side of the case. Only the questioning of the three dissenting Commissioners extended the case to a scant two days. The questioning of three of the four Commissioners in the majority occupied scarcely eleven full pages in the 607-page record. The fourth Commissioner's questioning was directed principally toward discrediting an FCC staff member, and assisting ITT counsel's effort to demonstrate the absence of any possible antitrust implications of the merger.
>
> The most notable peculiarity of the "oral hearing" was the total absence of any party whatsoever representing the public. . . . There have been numerous references in the trade press to the fact that a substantial minority of this Commission has been fully prepared to decide the case without even waiting to hear from the Assistant Attorney General (Antitrust).[6]

In fact, the commission did decide the case without permitting Assistant Attorney General Donald Turner to intervene on behalf of the Justice Department. At 10:00 A.M., on December 21, 1966, a four-to-three majority met, voted, and approved the merger, despite the fact that at 5:00 P.M. on the previous night the Justice Department had expressed concern about the anticompetitive issues of the case and asked to intervene. Eventually, however, Chairman Hyde decided that this had gone too far and voted to rescind the decision until after a formal hearing could be held with Justice Department participation. In June, 1967, the commission again approved the merger but the Justice Department challenged the decision in court (in a case amusingly styled *United States of America* v. *the Federal Communications Commission*); in January, 1968, ITT gave up and withdrew its offer to ABC's shareholders.

ABC-ITT forced Johnson, and the other dissenting commissioners, Kenneth Cox and Robert Bartley, into sharp philosophical disagreement with Hyde and the whole political infrastructure that he represented. In the view of the dissenters, the mission of the FCC was affirmatively to control the course of events in the broadcast industry. Its responsibility was to dictate the terms on which broadcast licensees could hold their lucrative franchises. The agency's "constituency" was "the public." Though the public was in fact a wholly abstract concept and though it never made its will known to its agents on the commission, its interests were clear enough in most instances. In any event, it was up to the commission to ascertain independently what was in "the public interest." That was the theory Congress had acted on during the 1930s when it created the FCC and other regulatory agencies. The Communications Act itself said so.

In the particular case now before it, the agency should not approve the merger, unless it found that the merger would serve the public interest. Again, given the political ideals by which they set their lights, it was not hard for the dissenters to decide this question. How, they wondered, could it serve "the public interest" to place ABC, this vital instrument of democracy, one of the nation's three television networks, under the control of a burgeoning conglomerate corporation, already one of the largest companies in the world? When it was recognized how great a stake ITT would be given in the way in which ABC-TV news programs would portray events in foreign lands, in particular Latin America, where ITT had large investments, the need to refuse permission for the merger seemed especially clear. (Four percent of ITT's assets were actually insured by the Agency for International Development [AID] under legislation that ITT lobbyists presumably had fought to obtain, and that ABC news might be useful in helping to keep.)

Finally, the dissenters felt that all questions about the impact of ITT control on the integrity of ABC news were resolved— against approval—when ITT's senior vice president for public relations arranged confrontations with reporters covering the case for the Associated Press (AP), United Press International (UPI), and *The New York Times* to push for more favorable coverage of the case. The ITT official was especially adamant in dealing with *New York Times* reporter Eileen Shanahan; she subsequently testified to the FCC that he had tried to force her to reveal the text of a story while she was in the process of writing it, and that he had warned her to consult with her publisher before she wrote "anything further about Commissioner Johnson's opinions." (His implication, Shanahan felt, was that the *Times* would want to consider its own economic interests before promoting the reputation of an official whose policy views might endanger the newspaper's own broadcast holdings.)

But Chairman Hyde and the forces he represented were not disturbed by these considerations. To them, the FCC's constituency was not some abstraction called "the public." It was the industry, the trade representatives, the congressional committee chairmen and staff members, and the trade publications with whom agency officials had routinely interacted over the past four decades, and with whom it would be necessary to deal, presumably, in the foreseeable future. The agency's mission was, in the view of the majority, also clearcut. The broadcast industry was, after all, an industry, and it was the agency's task to help keep it "healthy." This meant keeping the operations of the actual existing corporate entities that constitute the industry going at a profitable and stable pace. Mainly, this job involved not interfering with the private business judgments made by corporate officials. If ABC's president, Leonard Goldenson, thought a merger with ITT was needed to save his company from bankruptcy, how could regulators responsibly stand in his way? (And, conversely, if a Goldenson did not want a threatened merger to take place, as happened when, after the ITT merger collapsed in litigation, Howard Hughes contemplated a tender-offer to ABC shareholders, the commission felt that its duty was to loyally use every procedural means at its command to block the acquisition and this is what it did.)

There is no reason to believe that Chairman Hyde's attitude, or that of his supporters, was traceable to corrupt pressures of any sort. Nor is there reason to think that the White House itself pressured the commission or the Justice Department—though the services of the White House were solicited, and Justice officials more pliable than Ramsey Clark and Donald Turner might not have stood up to the pressure. The position for which Hyde spoke was as sincere and even as grounded in ideological considerations as was that of the dissenters. It was based on principles derived from forty years of experience with the political economy of American broadcasting, just as Johnson's populist principles were derived from his experiences as a student and a professor in major universities, as a clerk for Supreme Court Justice Hugo Black, and as a practicing liberal reformer.

Indeed, what was most remarkable about the commissioners' behavior was the depth of their sincerity—and their corresponding insensitivity to how isolated they were in their views. In fighting bitterly—and, as it turned out, vainly—to preserve Leonard Goldenson's freedom to merge with a corporate partner of his choice, the agency was acting out of habit. It was doing what came naturally to it in the solitary environment to which it had become accustomed, and to which an inert press and an apathetic public had traditionally left it. The old hands did not realize that ABC-ITT was a bigger case than usual—from the point of view of people who took seriously populist ideological concerns about the integrity of democracy. They did realize that Nicholas Johnson's 124-page dissenting opinion had focused far more than the usual measure of public interest on the case. But they were unable to comprehend the populist fears Johnson's critique had aroused (anymore than ITT's clumsy public-relations executives were able to understand these fears in their efforts to browbeat reporters over a case where the main issue was whether or not ITT could avoid dictating news policy to ABC). Much less did they attribute any political strength to populist sentiments.

In sum, Hyde's ideological blinders were such that he could not see that in sticking with ABC on this one case, he was endangering his own command over affairs at the FCC. He was threatening the values and the constituency he wanted to serve in a case that he was ultimately bound to lose.

The chasm that separated the values of the FCC infrastructure from the populist views of the agency's mounting array of critics became even clearer in the next major confrontation between Hyde and Johnson. This was a genuine landmark, the single most important case in American history affecting public access to bureaucratic decision making. In 1968 it was already before the FCC for the second time; the commission's first decision had been reversed by the U.S. Court of Appeals for the District of Columbia Circuit. At the commission the case was known as *In Re WLBT*. On appeal in the court, it was called, *Office of Communication of the United Church of Christ* v. *the Federal Communications Commission*.

WLBT: Crisis of the Old Order

WLBT was one of two VHF television stations serving Jackson, Mississippi. Licensed to the Murchison brothers of Texas, WLBT, from its first moments on the air, had provoked complaints to the FCC from leaders of the Jackson black community. The complaints depicted a pattern of segregationist partisanship, coupled with a refusal to give reply time to pro-integration responses; the station apparently even had the habit of cutting off network broadcasts when black leaders such as Thurgood Marshall appeared on camera. WLBT also avoided showing local blacks on the screen, even though they constituted 47 percent of the population covered by its broadcast signal. Newscasters had on occasion contemptuously identified local black citizens by their first names only, and words like "nigger" and "negra" were heard over the airwaves of WLBT's Channel 3.

Eventually fed up with the FCC's refusal to act on its own against these practices, the black leaders of Jackson obtained the assistance of the United Church of Christ in New York. In 1964 the church and the black community of Jackson filed with the FCC a petition to deny renewal of WLBT's broadcast license, scheduled to expire that year.

Even more than ABC-ITT, the United Church of Christ petition portended bitter conflict between the two ideologies competing for control of the FCC. To those who believed the populist theory that the FCC was supposed to control the industry affirmatively, the statutory requirement that station owners apply every three years for renewal of their licenses was no mere technicality. On the contrary, this was the basic mechanism through which public control over broadcasting was maintained. Renewal therefore was to be granted only if the applicant's broadcast record showed that it had served and would continue to serve "the public interest." As stated by Chief Justice Warren Burger, who as a judge on the Court of Appeals for the District of Columbia Circuit, became the decisive participant in the WLBT drama, "Like public officials charged with a public trust, a renewal applicant . . . must literally 'run on his record.' "[7]

Self-evident as Burger's proposition may seem to many, it was anathema to Chairman Hyde and his traditionalist colleagues. They were, after all, loath to deny a major broadcast corporation like ABC the right to *transfer* its licenses when it wanted to. But they could not begin to contemplate actually failing to *renew* a broadcast license, thereby destroying a valuable property outright. The Communications Act explicitly decreed that licensees were to have no legal property right in their franchise. But it was the most fundamental unwritten rule of FCC practice that once granted, a broadcast license did in fact confer a *de facto* property interest. Although all stations had to go through a complex and somewhat expensive ritual of applying for a license renewal every three years, never, never was a broadcast licensee supposed to lose its lucrative franchise—at least not on the ground that its programming substantively failed to serve the public interest. This rule was not written down anywhere, but it was well-understood within the broadcast infrastructure. And no breach of the rule had ever been seriously threatened—that is, until the WLBT case came along.

The commission was not unaware that WLBT's outrageous behavior threatened its traditional hands-off policy. It tried to avoid the threat with a compromise. Although the petitioners were denied official standing to participate in the renewal proceeding, their claims were accepted as valid. And WLBT's license was renewed for only a one-year term. This probationary grant was conditional on an order that the station adhere strictly to the fairness doctrine, that it initiate contacts with black leaders, and that it "immediately cease discriminatory programming patterns."[8]

But the petitioners were unsatisfied. They took an appeal to the court of appeals, where their case was heard by Judge Burger. Burger was appalled at the FCC. He reversed the ruling of the commission, ordered it to rehear the matter, and gave the petitioners standing to participate in the hearing. This part of his ruling was revolutionary, for it meant that any group of citizens had a legal right to enter a bureaucratic proceeding— and, therefore, subsequently to challenge the agency's decision in court if they so chose. Burger said that if the allegations turned out to be true, that "would preclude as a matter of law the required finding that renewal of the license would serve the

public interest."[9] The judge added that experience had under-
mined the old New Deal faith in entrusting the public interest
to the exclusive discretion of an administrative agency:

> The theory that the Commission can always effectively
> represent the listener interests in a renewal proceeding
> without the aid and participation of legitimate listener
> representatives fulfilling the role of private attorneys
> general is one of those assumptions we collectively try to
> work with so long as they are reasonably adequate. When
> it becomes clear, as it does to us now, that it is no longer
> a valid assumption which stands up under the realities of
> actual experience, neither we nor the Commission can
> continue to rely on it.[10]

The commission was shocked by Burger's opinion, which
must rank as one of the more extreme indictments on record of
one federal institution by another, certainly by an appellate
court. But the agency appeared to be more angered than intimidated. As in the ABC-ITT case, Commissioner Hyde could
not understand the clash of ideologies, much less appreciate the
growing strength behind the populist theory articulated by
Burger and the dissenting commissioners. The FCC did not
seem really to believe that it had to take the court seriously.
When the case came back to the commission, the agency
promptly put the burden of proof on the petitioners in the im-
pending rehearing, even though the court had explicitly ordered
that the burden of proof should rest with WLBT. Agency
officials subjected the Jackson blacks and their allies to a bar-
rage of petty harassments, as the case moved through the hearing to the review by the commissioners. During the argument,
Hyde and his majority sat stonily while the attorney for the
church complained of the examiner's refusal to accept much of
the evidence offered by the petitioners, and of his refusal to believe most of what he had accepted. A five-to-two majority
granted WLBT renewal of the license, this time ruling that the
injustices claimed by the petitioners—which they had accepted

as valid in their previous decision—had in fact never occurred at all.

The New York Times and the *Washington Post* responded with front-page coverage of the blistering dissent filed by Commissioners Cox and Johnson, which observed that

> What was once an unfortunate—though understandable and corrigible—attempt by the agency to ease its administrative chores has become a disgrace to the administrative process . . . [an] obstruction to participatory democracy and the efforts of American government to establish confidence among Negro and other citizens. . . .

On his own motion, without even waiting for the church to appeal, Burger ordered the commission to send up the record of the case. (In making his original remand back to the agency, he had taken the highly unusual step of formally retaining jurisdiction; this ensured that he would have the final say in the case.) Burger, who by this time had been appointed Chief Justice of the Supreme Court, did not send the parties back to the FCC for another go round. He ordered the commission to terminate WLBT's license and to put the franchise up for competitive applications. In a line to which special attention was paid by news commentators, he noted the agency's "curious neutrality-in-favor-of-the-licensee." Burger held that "it will serve no useful purpose to ask the Commission to reconsider . . . under a correct allocation of burden of proof. . . . The administrative conduct reflected in this record is beyond repair."

These were harsh words, but they should hardly have come as a surprise to the FCC. The commission seemed almost to invite the court's attack. Hyde permitted, perhaps even encouraged, displays of hostility to the petitioners, the kinds of hostility routinely used to deter would-be intervenors in the agency's affairs—as if this were a routine case, and as if these particular intervenors did not have a court order backing up their claims. To rationalize their defiance of the court, the majority relied on routine arguments cranked out by the opinion-writing bureau. Rife with contradictions and crude evasions, this document constituted an appealing target to the dissenters, critical reporters, editorial writers, and to Burger himself. No one within the infrastructure surrounding the FCC appeared capable of nudging the agency off its course, though few could have doubted that the case was bound to end unhappily.

For reformers, the *WLBT* case was proof that their cause was steadily gaining momentum. Newspaper front pages and federal judges were now paying attention to the scandalous state of affairs at the FCC. Impressed by the writings of these critical observers, charitable institutions and individuals began funding "public-interest law firms" to expand the populist campaign initiated by the United Church of Christ. Within a year, lawyers representing local groups like the Jackson black community were challenging the renewal of stations in other cities; the result was a series of innovative settlements, in which the stations agreed to provide service to hitherto neglected minorities. Other, largely national, groups began presenting claims on behalf of consumer, environmental, and political interests. The court of appeals in Washington continued to give the cases brought by this corps of public intervenors a sympathetic hearing. Occasional "counter-commercials" began to be heard on radio and television in response to demands for fair presentation of contrasting views by the new public interest lawyers that were challenging the FCC. Fitful bursts of public antagonism to the broadcast media and official attacks by the White House on network news coverage created a menacing backdrop for the increasingly reformist atmosphere at the FCC. For the first time in twenty-five years of federal regulation, the masters of the broadcasting industry were nervous that they might not be able to keep FCC regulation a domesticated servant.

Populism at the FCC: Concluding Observations
The industry had long ago acquiesced in a political stalemate. In principle, it was subject to pervasive government controls, defined by New Deal legislative draftsmen and broadly con-

strued by a New Deal Supreme Court. But, in fact, these controls, and the entire populist concept they reflected, soon began to enjoy an almost exclusively verbal existence. This concept had been devoid of any political content for so long that the regulators charged with overseeing it no longer believed in it themselves. By the late 1960s, they were unable to believe that anyone else of political consequence believed in it either. The requirement that broadcast mergers, renewals, acquisitions, expansions, or other activities serve the public interest had become a ritual, mechanically noted by the opinion writers on the FCC staff.

The broadcasting industry had never liked the broad grant of regulatory power written into the Communications Act (except when, in the late 1950s, they discovered how to use this power to suppress the potential competition of the cable television industry). But as long as the practical effect of the statute was innocuous, few people in the industry showed any interest in lobbying for a change in its terms. Suddenly, however, the upsurge in reformist agitation after the ABC-ITT and WLBT cases excited fears that life might at last be breathed into the Communications Act.

The anxious broadcasters blamed their difficulties on Nicholas Johnson. Virtually every week *Broadcasting* magazine ran several editorial paragraphs denouncing Johnson. The editors frequently urged broadcast lobbyists to redouble their efforts to find a way to push him off the FCC (FCC commissioners enjoy the statutory protection of a fixed seven-year term). Johnson was excoriated in far more extreme terms than his dissenting colleague Kenneth Cox, because he alone had put his critique across to a public beyond the closed environment of the FCC infrastructure. His views were therefore potentially more damaging than Cox's. He was continually denounced for spicing his opinions and speeches with demagogic rhetoric. It was alleged that he maintained improper contacts with reporters and editors from the national media. Attempts were even made to force him to abstain from cases involving issues he had discussed in the numerous magazine articles that appeared under his own name. Johnson was not, however, deterred from publicizing his assault on the commission in forceful and flamboyant terms. This, he believed, was his only hope for converting the FCC into an instrument that could realize the populist values inscribed in the Communications Act.

It would be grossly premature to decide that the days of the *ancien régime* at the FCC are numbered. Dissenting commissioners, the press, and the courts may have dented the battlements, but the walls and foundations remain. As is true of most other New Deal agencies, political obstacles make basic structural change seen far beyond the horizon. Even the "rococo additions to the existing structure" that reformers have won thus far could easily be lost. If instability persists at the commission, Congress might be stirred to produce some clarifying amendments to the Communications Act. But, given the still-embryonic state of public concern, such changes are more likely to reflect the wishes of the National Association of Broadcasters than those of Commissioner Nicholas Johnson.

Moreover, the turbulence at the FCC may be subsiding. Since 1969, the agency has had a new chairman, Dean Burch, who has provided a more deft brand of leadership than his predecessor. Burch was Barry Goldwater's Republican national chairman in 1964. On the major national issues of the 1950s and 1960s, he would have to be regarded as an extreme conservative. But he has maneuvered the FCC along a relatively more moderate course. Unlike Hyde, he is not a product of the broadcast political infrastructure. He manifests no special allegiance to or affection for the broadcasting industry. Whatever his personal views on policy, Burch clearly understands the logic of the populist critique of the FCC. He has prodded the agency partially to forswear its protectionist antipathy to cable television. In handling the spate of license renewal and fairness doctrine challenges that followed on the success of the WLBT petition, he has generally ruled against populist intervenors. But not always. And he has seemed to take challengers' claims seriously. Finally, he has countered Nicholas Johnson's dissents with quotable concurring opinions of his own. In short, the days are gone when the FCC's highest official is himself the best argument available to the agency's critics. Burch has bent commission policies enough to meet some of the critics' arguments, but in doing so he has lessened the chances for more radical change.

In any event, whatever becomes of the FCC, the conflict there offers an instructive view of the current status of the populist ideal. As a relic of past reform enthusiasms, the FCC typifies the political milieu created by most of the grand regulatory designs of the New Deal and the Progressive era. The regulatory environment is dominated by two ironic contrasts. First, there is the gap between the populist goals written into the Communications Act and the zealous insularity that guides the agency's performance. Second, and perhaps more startling, is the contrast between the virtual absence of political force behind this ideal, and the amazing *breadth* of approval it enjoys, both in popular and ideological terms; there are, after all, few causes that unite an apparent radical like Nicholas Johnson with a supposed conservative like Warren Burger.

Despite the efforts of these reformers, and despite the general rebirth of public concern about the integrity of regulation, the broadcasting industry is still in control of the governmental machinery most necessary to its fortunes. This machinery includes the agency and the relevant outposts of congressional power. Ringing this infrastructure are the dissenting commissioners, the courts, the press, and the do-good public-interest groups. Under prevailing circumstances, they can only expect to play a defensive role. Ordinarily, they cannot invoke the FCC's vast legal powers to direct affirmatively the course of the industry's development. In general, the most they can hope for is a chance to halt egregious abuses caused by the industry's own power to manipulate commission policy affirmatively. Through their familiarity and command over the verbal superstructure of communications policy, they can delay, object to, and expose. They can stop ITT from taking over ABC, but they cannot take NBC away from RCA. (Although in the brief populist heyday of the late New Deal, the FCC did succeed in diverting one of NBC's two national radio networks, and forcing its sale to interests that were eventually consolidated as ABC.) Now, however, the reformers' only resources are the cogency of their arguments, the eloquence of their rhetoric, and the prestige of their offices (this includes the kinds of prestige connoted by the by-line of a reporter or the masthead of a public-interest law firm). They depend on their ability to persuade other officials and influential figures, and ultimately on their capacity to persuade the public.

For its part, the public can usually be counted on to approve of the populist objectives of this ideocratic coalition. But only rarely, and then temporarily, will public concern reach a pitch high enough to endanger the reelection prospects of politicians. Still, even mere public approval is not without political value. Such approval indeed is essential to attaining the defensive, short-run objectives of a muckraking news article or a strongly worded court reversal. Such initiatives will deter the individuals and institutions at whom they are aimed only if they inspire— or are believed to inspire—public acclaim.

But to achieve change of any duration in the political structure of regulation, FCC reformers will need more than passive approval. At this moment, the prospects for stirring intense popular enthusiasm for FCC reform are dim. They should not, however, be dismissed, especially in view of the success similar agitators have had in other policy areas. Once a set of institutional arrangements has lost its legitimacy in the public's eye—as the present state of broadcast regulation has —political lightning can strike it at any time.

The larger question—or at least the question largely unanswered as yet—is what the reformers would do with a massive outpouring of public support. What proposals would they fashion to answer the public demand for change? Right now the main model available, or the only one that seems at all appealing to reformers at the FCC, smacks of the old New Deal hope, the grand design concept of public control. The principal recommendations one hears invariably emphasize giving the agency more legal power to determine what is in the public interest and more power to take broadcast licenses away from operators who don't meet FCC programming standards. The only switch from the New Deal formula is to expand statutory sanction for public intervention in these broader determinations —though extra guarantees of this sort are largely superfluous since Justice Burger's sweeping *WLBT* decision.

If public support for populist FCC reforms does materialize, the process by which any such basic changes will come about will be one of stagecraft. And it will be managed by a coalition of individuals and institutions who play an active, though essentially peripheral, role in the present regulatory environment —reporters, judges, reformist bureaucrats and legislators, professors, foundations, and professional do-good groups.

It may seem strange that the cause of vindicating populist ideals in our democratic society has to be entrusted to an elite such as the "ideocracy." In practice, however, there is no choice. The populist ideal may appeal broadly to the American people, and it may be designed to serve their interests as well as their most deeply cherished values. But the politics of actually achieving populist goals has always placed a special emphasis on an activist vanguard. The populist vanguard, moreover, has always been disproportionately (though not exclusively) recruited from relatively elite sectors of the population.

6
The Genteel Populists

"No democracy can live without a leisured class capable of thinking on the problems of government," a political scientist at Princeton observed in 1889. His name was Woodrow Wilson. Such frankly elitist sentiments may seem curious coming from someone who, two decades later, would be elected president on the basis of the most radical populist campaign in the nation's history. In 1912 Wilson campaigned to liberate the White House from "big business interests," whose power, he charged, had become "so great that there is an open question whether the government of the United States with the people back of it is strong enough to overcome and rule them. . . ."[1] But the contradiction was only a logical, not a political one. The constituency Wilson led to victory in 1912 was populist in its outlook, but by no means poor. As has been confirmed by every study of the social composition of the Progressive movement, Progressive leaders usually tended, like Wilson himself, to belong to highly educated, professional families with conservative leanings. They entered politics from a background of inherited wealth and business connections.[2]

These genteel reformers did not see in regulation and direct democracy the means of improving their own lot or that of their immediate constituency, nor did they seek to improve the general prosperity of the nation (which was in any event enjoying a dazzling boom). Their motives were abstract, altruistic, even aesthetic. They wanted the new economic machine to run in accordance with old democratic principle—with the populist ideal that the interests of the public should never be subverted by private power. Their point was to see to it, as Teddy Roosevelt believed he had done with his victory over the Northern Securities merger, "that the most powerful men in this country were held to accountability before the law."[3] As Henry L. Stimson elaborated in explaining why he left his Wall Street law firm to serve as a United States attorney and prosecute corporations under new regulatory laws:

> [It] has always seemed to me, in the law from what I have seen of it, that wherever the public interest has come into conflict with private interests, private interest was more adequately represented than the public interest.

Of his work on behalf of this new client, the public interest, Stimson said,

> There has been an ethical side of it which has been of more interest to me, and I have felt that I could get a good deal closer to the problems of life than I ever did before, and felt that the work was a good deal more worthwhile. And one always feels better when he feels that he is working in a good cause.[4]

Noblesse Oblige

The contemporary ring of Stimson's confession must intrigue anyone acquainted with the recent ferment that overtook the legal profession in the late 1960s. His anxiety that the "private interest was more adequately represented than the public interest" matches with remarkable precision the anxiety of the new populist point of view. The same speech could easily have been made by any of the young lawyers clustered with Nader and in satellite "public-interest law firms" around Dupont Circle in Washington, D.C., or by their more cautious colleagues who have induced private law firm employers to work on individual public-interest projects.

The new movement has not yet produced a figure comparable in professional stature to the Progressives' Brandeis. But Brandeis's own career underscores how dramatically similar are the sentiments and the strategies that link new populist leaders like Philip Moore to that earlier genteel crusade to vindicate the populist ideal. Brandeis took time off from a glittering, corporate practice in 1897, when he was forty-one, to stop efforts by the Boston Elevated Railway Company to procure franchises he felt would "if, enacted, sacrifice the interests of the public to that of a single corporation." Brandeis lost that battle, but went on to victories in larger causes, which ultimately made him a best-selling author, presidential adviser, and finally one of the nation's truly great judges. A letter written by the young Brandeis to the president of the Boston Elevated during his first battle for the public interest is full of the spirit that animated his subsequent career as a reformer:

> I was told today by a common friend that you stated to him that I was retained by the Municipal League to oppose the Boston Elevated Railway Company's bill, and was paid for so doing. The statement is absolutely without foundation. I have been retained by no person, association, or corporation, directly or indirectly in this matter, and I have opposed it solely because I believe that the bill, if passed, would result in great injustice to the people of Massachusetts, and eventually great injustice to the capitalist classes whom you are now representing, and with whom I, as well as you, are in close connection.[5]

Brandeis was evidently stirred by a brand of noblesse oblige, but one that compelled service not to concrete, identifiable entities or people, but to *the* people, to an ideal of the good society. This feeling is most similar to the ideals that led young men in other lands and at other times to join the army. For explicit contemporary echoes of this progressive sentiment, one need not look far. John Gardner, who has been engaged for two years with moderate success in becoming a patrician Ralph Nader, provides a good example. Gardner could have lifted the following harangue, which appeared on a recent "Op. Ed." page of *The New York Times,* from Wilson's *The New Freedom*:

> It isn't a pleasant thing to admit that in this great nation elective offices can be purchased, that votes of Federal, state, and local officials are bought and sold every day; that access of the people to their government is blocked by a Chinese Wall of money.
> It isn't pleasant but it's a fact—and, today, a dangerous fact.
> Americans in every walk of life are increasingly skeptical about their political and governmental institutions. They doubt that these institutions, which are supposed to serve them, are in fact doing so. And that withdrawal of confidence bodes ill for the Republic.
> People need to feel they have access to their government. They need to believe their government is responsive. They need to feel it can be called to account. But wherever they look they find that "the access of money to power" is blocking the access of people to power.[6]

Accountability, responsiveness, access, corruption, even "power-to-the-people"—the standard clichés, goals, and evils of the new populist litany pervade Gardner's rhetoric. If the *Times*'s (presumably affluent) readers were disturbed by his indictment, it was not, in all probability, because it threatened their interests, but because it was not "pretty," as he put it—it affronted their moral sensibilities. The same could be said of the *New Yorker* readers who responded with an unprecedented flood of approving letters to the editor, when Charles Reich first laid bare the "anatomy of the corporate state."

> What is the nature of the social order within which
> we live? Why are we so powerless? Why does our state
> seem impervious to democratic or popular control? . . .
> Our present social order is so contrary to anything we
> have learned to expect about a government or a society
> that its structure is almost beyond comprehension. Most
> of us, including our political leaders and those who write
> about politics and economics, hold to a picture that is
> entirely false. . . . The corporate state is an immensely
> powerful machine, ordered, legalistic, rational yet utterly
> out of human control, wholly and perfectly indifferent to
> any human values. . . . The corporate state is a complete
> reversal of the original American ideal and plan. The
> state, and not the market or the people or any abstract
> economic laws, determines what shall be produced, what
> shall be consumed, and how it shall be allocated. . . . The
> state is subject neither to democratic controls, constitu-
> tional limits, or legal regulation.[7]

Enthusiasm for Reich's thesis could not have come from any
sense of victimization on the part of his audience, at least not
in any objective or economic sense; the corporate state has,
after all, done well enough by subscribers to the *New Yorker*.

And it is the same constituency that contributed $200,000
to John Gardner's Common Cause in its first year and more
to Ralph Nader's "Public Citizen" campaign. Neither of these
sums shows a particularly broad base of active support for
the recipients' causes. Moreover, Nader was originally so dubious about the breadth of interest that could be mobilized
to support his work that he persistently declined proposals to
launch a mass-membership type of fund-raising campaign.
Joseph Onek, a founder of Campaign GM and now director of
the Center for Law and Social Policy, tried as early as 1968 to
interest him in the idea but did not succeed until Nader was
goaded into duplicating Gardner's apparently successful strategy. The bulk of Nader's financial support comes from campus
and other audiences who pay up to $3,500 per lecture to hear
him in person. Additional funds for the cadre of public-interest
law firms that represent them in litigation are supplied by a

small number of relatively adventuresome foundations, among which Ford, Rockefeller, the Stern Family Fund, New World, the Field Foundation, The Norman Fund, The New York Foundation, and Carnegie have been the leaders. Seed money for Common Cause went to Gardner in large personal contributions from Henry Ford and David Rockefeller, along with funds raised by Dreyfus Fund Chairman Howard Stein.

Apart from the concern of Nader and Gardner with the integrity of federal regulatory institutions, the new populists, like the Progressives, have focused on bringing the electoral system more closely in line with the populist ideal of direct democracy. Here again leadership and active support have come from the higher strata of the society. The amendment to replace the electoral college with a direct-election system for selecting presidents was drafted by none other than the American Bar Association (ABA). The ABA treated electoral reform as a major cause, as did *The New York Times,* the *Washington Post,* and a variety of other well-situated institutions. The cause of reform of the nomination process, which proved dramatically more successful than the move to abolish the electoral college, has been supported mainly by a similar elite constituency on the left of the Democratic Party—a decentralized constituency that has local roots in many states, but is, nevertheless, a cohesive, well-educated, and relatively well-to-do coterie.

Still another index of the social character of this political reform constituency is the surprising amount of campaign financing that was available to the candidates who were its heroes. Some observers were shocked in 1970 when Herbert Alexander's Citizens' Research Foundation revealed its figures on money consumed by the presidential campaigns of 1968. Senator McCarthy's quixotic, bootstrap crusade was shown to have raised and spent over $8 million, four times as much as the Humphrey campaign raised before the convention and almost as much as Humphrey and the regular Democrats raised during the election campaign itself. Despite the equally quixotic image of George McGovern's campaign, he was able to report a more than respectable total of approximately $25 million even after McGovern's soak-the-rich tax plans and bleak prospects frightened off some large contributors, like Howard Stein, who had favored McCarthy (such fear may have been magnified by the new disclosure law, which assured that the victorious Republicans would be able later on to identify those who had supported their enemy). Some of McCarthy's large donors proved to be against inequality at home as well as war abroad. And mailings produced an unprecedented response of $25, $50, and $100 contributions. Ironically, McGovern's populism stirred broad and active support from within the upper-middle-class constituency represented on the various mailing lists that went into his finance operation's computers—even though his program yielded mainly indifference and even hostility from the middle and lower-middle classes whom it was originally supposed to benefit. Indeed, one of the most important—and least noticed—sea-changes of the decade in the country's political structure was the dramatic demonstration by McGovern, Gardner, and Nader that substantial money could be raised for the pursuit of new populist politics.

But the most ironic demonstration of the tie between riches and populist interest in democratic reform came in 1971, when it was revealed that a secret conference of liberal millionaires had been organized by John Gardner and Howard Samuels; their objective, never realized, apparently because news of the meeting became public, was to agree to boycott all candidates who did not support legislation to achieve fundamental reform of, of all things, campaign finance.

Farewells to Reform: The Farmers

If John Gardner's public writings are any indication of what he might say in addressing a secret meeting, then the contributors who convened at his behest may well have heard rhetoric much like that which the 1892 national convention of the Populist Party heard when their platform was read out: "Corruption dominates the ballot-box, the Legislatures, the Congress, and touches even the ermine of the bench. . . ." Those original Populists would no doubt have been dumbfounded by the setting of the posh Hotel Pierre at Sixty-First Street and Fifth Avenue, where the 1971 campaign finance reformers gathered. Yet there is no reason to doubt the sincerity of John Gardner's commitment to attack electoral corruption, anymore than there is any basis for cynical speculation about Louis Brandeis's commitment to squelch the greed of the Boston Elevated, in 1897, just five years after the Populists launched their first national campaign.

Indeed, it is good for the cause of populism that the Brandeises and Gardners have picked up its banner. For the Populist Party's first national campaign turned out also to be its last. And, what is more important, though populist rhetoric was soon thereafter embraced by the Democrats' new leader William Jennings Bryan, the agrarian constituency that activated both the Populists and the Bryanite Democrats was already, by the time men like Brandeis were rallied to their standard, growing disenchanted with the populist ideal itself. In the first decade of the twentieth century, agricultural politics had chosen for itself a truly revolutionary course. A new network of pressure groups sprang from what once had been a base for the ideological politics of populism. At length there emerged a virtual private government with internal autonomy and external command over governmental authority unmatched by any other commercial interest in the country.

The feudalization of agricultural politics is a tale that has been well-told a number of times. Only the briefest summary is necessary here. In the first decade of the twentieth century, a novel institution known as the "county agent" appeared in farm counties across the nation; the job of the county agent, as then defined, was to instruct local farmers to use scientific farming techniques. In 1914 Congress gave the county agent system federal financial backing, though the agents were also still expected to raise local funds. In order to solidify their influence, the agents, with strong encouragement from USDA, created tight organizations composed of their local clientele; these organizations, which seem from the first to have been dominated by the richer and more skillful farmers in each community, were called farm bureaus. By the end of World War II the local farm bureaus had united to become the National Farm Bureau Federation (NFBF).

The NFBF (which only last year induced President Nixon to replace his agriculture secretary, Clifford Hardin, with a controversial bureau candidate, Earl Butz) showed its great power soon after it was formed. As Populists in 1890, farmers denounced the wild gyrations of the world commodity markets, and blamed their uncertain plight on the monopoly power of the railroads and other capitalist enterprises. By 1920, they were facing an additional difficulty—a persistent excess of farm products over the urban public's demand for them. These economic facts, plus the political fact that farmers were showing up as a smaller and smaller portion of the electorate in each census, seemed to portend a bleak future. And for smaller, poorer farmers, the future did often prove to be a grim struggle for existence.

But the power—and wealth—of the Farm Bureau constituency grew as their numbers decreased and their natural economic position worsened. Instead of opposing the idea of antimonopolism, they set out to use the government to establish monopoly power for themselves. During the 1920s they got the newly formed farm bloc in Congress to pass two ambitious schemes for government-sanctioned price fixing, the equalization fee and the export-debenture plans. These were vetoed by Calvin Coolidge, but a decade later their basic concept was embraced by the New Deal. The 1933 Agricultural Adjustment Act (AAA), drafted in the Farm Bureau's Washington headquarters, explicitly declared that it was a goal of national policy to guarantee farmers an amount for their goods equal to the purchasing power of the dollars earned by farmers in the years 1909–14 ("parity"), the period of their greatest prosperity. The AAA sought to attain this goal through a complex variety of inducements to individual farmers in exchange for their promise to limit production. The system for administering the production controls was complex and radically decentralized, providing local committees of farmers with a substantial policy-making role. The Supreme Court invalidated the act, but it was soon replaced by a virtually identical one, the Agricultural Marketing Agreement Act. This was sustained by the more hospitable Supreme Court of the later New Deal years.

The balance of power between producer and consumer struck by this system of marketing controls is illustrated nicely by a current controversy involving tomatoes. The main actor in the tomato drama is an institution called the "Florida Tomato Committee." This is a group of twelve tomato growers "appointed" by the secretary of agriculture on the "nomination" of the tomato industry itself; its job is to make "recommendations" to the secretary about what regulations he might adopt limiting the grade, size, quality, and amount of tomatoes grown within the committee's jurisdiction, which in this case includes all domestically produced tomatoes. In fact the secretary usually rubberstamps the recommendations of this committee and of the many similar industry committees as well.

In the late 1960s the tomato industry began to face growing competition from higher quality, lower cost tomatoes coming across the border from Mexico. The domestic growers had a ready response to this threat. The Florida Tomato Committee simply issued a recommended regulation, which was immediately approved by USDA. This innocuous-seeming rule forbade the sale of "mature green" tomatoes unless they are 2 9/32 inches in diameter; at the same time it forbade the sale of "all other" tomatoes unless they are 1/4 inch larger—2 17/32 inches in diameter. The effect of the rule was to exclude virtually all Mexican-grown tomatoes from the American market. The reason is that Florida tomatoes are green at maturity (and have to be gassed to look red on supermarket shelves). Mexican tomatoes are pink at maturity; very few of either kind of tomato, which are botanically identical except for their color, grow to boast a 2 17/32-inch diameter.

The Florida farmers had not only exercised the monopoly power and public authority which the Agriculture Marketing Agreement Act had put at their disposal, they had gone further and used the statute to arrogate to themselves the power to enact a private protective tariff. The growers were not shy about their motives (they had no reason to be, for their wishes were almost always regarded as commands by reviewing authorities in the USDA). The following remarks were among those recorded in the minutes of the committee meeting at which the new rules were adopted:

> The reason behind it is that we can cut a lot of Mexican tomatoes. . . . Let's face it, we are trying to cut out more of the Mexicans than we are of ourselves.
> Let this in, this marketing order for a couple of weeks, so they can get a taste of what we can really do with a marketing order.
> Well, the thing we are looking at will be of help to the Florida growers. It will eliminate our competition, and that's what we're trying to do. Let's face it. We're trying to eliminate our competition. . . .[8]

In "trying to eliminate [their] competition," the Florida growers were notably successful. Within one month after the regulation went into effect in the spring of 1970, Mexican tomatoes, which had gained up to 70.6 percent of the American tomato market, slipped to 24.0 percent. The impact of the regulation was also felt by consumers. By the winter of 1971, the Consumer Price Index showed that prices for tomatoes had jumped over 40 percent more than prices of all other foods consumed at home. In the midst of runaway inflation that ultimately forced the government to impose price controls on most products, these Florida tomato farmers had induced the government to help them send their prices spiraling up almost half again as fast as other food products. It should be added that the prices of many other food products are kept at artificially high levels by similar production control and price-support mechanisms under the AMAA and other protective farm legislation.

Evidently, the forces of organized agriculture, that could not beat the monopolists and fixers in the 1890s, had joined 'em, and quite successfully. Many Americans are aware of this by now. Indeed, people have come to understand that the cartel machinery that governs the political economy of agriculture was put into place behind the grand design rhetoric of the New Deal. But there is one thing we tend to overlook when we consider the feudal manner to which "Agriculture, Inc." has become accustomed. Not only has American politics gained a formidable concentration of power, it has *lost* a once-important constituency for populist idealism. There are a few aspects of contemporary government more incompatible with the tenets of that ideal than the complex which includes USDA, the NFBF, and the lesser farm lobbying organizations. Some liberal Democrats might object to this position. They might approve of the National Farmers Union, generally thought to be the more "liberal" farm lobby, which tends to represent the primarily wheat-growing interests of the plains states, and to some undefined extent, also the interests of farmers smaller and less rich than the Farm Bureau's constituency. But the Farmers' Union is a more vociferous advocate of price supports and other monopolistic devices than the bureau, a stand which no doubt reflects its constituents' needs, but which also clashes with the interests of consumers and with the requisites of the populist ideal.

Farewells to Reform: The Workers

Substantially the same story can be told about the evolution of the American labor movement, though labor has not forsaken the populist ideal as completely as the farmers have. The first stirrings of a national labor movement occurred in the 1880s, just when antecedents of the Populist Party were agitating on the farms. The organization called itself the Noble Order of the Knights of Labor. The knights never turned their vast membership of the 1800s into a splinter political party as the Populists did. But that was the direction in which their rhetoric would surely have led, had the organization survived. Their commitment to the populist ideal and its attendant conceptual paraphernalia—that the interests of all workers, and indeed, all "the people" including consumers, were harmonious and could be mobilized to combat a tiny capitalist elite—mirrored that of the Populist Party itself. In the composition of its membership, and especially of its leadership, the Noble Order of the Knights whose ranks were sprinkled with middle-class representatives, anticipated the Progressives more perfectly than the Populists did. The knights, however, proved an ephemeral presence in industry and politics. By 1900, they were gone, and they left behind few enduring institutional changes to attest to their once formidable presence.

Like the Populists, the knights were replaced by an organization that followed a pluralist strategy for improving the lot of their constituents, the American Federation of Labor (AFL). Indeed, the AFL was at first far more advanced and self-conscious about its pluralist goals and its contempt for populist ideology than the infrastructure that evolved from the county agent system. In 1898, the AFL had 278,016 members, only one-third that of the knights' peak membership. But by 1914, this figure had jumped almost ten-fold, to over two million members.

The AFL organized workers and sought higher wages for them. It did not promote democratic ideals, or any other kind of ideals. Samuel Gompers, its leader, is famous for his answer to the question, "What are the goals of your organization?" "More!" he replied. For movements like those of the Populists or the knights, Gompers had only the greatest contempt. "Each 'ism" he once said,

> has stood but as an evanescent and iridescent dream of
> poor humanity groping blindly in the dark for its ideal;
> and it has caused many a heart wrench to relegate some
> idealism to movements which do not move, to the dead
> ashes of blasted hopes and promises.[9]

If Gompers' syntax here was garbled, his point was not. Though
generally counted as an ally of the Progressives, he was somewhat unreliable. He was, for instance, a good deal less interested in fighting monopoly by corporate business than he was
in promoting monopoly power for his own members; at the
Chicago Conference on Trusts of 1899, a critical link in the
chain of events that transmuted the agrarian populism of the
1890s into the broader-based Progressive movement, Gompers' speech was not what the audience had come to hear. His
main message was that organized labor looked "with apprehen-
sion at the many panaceas and remedies offered by theorists
to curb the growth and development or destroy the combinations of industry."[10] (More in line with the spirit prevailing at
this gathering of the Progressive faithful was the attitude of the
Knights of Labor, by then a mere shadow organization; their
speeches had such titles as "The Social Enemy" and "The
Trust as a Conspiracy Against Civilization.")

To be fair to Gompers, it must be added that his distaste
for antitrust legislation was grounded in a refined understanding of the power configurations that would control the administration of such statutes; he noted that "panaceas and remedies"
would very likely become in practice "the very instruments employed to deprive labor of the benefit of organized effort."
Gompers here was referring to Richard Olney's use of a Sherman Act injunction to crush the socialist Eugene Debs' Pull-
man strike in 1894 and he was anticipating the legally more
extravagant antitrust attack on the Danbury Hatters that the
Supreme Court upheld in 1908.

In any event, the goal of organized labor, like that of organized agriculture, was internal political autonomy and external
market power. This goal was realized, again, as in the case of

agriculture, under the populistic aegis of the New Deal. Then the AFL and the new Congress of Industrial Organizations (CIO), obtained the Norris-LaGuardia Act, the Wagner Act, and the *United States* v. *Hutcheson* decision from the New Deal Supreme Court. Together, these legal changes conferred on organized labor the same status conferred on organized agriculture by the combination of the AMAA and the Capper-Volstead Antitrust Immunity Act which the Farm Bureau and its allies among the packers and processors had obtained in 1922. The unions got substantial freedom from antitrust restraints, and a variety of governmental inducements and sanctions to aid them affirmatively in organizing and bargaining collectively. The National Labor Relations Board (NLRB) began largely as a captive of the labor movement (though it was to become less captive in later years). Its job was to shelter organized labor in its efforts to attain the total unionization of the working class and it was impressively successful in realizing that goal. As in the case of the Nixon inflation control mechanisms, World War II legislation did not put labor under the Office of Price Administration (OPA), but gave it its own wage-control apparatus, the National War Labor Board, which had the conventional tripartite structure involving labor, business, and "public" representatives. (The political power reflected by this special treatment did not, however, quite seem to match that of organized agriculture. The latter succeeded in obtaining from Congress, among other things, statutes guaranteeing freedom from controls until prices rose above 11 percent of parity— a standard that pushed some agricultural prices over consumers' ceilings and obliged the government to pay subsidies to producers caught in the middle.) [11]

Along with its new economic and political power, labor acquired the image as a bulwark of progressive policies beyond its own immediate interests. This reputation was linked to its close alliance with the national Democratic Party. Even after 1968, when many upper-middle-class liberals were distressed by labor views on military, race, and civil-liberties issues, open antilabor sentiments seemed philosophically as well as politically unthinkable. And the reputation of the unions as a political base for progressive policies lives on.

For the most part, this reputation is deserved. Except for the churches there is no organized interest of any consequence, other than the unions, that uses its power for ends other than the immediate economic welfare of its own constituents. The construction trades may now be barring their doors to blacks (as well as anyone else who does not happen to be a close blood relative of existing members). But the civil-rights movement of the early 1960s could not have succeeded without strong union support. The United Auto Workers (UAW) financed the 1963 March on Washington. The AFL-CIO put all its lobbying resources, in many ways unmatched by any other interest group active in Washington, at the disposal of the Leadership Conference on Civil Rights to help pass the Civil Rights Act of 1964. One of the sections that the House Judiciary Committee added to President Kennedy's civil rights bill was Title VII banning employment discrimination; supporting that amendment, AFL-CIO George Meany testified specifically in favor of banning discrimination by unions as well as by employers. Beyond civil rights, the unions have always led the fight for welfare legislation, from Medicare to the Economic Opportunity Act of 1964 to the child development program vetoed by President Nixon in 1971.

Labor has even, on occasion, made its weight felt or at least raised its voice on behalf of consumer causes. The AFL-CIO's political action arm, the Committee on Political Education (COPE), made the Fair Packaging and Labeling Act of 1966—one of the new populist movement's first legislative initiatives—one of the test measures used to evaluate the records of members of Congress. The day Leonard Woodcock was sworn into office as Walter Reuther's successor (after Reuther died in a 1971 plane crash), he dramatically appeared at Detroit's Cobo Hall, where General Motors management was grimly hosting an annual shareholders' meeting dominated by strident spokesmen for Campaign GM. Woodcock took the microphone and delivered a brief address supporting Campaign GM. More recently, both the UAW and the AFL-CIO have become the prime movers behind the current effort to enact a national health insurance program. In the summer of 1972, Woodcock made a dramatic proconsumer gesture when he joined in Ralph Nader's suit to force the Nixon Administration to hold public hearings on the auto industry's application for price increases. Woodcock reasoned that higher prices would mean fewer sales and, hence, fewer jobs.

However, despite the major role which organized labor plays—and will no doubt continue to play—in an array of welfare, civil rights, and even consumer causes, the unions are not on the whole a reliable supporter of the populist ideal. They are, after all, devoted to putting cash in the pockets of their members. They must therefore regard politics as a means to that end—just as representatives of the Farm Bureau or the oil industry regard it. To the union man politics cannot be primarily an arena for the playing out of democratic rituals, though these rituals may be seen, in important instances, as useful supports for union objectives. Where populist standards clash with labor's economic interests, it is obvious and understandable that the latter must come first.

Even more important, organized labor is now a full-fledged participant in the pluralist system of interest-group bargaining; its wealth and organization are powerful counters with which to influence the behavior of institutions and officials at all levels of government. Because of this power, labor does not really have an interest in promoting the populist image of democracy among the electorate. A regulatory system that everywhere subordinated producer interests to consumer and other public concerns would threaten the economic security of many important labor groups. A political system that conformed to populist standards would leave organized labor on the whole less potent than it is now. This was true even in the early postwar years when liberal and labor objectives were far more nearly coincident than now.

But now the natural friction between labor interests and populist ideals is growing continually more pronounced. As Frederick Dutton recently observed, "Organized labor is actually now much stronger as a lobbying bloc than as an electioneering force. . . . Labor's main influence currently comes from the substantial campaign contributions it makes." Dutton observes that the unions gave a reported $700,000 in the 1970 (off-year) elections in California alone, and that during 1968 campaigns they contributed cash and services valued at more than $18 million.[12]

For all these reasons, it should not be surprising that cartel protections administered by the ICC are sustained as much by the railroad unions and by the International Brotherhood of Teamsters as by the railroad and trucking companies; that the similar cartel created for the major airlines when the CAB was created in 1938 was promoted by the pilots' union as well as by the airlines; or that when Thurman Arnold set out to liberate the housing industry from trade restraints that help keep housing supply behind demand, he failed because he could not reach the main culprit—the powerful building trades unions. Labor is often a crucial silent partner in anti-populist coalitions. For example, when the Congress was considering whether to rescue Lockheed Aircraft from bankruptcy, John Kenneth Galbraith warned the legislators that an affirmative decision would "serve no purpose except to show the country that the military-industrial complex was alive and well in Washington." A majority of the representatives ignored Galbraith and his allies and bailed the company out. It is certain that they would not have done so if organized labor had not made the cause of Lockheed (and, naturally, its work force) a high priority cause of its own. Similarly, the outcome of the fight against the SST would never have been in doubt if labor had not provided strong backing for the project.

And when issues of general political reform are raised, labor must often also find its interests on the side of the status quo.

Should the unit rule be abolished in choosing delegates to Democratic national conventions, right down to the level of precinct caucuses and state conventions? The UAW showed that it had its doubts, when some of the union's delegates to the 1968 convention voted against a major party reform resolution because it contained such a provision. These auto workers liked the unit rule because it allowed them to monopolize the delegations from Detroit and its environs to the state nominating convention. Or should the electoral system be revamped by providing for a direct popular vote with a run-off election when no single candidate in the first round gains 40 percent of the vote? The unions could not look upon such proposals with equanimity, if it meant—as it would have to—that nationally popular individual candidates could run for president without the backing of one of the major party conventions. Should the source and use of all federal campaign funds be fully disclosed, and should this requirement be made at last enforceable? This important populist objective can hardly be expected to be near the top of the list of legislative priorities for the AFL-CIO's COPE.

In fact, when the 1972 campaign finance reform legislation was before Congress, COPE's main priority was to use the bill to *increase* the legal opportunities available to unions *and* corporations to make influencing-conferring campaign contributions. Furthermore, by means of what Common Cause's chief lobbyist, Fred J. Wertheimer, called "a brilliant strategic coup," COPE succeeded in inserting into the new reform law a generally overlooked provision that had precisely that regressive effect.

Labor was not significantly concerned with the issue of expanded disclosure requirements. It was the press and most legislators who focused the issue as the main point of the bill. Traditionally, the unions continued to contribute to campaigns through special funds to which individual union members made "voluntary" contributions; to a large extent these funds had been registered with the government under laws already on the books in 1972. The unions understood that the disclosure requirements of the proposed law would not significantly change their status. What concerned labor was not disclosure, but the maintenance of their "voluntary" fund technique of making contributions. The continued use of these funds had recently been threatened by a shift in prosecutorial policy in the Department of Justice; the department had won new rulings that closed loopholes in the old law formerly exploited by the unions. By engaging a respected moderate Republican, Orval Hansen of Idaho, as sponsor, COPE succeeded in having its own amendment—drafted by its own lobbyists—inserted in the bill. The amendment overruled the Justice Department's victories in court and immunized the unions' voluntary funds from further attack.

At the same time, the Hansen amendment incidentally, but necessarily, opened the door to *corporate* "voluntary" funds consisting of contributions from their executives. This technique had not previously been used widely by corporations interested in buying influence in government. But in the 1972 campaign, because of COPE's adroit manipulation of legislation intended to reform campaign finance procedures, corporate voluntary funds for their executives appeared in far greater numbers than ever before.[13]

A footnote to the episode bears mention here: in amending the campaign finance reform bill, COPE had overlooked an obscure provision in the old law, not involved in the Justice Department's prosecutions, that forbade *any* political giving, whether voluntary or not, by government contractors or their employees or officers. COPE chief Andrew Biemiller and his astute staff had overlooked this potentially far-reaching provision for a simple reason: up to that time the Justice Department had never enforced it. But Biemiller became concerned when Common Cause won the right to invoke the neglected section of the act in a private civil suit against TRW, Inc., which held about $230 million in federal government contracts, and which had also given $475,000 to members of congressional committees of special interest to the corporation in 1970. If Common Cause won this innovative suit, the unions as well as corporate adherents of the voluntary fund technique of contributing would be affected; virtually all major unions hold contracts with the government through the Labor Department and other agencies. Common Cause staff member Kenneth Guido was informed by COPE officials that they were concerned about the case—"but if we have to," they said, "we'll change the law."

Their confidence would seem to be well-grounded. After all, they already had changed the law once before when it had proved necessary. Moreover, a Republican congressman had introduced a bill in Congress to amend the section under which Common Cause's TRW lawsuit had been brought, and the Justice Department was supporting the bill this time.

Populism and Poverty

In sum, labor and agriculture have become too well-organized, too adept at manipulating the political system to support consistently its democratization along populist lines. Following in their footsteps is a newer potential entry into the process of group competition: the poor. They surely do not have the power of the agricultural interests and organized labor. But, even so, the poor and their spokesmen cannot in general be looked upon as allies of the new populism. They do not seek to improve democracy in any abstract sense. They want more wealth and more power for their constituents. And in this they are no different from the labor unions and agricultural cooperatives. The National Welfare Rights Organization (NWRO), the most promising instrument for the interests of the poor now functioning on the national political scene, wants, in blunt terms, to capture the legislative and administrative arms of the welfare system in the same way that the shipping unions and companies have captured the apparatus that regulates and subsidizes the nation's merchant marine.

In May of 1971, the Center for Law & Social Policy, one

of Washington's most aggressive and successful public-interest law firms, hosted a large conference on the problems of and prospects for public-interest law at Airlie House in Warrentown, Virginia. The meeting, attended by leaders of the burgeoning public-interest law movement from across the country, turned into a donnybrook. Most participants were environmental and consumer lawyers; their main concern was to compare notes on their legislative tactics, successes, failures, and objectives. In particular, they wished to discuss the major problem hanging over their movement—how to create alternatives to the foundations as a secure source of funding. This discussion never took place, however. The relatively few blacks in attendance did not let it proceed. Instead, led by George Wiley of NWRO, they excoriated as "racist" and "elitist" the organizers of the conference and others whose work was primarily concerned with consumer and environmental cases. Wiley's charges seemed often irrational, but nonetheless unsettling, to the white liberal lawyers. And the core of his position was certainly valid, from the standpoint at least of his own constituency: you rich white professionals, he charged, have deserted my poor, mostly nonwhite constituents. You have sought safety in the pursuit of innocuous ideals that win the applause of the affluent majority. You ought to be down in the trenches with us—helping to change illegal welfare regulations and to write new welfare statutes, to get permits for demonstrations, and to stop official harassment, or helping NWRO chapters to stay out of trouble with the IRS.

Few at the Airlie House conference disputed Wiley's major premise—that the needs of welfare recipients should take precedence over the relatively abstract ideological goals to the realization of which these white liberal lawyers had chosen to devote their professional careers. On the other hand, few believed that Wiley's objectives were in any meaningful way in conflict with their work as public advocates. The poor, they felt, do not need lawyers like Ralph Nader. The poor mainly need organizers like George Wiley, who plays a role that their race and class if not education bar white ivy league lawyers from assuming. But, as poor blacks set out to join the pluralist struggle, populist idealists can and should expect no new support in their own struggle for influence.

Populists and Pluralists

George Wiley's anger at the idealistic white lawyers echoes the attitudes of Samuel Gompers and the agricultural and bureaucratic leaders who formed the first farm bureaus. As the groups these people led came to understand how best to promote their own interests, they abandoned their sponsorship of general populist reform. The result has been that the populist ideal has never been able to depend on deprived but organized groups (or organizable groups) for political influence. But despite its orphaned status, populism as an ideology has shown "stamina," to borrow a phrase from Ralph Nader. This resilience has been largely—and increasingly—due to the William Allen Whites and the John Gardners, to the compact and relatively well-to-do constituencies that show active concern for the fate of populist principles, and finally to the broad, if passive, favor that populist causes enjoy with the public at large.

If viewed as a whole, therefore, the American political system does not look too different from the political picture sketched of the FCC. Two distinct species of politics uneasily cohabit its institutions. The routine business of the system is conducted in pluralist terms by pluralist entities. Their pervasive influence over much of government, especially over legislative committees, administrative agencies, and the mechanisms of campaign finance and organization is, as Grant McConnell has put it, an "open secret," a brazen but fundamentally unchangeable contradiction of the simple populist ideal prescribed by civics textbook principles. This populist ideal itself generally languishes, except insofar as it is promoted by narrow leadership groups, whose motives are ideological and altruistic (at least with respect to any specific *group* interests—populist leaders may of course be motivated by *personal* ambitions for power and glory). These leaders are drawn from those professional and educational backgrounds that take political ideals seriously. In practice, this means that many of them come from the same relatively elite social or educational backgrounds that provide an active constituency for financial and organizational support. Their areas of strength tend to be different from those of pluralist participants in the political struggle—the media, the courts, and the overt parts of the election process. Within established governmental structures, populist partisans operate at a continual disadvantage, though they often vie for control, and sometimes even win it.

Thus, American government is not purely pluralistic, as political scientists maintained during the postwar era. Nor is it enough to call it "polyarchal," a concept introduced by Robert Dahl and Charles Lindblohm in 1953 in their *Politics, Economics, and Welfare*. This book remains the most subtle account of academic pluralistic theory. These pluralists portray the system as being composed of many autonomous and independent leadership groups. This conclusion makes the policy seem wanting by the strict democratic standards of populist theory, but more democratic than the "oligarchic" elite-run systems described by the antidemocratic European theorists who dominated early twentieth-century social thought in the West—Pareto, Mosca, and Michels. The problem with the Dahl-Lindblohm polyarchy image is that it equates two radically different kinds of leadership groups. It fails to distinguish George Meany from Ralph Nader, the National Association of Manufacturers from the National Committee for an Effective Congress, the New York State Insurance Rating Bureau from the Consumers Union.

The fact of the matter is that the system is somewhat more democratic than Dahl and Lindblohm perceive, though it is often only fleetingly so. The phenomenon of populist leadership is often ignored in analyses of the nation's political structure precisely because populist leaders have such a precarious and superficial hold on political influence. They are, paradoxically, *elites without power*—if power is understood to be the solid base of money and organization that genuine interest-group representatives command. But, though they lack power in this sense, they cannot be dismissed outright. They do have influence and occasionally they do prevail. Their success at creating and exploiting opportunities is largely dependent on their individual abilities. To a far greater extent than is true of organized interests, the Moores and Naders and Brandeises themselves—their skills and their strategic judgments—bear much of the responsibility for vindicating the populist democratic faith that most Americans still consider the true source of legitimate public authority.

7

The Reformer's Dilemma: Populism or Paternalism?

Ironically, populist leaders, now as in the past, do not think of themselves as an elite. Indeed, they do not consider their political role, crucial though it is, in any systematic way. The image of politics that they carry into battle is neither the pluralist construct of competing interest groups nor this book's three-tiered model of elite agitators/active constituents/passive but approving public. Their experience and instincts have acquainted them intimately with both these political worlds. But when they consciously contemplate the structure of politics, they tend to see things in the same simple terms of their propaganda.

The Self-effacing Elite
In the Populist propaganda model, the world consists of "the people" on the one hand—also known as the public, the masses, the majority, ordinary citizens, and so forth—and "the interests" on the other—also known as the special interests, the corporations, the privileged few, and the rich. Of course, nobody would admit to views so simplistic. But the fact is that through-

out the twentieth century populist leaders have consistently shaped their actions and based their programs on a view as simplistic as this. They would be appalled to think of themselves as an "elite." In intramural arguments, the surest and weightiest epithet with which to discredit an opponent or his arguments is "elitist." (Recently, in preparing a chapter for a book published by Ralph Nader's Corporate Accountability Research Group, I used the word "elite" to describe the role public-interest lawyers play; editor Mark Green struck out the term everywhere it appeared in my manuscript and replaced it with "corps," a euphemism he assumed I would consider "more judiciously chosen.")

Critics of corporate power often ridicule corporate managers for describing themselves as helpless instruments of public market preferences. In fact, of course, these managers are skilled leaders who command not only their own enterprises but entire sectors of the economy. Ironically, however, the self-effacing outlook of populist idealists perfectly mirrors the false modesty of the corporate managers. United States Steel Chairman Roger Blough can decide whether to meet Japanese competition by improving his plants' efficiency or by lobbying for import quotas. Ralph Nader, however, exercises equally consequential discretion when he decides, for example, to concentrate his resources in battles on Capitol Hill for a new consumer protection agency rather than on litigation in the courts to stop abuses by the old agencies.

But the failure of populist leaders to see themselves as an elite in drawing up their strategies and goals for reform is not merely ironic or amusing. It is a blind spot in their social vision and it has serious and destructive consequences for their cause—much in the way that the New Dealers' naive optimism had destructive consequences for their reform designs. By reifying their own propaganda—and therefore seeing themselves as bloodless extensions of the public in its struggle against the interests—new populist leaders misrepresent both their political and their moral environments.

To see politics as a struggle between the many who are good and the few who are bad is to understate the political obstacles to reform. It may be useful in terms of propaganda to depict legalized rate fixing at the ICC or federal largesse for Lockheed as the results of corporate conspiracy. But ignoring the political role of multiple small firms, dependent communities, and/or labor organizations in sustaining these conditions will not help to eliminate them. In general, systems of private power involving multiple units and levels of dependencies are better equipped to withstand or to subvert a tide of reformist sentiment than are systems composed of a few very large corporations. It is not by accident that agricultural interests have blunted the strong environmentalist drive for the prohibition of DDT and other pesticides at both the congressional and administrative levels, and have been defeated only by public-interest lawyers in court; in contrast, the automobile industry has watched stringent safety and emission control standards pass overwhelmingly in the Congress.

If populist propaganda creates too rosy a view of how potent the political opposition may be, it also obscures the harm populist measures may themselves cause. Or more accurately, the paradigm of the people-versus-the-interests is too simple in its refusal to calculate the costs of a particular proposal for reform, and to identify who will bear those costs. Some of those who have conducted recent *jihads* against imagined or real environmental dangers—such as, for example, those involving power plant siting—have shown no more anxiety about harming the defenseless poor than did urban renewal schemes of the 1950s.

The mythology of conspiracy sometimes encourages a tendency to view as crusades against corporate *power* what may in fact be celebrations of the idiosyncratic *values* of populist leaders themselves. This can most easily be seen in the game of denouncing advertising as an insidious corrupter and even creator of bad public values. As in the case of so many other populist and even anti-populist points of view, John Kenneth

Galbraith has put the matter more articulately than anyone else. In the revised 1971 edition of his *New Industrial State* he refused to qualify his assertion that consumer demand is dictated by business needs, not by consumer needs. Galbraith called this notion—in *The New Industrial State*—the "revised sequence." The old ideal of consumer sovereignty is obsolete, he says. Instead, the "sequence" of decision does not start with consumer needs and end with producers seeking to accommodate those needs. Rather the reverse:

> [The] producing firm reaches forward to control its markets and on beyond to manage the market behavior and shape the social attitudes of those, ostensibly, that it serves. . . . The mature corporation has means for managing what the consumer buys at the prices which it controls.[1]

A decade earlier, in *The Affluent Society,* Galbraith had made the same point, though there he gave it a different label: the "dependence effect." This notion referred to the elimination of "independently determined consumer wants" by the "forces of advertising and emulation," with the results that "production creates the wants it seeks to satisfy."[2]

Galbraith's extreme dogmatism on this point has been received enthusiastically by much of his lay audience, partly because it is precisely what they want to hear. His professional critics, however, have charged that these elaborate formulations are merely a slick cover for his class prejudice against middle-American tastes. The charge is surely correct. He revealed his true feelings two decades ago in his first major work, *American Capitalism: The Concept of Countervailing Power,* when he attacked the "unseemly economics of opulence," and told economists to stop worrying

> about partially monopolized prices or excessive advertising and selling costs for tobacco, liquor, chocolates, automobiles and soap in a land which is already suffering from nicotine poisoning and alcoholism, which is nu-

tritionally gorged with sugar, which is filling its hospitals and cemeteries with those who have been maimed or murdered on its highways and which is dangerously neurotic about normal body odors.[3]

Then Galbraith was saying, "If that's what the fools want, let them go ahead and pay a little extra for it." Now he (as how many other populist liberals?), finds that it sits easier on his democratic conscience to blame it all on Madison Avenue and to maintain that the people do not really "want" these vulgar things, after all.

Unfortunately, though Galbraith may deceive himself and the many like-minded liberals who find this style of argument congenial, he cannot fool the people whose style of life he means to impugn. Nor will middle-class observers miss another, more offensive point; that he considers the consuming public dumb enough to be easily taken in by the crude appeals of the ad men. Thus, his unconscious snobbery is politically self-defeating as well as morally objectionable.

Some new populist spokesmen have shown considerable sensitivity to the potential for conflict between their actual preferences and their middle- or working-class espoused interests. Ralph Nader in particular apparently tries to avoid offending these constituencies. Although he frequently attacks corporate advertising, he avoids, at least for the most part, Galbraith's bombast about corporate manipulation of societal values. His target is deception, something that all people can unite to oppose. And his charges are usually specific. Thus, Nader has actually succeeded in changing public tastes and moving them away from the predilection for trivia which the Galbraiths have traditionally decried. Consumers of cars now are said to show more interest in economy, safety, and durability, and less interest in speed and glamor than they did before 1965; Nader's allegations have driven at least one product, the Corvair, off the market altogether. In a more recent, and less well-known case, a report from Nader's Center for Auto Safety in Washington induced Volvo (as in "ten of eleven Volvos sold in the last eight years are still on the road") to increase its negligible six-month warranty protection to the full year that is standard for most other makes. Nader has managed to give the impression that his contempt is for specific corporations, not for the people who enjoy the corporations' products.

Nader has also taken pains to avoid clashes with labor. Only very rarely has he criticized the anticonsumer positions taken by organized labor representatives in Washington. Nader generally has been oddly reticent on the subject of protectionism, an area where consumer interests currently face a threat more severe than any since the days of the Smoot-Hawley tariff in 1930. Perhaps, Nader senses the depth of protectionist sentiment among workers and their leaders in many industries, and he is reluctant to challenge them. In most of his public statements on this issue he has attacked multinational corporations for moving their manufacturing operations overseas—a somewhat bizarre tactic, even a betrayal of his own constituency, since corporate emigration tends to bring lower costs and hence lower prices for consumers.

The Reformers' Open Secret

Ralph Nader's waffling on the tariff issue—which would surely draw the scorn of old antitariff Progressives like Robert La-Follette or Albert Beveridge—reflects a strain of political and philosophical ambivalence evident in the thought of many sensitive leaders of the new populist movement. They recognize with dismay that their ideology—populist democracy—and the interests of their constituency—the "general public"—sometimes clash with the needs of traditional beneficiaries of liberal affection—the workers, the blacks, and the poor. In such situations, the typical new populist leader may become seriously disturbed. Is it "elitist," he wonders, to favor the "public," which usually means "consumers," when black textile workers or inefficient family farmers are on the other side of the issue? When he is unable to face up to the logic of his usual defense of "the public interest," as Nader may be on the tariff issue, or as the many reformers attracted to the new cause of raising agricultural subsidies for the beleaguered small farmer are, the populist may abandon his role and support these "special interests"—covering his confusion with an irrelevant blast at some alleged corporation machinations. In such instances a knowing reference to "the conglomerate menace" is always especially handy.

The populists' confusion reflects the gap between the complexity of their actual political role and the prescriptions of the simple model in their propaganda. Their propaganda teaches that, as heirs of the populist tradition, it is their high calling to be defenders of deprived groups in society as well as servants of the abstract principles of populist ideology. Yet neither logic nor politics dictates that conclusion. This fact is tacitly recognized by the shrewder participants in the new populist movement. But it is faced frankly by few. And it is not openly discussed at all. The result is a hidden fault of moral and political insecurity that runs through the new populist creed.

Grant McConnell once called the pervasive influence of private power over government the "open secret" of American democracy.[4] But the reformers have their own "open secret" —the moral ambiguity of their own commitment. What can justify a self-appointed elite, predominantly from privileged social strata, battling for a set of abstract and to some extent subjective ideals? Is such a crusade a mere superfluity in a pluralist democracy? Is it perhaps even antidemocratic?

Neither scholars nor activists have honestly examined this question. But the movement would do well to face the issue squarely. It is comforting to believe that one's only enemies are tycoons and robber barons. But the reality of populist politics is more subtle and complex. Its adherents would be more at ease with themselves and more effective in their work if they admitted that theirs is a crusade for a vision of the whole society, not for the material betterment of any particular group. At times this realization would dictate that their idealism and the needs of relatively deprived groups must clash. Sensitivity to the possibility of such conflict might dilute the arrogance and sanctimony that unfortunately characterizes some recruits to the new populist cause. Moreover, in particular cases, it might—and should—induce moderation in the pursuit of populist goals. Perhaps underground power transmission cables are not so important, since they will raise electricity costs for the urban poor. Perhaps the electoral college should be tolerated—even though it violates populist principles—because blacks in the cities need the extra leverage they have under the present system, or because workers need the leverage their unions have at the National Democratic Convention (which would lose much of its significance under a direct election system). Perhaps small farmers should be subsidized and be allowed to engage in monopolistic price fixing, if lower consumer prices would drive them into the urban proletariat.

After all, by what reasoning can consumer interests be said to be the only valid criterion for structuring economic arrangements? Social theorists have never critically examined Adam Smith's postulate that the betterment of the consumer is the only proper end of all economic activity.

And in another philosophical vein, perhaps the pluralists are right. Perhaps the formal requisites of populist democracy are irrelevant to the achievement of distributive justice. Perhaps the proper path to reform is not through defense of the mythical public interest against the organized special interests, but through assistance in the organization of those interests that are not now equipped to compete in the pluralist struggle. This, in essence, was the position taken by George Wiley in his bitter attack on the elitist Galahads at Airlie House. Instead of winning symbolic court victories for the "public," he said, you should all be serving as house counsel to my struggling organization, helping to bend the law and the system generally to the needs of my constituents the way "private" lawyers do for interests that have already organized for their own aggrandizement.

Few would disagree that abstract populist principles should give way before the concrete needs of deserving special interests. But certainly their conflicts with the poor or the workers should not induce populist enthusiasts to abandon their cause. Their movement may not always be on the side of the angels, but there is justification to be found in other considerations.

A Rationale for Reform

It is indeed entirely justifiable, for example, for environmental advocates who litigate to stop the SST, and thereby perpetuate joblessness in Seattle, to consider themselves lawyers for the "public interest." All that is necessary is that they do not confuse the public interest in such cases with the "correct position." The truth of the matter is that they represent *a* public interest, a significant point of view, which ought to be represented in the decision process, but which cannot command enough wealth or organizational resources to assure the necessary political response. Whatever the decision ultimately is, important social interests that have only a "public" or unorganized constituency behind them deserve a hearing. That critical function—the representation of public, unorganized social interests—fills in the gaps left by the arbitrary patterns of pluralist politics. It is justified, in other words, by the morality implicit in pluralist theory itself. Plainly, such representation deserves to be continued and to flourish, even where its promotion in individual cases seems to conflict with relatively deprived special interests.

Furthermore, the populist mode of politics is not merely a surrogate for a "perfect" pluralist system in which all significant interests are organized and able to defend themselves. Such a system is, of course, not attainable in practice, nor even, probably, in theory. But even if it were, it would be a guild society, a polity frozen into rigid patterns, in which no element having any significant influence would be able to see beyond its immediate interests. For example, one can feel sympathy for workers who might be dislocated by the dismantling of Boeing's airframe facilities in Seattle or by the imposition of air quality controls in Detroit. But society must, at times, make painful political decisions that involve dislocations in order to produce at least marginal improvements in the welfare of the general public. Any society incapable of making such choices would not long remain a very satisfactory one. This function of keeping the channels of criticism and change open is an additional justification for the conduct of populist politics in a democracy. The exceptional influence of populist ideology in this country may be an important reason the United States is often peculiarly successful at expressing and accommodating public demands for change.

It may also be true that keeping the polity functioning in rough accord with direct democratic dictates does serve in a general way to benefit disadvantaged groups. In such a democracy those interests that have superior wealth and organization would be able to use the government for their purposes more effectively than the disadvantaged and unorganized could. But the strong would be even stronger, if, without changing the economic and social structure, the instruments of political democracy were discarded. In a genuine corporate or fascist state, the rich and the organized would be even better off than they are. Expanding the area for the play of populist democratic principles in America will not equalize the distribution of political and material resources (as a genuinely socialist dictatorship might do), but it will keep them more fairly distributed than they would be in authoritarian regimes such as contemporary Greece or Spain.

Finally, putting all this theoretical speculation to one side, we should remember that, as a practical matter, many important social interests and views have no chance at all of being heard through the pluralist mechanisms that dominate democratic government. There has to be some recourse to the public—in the populist sense of the term "public"—to make democracy work—even in the pluralist sense of the term "democracy," which requires only that all social interests be "represented." It should be emphasized, however, that this argument does not envisage a public that has "control" in any substantive sense. The organized interests will inevitably control or at least dominate the substantive content of policy.

To refine the point from a different perspective, the "public" is not the simple majoritarian concept sometimes found in conventional populist democratic theory. During the 1920s, while the nation was catching its breath from the two decades of populist reform that preceded World War I, Walter Lippmann attacked the populist doctrine that virtue and sound judgment could be ascribed only to policies that 51 percent or more of the electorate had formally approved of. Lippmann's critique, which emphasized the structural impediments to meaningful public judgments, has been considered devastating since he first propounded it.[5] And he was not unjustified. The doctrinaire majoritarianism he derided was in fact reflected not only in many examples of populist rhetoric but in actual proposals as well (such as initiative, referendum, and recall). To an extent, the notion continues to surface, as in the recent demand for a strict one-man, one-vote rule in presidential elections, which Alexander M. Bickel and others attacked in Lippmannesque terms.

But their critique of populist democratic theory is in large measure beside the point. It is true, as Lippmann alleged, that the public is in practical fact a "phantom" whose views on individual policy questions are difficult to ascertain and often even more difficult to enforce. It is also true, as the pluralists have more recently argued, that most of politics is dominated by organized interests—minorities, that is—in apparent contradiction of the populist requisite of public, or majority, control of government. But all this does not diminish the relevance of the populist ideal, or the value of populist politics. For the real function of the populist concept "the public" is heuristic. As deployed in political discourse, it is a myth. But it is nevertheless of great practical significance.

The concept of the public (or "the people," et cetera) exists as an object of appeal for interests and points of view incapable of pluralist competition on the "inside" of the organized political structure. The individuals and institutions of immediate relevance to most governmental decisions (or to formally private but socially significant decisions) are, almost always, very few. If anyone wishes to bring in views not represented at the bargaining table, his only excuse is that the public is being ignored and that the public interest is being trampled upon. Without that excuse, there would be no moral reason—and usually no political way—to broaden the terms and the arena of debate.

Often the would-be transgressor is threatened with public reprisal: "The American people," warns the populist congressman summing up a set of investigative hearings, "will not stand for the outrages which have been disclosed to this committee!" But such threats are more rhetorical than real; there is usually little the American people can or will do. Despite mass suffrage and a free press, the political mechanisms of public retaliation are too cumbersome to invoke. The possibility of actual reprisals at the polls exists in general as a background threat, usually very muted and contingent, a reminder to the powerful not to press their advantages too far or too brazenly.

It is often very difficult to justify in hard political terms the actions reformist officials sometimes take in behalf of some presumed "public interest." When evidence is adduced to buttress the contention that the public demands some reform or other, it is often meaningless in political if not analytical terms. For example, polls showed that overwhelming popular majorities approved a switch from the electoral college to a one-man, one-vote electoral system. But these polls did not reveal the *in-*

tensity of popular feelings on this issue, nor in any way indicate what the relationship was between the public's position on the electoral college question and its positions on other issues. Nevertheless, the momentous constitutional amendment passed the House by a huge margin, received rhetorical—if qualified—support from the White House, and was killed only in the Senate by a filibuster.

In sum, threats of public reprisal like that of our hypothetical populist congressman are often effective even though they are nearly always empty. When leaders make such threats they are engaging in a tactic that might be called "shaming." This technique has the effect of warning their antagonists that they are sinning against democracy. Although their conspiracy (whatever it may involve) may succeed, its architects will henceforth have to face their peers with sacrilege etched on their public records. Recently Elizabeth Drew astutely pointed out that Ralph Nader shows frequent signs of turning into a "national scold."[6] The fact is that Nader *is* a national scold, but this makes him neither unique nor ineffective. "Shaming" such as Nader engages in is both a natural expression of populist ideology and a technique of populist leadership, evident, for example, when John Gardner attacks political corruption or when Chief Justice Burger denounces the FCC. The ubiquity and surprising efficacy of shaming in public debate helps to explain why many populist causes, such as the ABA's move to abolish the Electoral College, attain far greater political success than the actual power behind them would appear to justify.

Of course every political year provides instances where public opinion does crystallize and focus on an issue clearly enough to *force* a change in policy, by threatening or showing genuine strength at the polls. But in general, when one considers the feebleness of the actual channels by which public opinion can form and then be translated into policy, it is a wonder that democratic governments are as responsive as they are. It is also a wonder that issues receive as much broad attention and discussion as they do, when so much of the real power remains with a narrow set of interests. The fact of the matter is that many public leaders, in and out of office, talk and even act as if the public had influence—which it does not. They do so in part, no doubt, because they fear that the public *may* become aroused and reward or punish them for their own record. But often they invoke the public and its supposed influence, because they believe that morally the public is entitled to have influence and that, if mobilized, the public would endorse and support their own views.

Without this populist notion that the public is entitled to know and to have the final say, there would be little discussion and interplay among the elites that structure American politics. Indeed, it is no accident that in Europe, where the populist tradition of American politics is not nearly so pronounced, the politics of democracy, at least where potent organized interests are concerned, is tighter, less flexible, and less reasoned than politics in the United States.

Walter Lippmann equated the populist insistence on the public's right to control policy with a one-dimensional majoritarianism that was (and is) evident in many expressions of the American populist mentality (as in the mania about polls reflected even by supposedly shrewd, conservative politicians). Lippmann preferred a politics of "civility," of reasoned discussion among informed and responsible elites, to the feckless mass crusades he associated with populism. But ironically, without the moral status the populist ideal enjoys in this country, disinterested but politically meaningful exchange would be reduced severely. It would give way to a pluralism without respite, in which policy—even in its formative phases—was no more than the sum of relevant organized pressures. This "derangement of powers" into the hands of special interests, untouched by any public constraint, was abhorred by both Walter Lippmann and his populist contemporaries.[7] But ironically, the democratic ideal that he mocked has been the nation's main defense against this specter which was their common fear.

Understood then in this heuristic sense, the populist concept of the public is both meaningful and valuable. Therefore, reform elites that strive to preserve and enhance public control of policy need not be riven by self-doubt. Public-interest lawyers need not feel intimidated by George Wiley's charge of elitism. Courts asked to challenge wayward bureaucracies or special interest legislation should not be mesmerized by the notion that judicial activism is undemocratic.

But if populist elites can thus justify their exercise of influence, despite their lack of affiliation with any actual economic interest, and despite their lack of any formal requisites of "accountability," the justification is yet a limited one. Since reformers act largely on the basis of their own preferences, their exercise of influence is defensible mainly because they have so little influence, and because what influence they do have is so dependent on public approval. If they had real power, their role could not be reconciled so easily with their democratic creed.

Hence, just as this conception of the populist role is more modest than that of early twentieth-century majoritarianism, it is similarly more constraining than the New Dealers' self-image as managers of a grand design for reform. The New Dealers took literally the message in their regulatory statutes, that it was their responsibility to define and enforce the public interest. In fact, of course, their relationship to public wishes, as well as their hold on power, was far more precarious than they dreamed. Since the New Deal bureaucracies have turned out to be inhibited by the power of their regulatees, liberals have cried out in pain and anger that those bureaucracies have refused to use their broad powers to defend the public interest. Such laments generally receive a sympathetic hearing, mainly because they are known to be futile.

For example, take the by-now familiar case of the reformers congregated about the FCC. Justice Burger's theory that the broadcaster is a "public official" whose license should be revoked whenever the FCC finds a programming record incompatible with "the public interest" may not seem threatening in the context of an outrageous case like the WLBT controversy. The petitioner's request to deny renewal of a license was not only based on this extremely serious charge, it was presented to a regulatory body known for its servility to its regulatory clientele. No one would picture the FCC as likely to become intoxicated with the powers of censorship implicit in the authority to destroy a major communications medium because of objections to program content.

But the rhetoric brandished by the FCC reform movement does not apply only to egregious and exceptional cases like *WLBT*. Nor does it furnish criteria for clearly determining how an egregious case of broadcast unfairness could be distinguished from a routine transgression. Reform groups like the National Citizens Committee for Broadcasting seem seriously to contemplate a regime in which license renewal would be tied to concessions to a host of community organizations each pushing its own conception of the programming needs of its constituency. Some reformers would like to see "quality" programming requirements—more documentaries, dramas, and concerts—imposed on the television industry and the television audience. Perhaps some believe that FCC commissioners themselves should oversee carefully the content of television documentaries to ensure that community needs are really being met.

There is scant basis in any conception of democracy for such extreme paternalism. Theory aside, such doctrines are dangerous from the practical standpoint. Imagine what would happen if organized community groups of all persuasions understood that they could command more favorable television coverage by challenging local stations' licenses before the FCC. The local police union, for example, might allege that the stations were giving demonstrators excessively sympathetic coverage. Doubtless they could produce an endless string of eminent witnesses to support their demands in a commission hearing. In all likelihood, however, the matter would never reach that stage; the police would tacitly let it be known that they would drop the challenge if the stations promised to turn their cameras off whenever officers roughed up a protester or two. It is no wonder that Nixon's communications chief has discovered promise in the traditional excitement of FCC reformers about the notion of local community participation.

But the dangers inherent in any serious attempt to apply the "public official" theory of broadcast licensing do not stem simply from the possibility that the doctrine might be invoked by the right as well as the left. The danger is simply that broadcast news operations would become even more timid and deferential to the best organized interests in a community than they are already.

At the national level, the consequences would be equally abhorrent. Now the only special interests that strive to influence FCC appointments are the broadcasters. But the line at the president's door would grow much longer if it were generally understood that the FCC appointment process influenced the content of television programming. It is disturbing that Texas oilmen give vast campaign contributions in exchange for favors to the oil industry. But it would be worse if some of them exacted, for their contribution, influence over FCC policy toward television news.

Despite these quite obvious perils, most enlightened citizens do not dispute the doctrines and activities of the FCC reformers. They even admire them, perhaps because they are sure the reformers' ambitions can never be realized. The particular stalemate into which the distribution of power between reformers and the industry has frozen FCC policy—whereby the reformers dominate the verbal substance of the law and the industry dominates its operational content—keeps innocuous the reformers' grand design pretensions.

The paternalist edge apparent in some of the rhetoric of FCC reform can be seen elsewhere. In the *Washington Post* of March 5, 1973, for example, Nicholas von Hoffman excoriated the public for rejecting Senator McGovern's appeal for tax reform:

The suckers would rather believe it's welfare for the poor rather than welfare for the rich that keeps their taxes high. . . . They'll string along with their obsessional delusion that they're rich, or they're going to be rich or their kids are going to be rich—and so they identify with the wealthy.

Nick von Hoffman thinks the public should want equality rather than wealth. Their views to the contrary are not merely disagreements but "obsessional delusions" that make them "suckers."

Such cocksureness about the rightness of reform is also discernible in the rallying cries for other new populist causes. Will stopping the Alaska pipeline speed the upward movement of utility costs for the urban poor? Will emission and safety restrictions for automobiles levy on auto purchasers a regressive tax of 10 percent or more of the price of a low-priced car? Is the price of compulsory air-bags a justified cost to impose, merely in order to stop risk takers from *voluntarily* disconnecting the ignition lock flashing lights and buzzer apparatus that is triggered in all cars made after 1974 whenever the car is started before seat belts are fastened? Do advocates of an end to economic growth intend to condemn all levels of society to their present standards of living, even the poor and lower-middle classes? (Do they really believe that they could succeed in implementing income redistribution as a meaningful alternative to growth, as Leonard Ross and Peter Passell have recently asked, when Congress refused to pass even President Nixon's miserable $2400 annual income guarantee?)

With regard to all but the last of these issues, the costs of adopting new populist measures will be more than offset by the gains, even for the poor. But in each case the problems of incidence and cost are complex and the answers are not clear. And in none of these cases have the reformers themselves shown much concern for the price that would have to be paid for their success by large sectors of the American public.

If the costs of reform do turn out to be high, and if they fall heavily on the masses, political backlash will follow in due course. A "public-be-damned" attitude toward economy may seem just as objectionable to consumers as industry attitudes were toward pollution and auto safety. But if the reformers lose the heavy presumption of public favor they now enjoy, their cause may be doomed. Reformers, unlike the auto industry, cannot afford to be unpopular. Democratic constraints are more binding for them than for their special interest antagonists. For, the reformers' ability, real and presumed, to elicit approval from the public is their only source of influence. Without it, they have nothing. They stand exposed as an elite of would-be do-gooders who deserve the contempt they are sure to receive from their enemies.

Harrison Wellford, one of Ralph Nader's most thoughtful lieutenants, has said, "We hold a referendum every time we ask for funds or send out a release or publish a book." More than most participants in the democratic process, Wellford and his colleagues need to ensure that most of these referenda have favorable outcomes.

This danger of falling into paternalism is a potential problem for populist reformers. Only in relatively few other instances have populist hopes advanced so far toward actual fruition. A number of similar regulatory statutes have been enacted, but most of them are already suffering from desultory administration and press and public indifference. The populists' main strategic problem remains the challenge of designing mechanisms to survive the pressures of regulated special interests. But before this strategic problem can be solved, populist leaders must overcome their squeamishness about conceding their own role as an elite.

Activists, reformist legislators, and officials must understand that in drawing up plans for new government initiatives, they must always take care to preserve and enhance *their own* influence. Even modest designs for the disciplining of special interests cannot work unless populist leaders are there to scrutinize, to criticize, and to keep the public informed. In many instances, no regulation is often better than bad regulation. In general, a proper concern for their own political welfare may convince new populist activists to redirect their priorities. They could spend more time building up their own long-term political strength, rather than focusing on dramatic but ephemeral triumphs on Capitol Hill.

A similarly frank assessment of their role in preserving democracy is required of the more established bases of populist influence—the press, the foundations, the universities, and the courts. These institutions do not share with the Project on Corporate Responsibility a basic anxiety about their own survival. But they do know well the feeling of prudential and moral doubt about their political role. Despite the sympathy for populist causes in many sectors of these institutions, they are generally inclined to see their prescribed role as that of the passive observer, above the battle.

Each institution maintains its own rationale for self-restraint. But they all boil down to much the same argument. In part, the concern is for the institution's own welfare; active involvement on behalf of reform may anger powerful interests and jeopardize a reputation for objectivity and impartiality, itself a vital political asset. Obviously, insofar as such fears are well-grounded, they are legitimate bases for policy.

On the other hand, part of the rationale for restraint, whether on the part of scholars or editors or judges, is a conviction that their services would be superfluous, even if they were offered. Unlike some populist activists, these institutions are deeply aware of their elite status. And they are not only skeptical of their own warrant for undertaking an active reformist role. They believe that such a role is not necessary. They believe that democracy is ultimately self-regulating. They continue to have faith in the New Deal assumption that governmental control of private interests is either a reality or a realistic possibility; or else they accept the more recent pluralist maxim that all worthy social interests will organize for their own promotion, and that, therefore, justice will ultimately be achieved through the operation of competing forces in the political market.

But these theories of democracy, impressive as they seemed when they were first unveiled in the 1930s and 1950s, now appear naive. The new populist notion, which is a restatement of the old Progressive notion, that democracy is *not* self-regulating, sits far more comfortably with the nation's experience as well as with the mood of the moment. To give this vision a chance to succeed, elite sectors of the policy that have traditionally enshrined democratic values must recognize an obligation to aid in actively promoting them.

8
Antipopulist Liberalism

At this point it seems appropriate to recapitulate briefly the points developed in the preceding chapters. I have tried to draw an ideological and political profile of the American populist tradition. The profile has yielded four main conclusions:

1. The populist ideal—the notion that power is illegitimate unless subjected to the effective sovereignty of the public —has fathered two recurrent themes in twentieth-century reform politics in the United States. One of these is "big government"—the goal of conferring on government the capacity to control major centers of private power; the second is "direct democracy"—the goal of removing impediments to direct popular control of government itself.
2. In somewhat different ways, this ideal has shaped three specific reform movements: the Populist-Progressive effort of 1890–1915, the New Deal during the 1930s, and the growing contemporary concern focused on consumer and environmental protection and on the integrity of the electoral system.
3. Though broadly approved by the American people the populist ideal is in practice mocked by the actual structure

of relations between government and centers of private power; in the everyday reality of politics, as Robert Dahl has put it, "minorities rule"—rather than the public.

4. Since the late nineteenth century, when populist rhetoric was the staple of the Knights of Labor and of the agrarian Populist Party, populist ideology has lost its original base among disadvantaged interest groups. Instead it has become the ward of tiny elites, in and especially out of political office. These populist-oriented elites come to their idealistic commitment through professional involvement with the mechanisms for depicting government—as scholars, newsmen, judges, reform legislators, and bureaucratic leaders. These elites lack the wealth and organizational requisites of power; their only source of influence is their facility to persuade the public to approve and indirectly support their efforts to stop abuses by powerful special interests.

This theoretical profile must now be brought up to date, and certain loose ends tied down. Before moving on to look in some detail at some major programs and achievements of the current populist movement, we must focus first on the antipopulist critique mounted by liberal politicians and intellectuals following World War II and then on the rebellion against antipopulist liberalism which gathered on the left and the right during the 1960s and paved the way for the current "new populist" movement.

The Contradiction in the New Deal

It is now fashionable on the left and the right to celebrate "the end of liberalism"—a phase that is itself the title of an influential recent book by Chicago political theorist Theodore J. Lowi.[1] However, to any observer of everyday politics, liberalism will seem anything but dead. Politicians, reporters, and voters use the term all the time, and they are pretty much in agreement as to what it means. Every serious contender for the 1972 Democratic presidential nomination openly fought for the honor of being considered a "liberal" candidate, a "truly liberal" candidate, or even the "most liberal" candidate. The fact is that, despite the traumas of the late 1960s, liberalism is very much alive.

But on the other hand, the ideological content of liberalism has changed a great deal. These changes have not always been clearly recognized because to most people being liberal means simply taking a certain political attitude rather than adhering to a consistent set of ideological axioms.

The postwar generation of intellectuals and political leaders has been especially slow to grasp the changes in liberal thought generated by the basic contradiction the New Deal nurtured at its very core. While its verbal self-image was populist, the political infrastructures it created—or perhaps, more accurately, extended—were profoundly antithetical to the populist ideal. Many of the New Deal reforms conferred great political and often considerable legal power on specific interest groups to dictate the terms of their economic relations with the public; at the same time, the affected interests obtained virtual political and legal immunity from meaningful public control.

But many observers did not acknowledge the conflict between the vision of society heralded by New Deal propaganda and the actual regime established by New Deal politics. On the one hand, Arthur Schlesinger, Jr. could believe that F.D.R. had realized Woodrow Wilson's fondest populist dream of "redressing the balance of social power" through governmental—that is, public—control of the corporations and the rich. On the other hand, Schlesinger could also acknowledge—and celebrate— the triumph of a kind of politics in which government is in fact a captive of the most powerful social interests; in advocating the election of the Democrats' Kennedy over the Republicans' Nixon in 1960, Schlesinger explained that the Democrats were preferable because only they could put together a "multi-interest administration." "What," asked Schlesinger,

is the essence of a multi-interest administration? It is surely that the leading interests in society are all represented in the interior processes of policy formation—which can be done only if members or advocates of these interests are included in key positions of government. . . .[2]

Unlike Schlesinger, most postwar political scientists were able to comprehend that the U.S. government could not at one and the same time dominate and be dominated by the "leading interests in society." But they concluded that an interest-dominated democracy was a way—indeed, the best way—of attaining distributive justice and material welfare.

Pluralism in Practice and Theory

Pluralism, as the new orthodoxy came to be called, was a practical as well as an academic credo. Pluralist theory described the realities of politics known to practicing liberal politicians, at least after the McCarthyist mania of the early 1950s expired. The constituents of the New Deal coalition—labor, blacks, liberals, some sectors of agriculture—functioned in accord with the pluralist model in presidential as well as congressional politics. Representative organizations, or leadership groups presumed to be representative, bargained, negotiated, and compromised. Interests were managed by party and bureaucratic professionals. A variety of business interests became aligned with the Democrats, especially the oil industry and the military and space contractors who profited from the increased spending in those areas authorized by the Kennedy and Johnson administrations. The economy grew, support for civil-rights legislation mounted, and everyone seemed to agree that some internal dynamic was driving the United States toward ever-higher levels of material welfare, social equality, and personal liberty. If the "affluent society" was boring, it nevertheless seemed hard to deny that "democracy is the Good Society in operation," as Seymour Martin Lipset put it.[3]

Affluence made the old populist fears about concentrated power seem trivial ("theoretical" in the pejorative sense), at the same time that it enabled liberals to believe that the New

Deal itself had brought about the nation's recovery from the Depression. In fact, the New Deal itself was an even greater failure in promoting recovery than it was in realizing the traditional populist reform goal of public control of special interests. Without the war, and its forced imposition on Roosevelt of Keynesian fiscal policy, there would have been no recovery. Unemployment in 1939 was nearly as catastrophic as it had been in 1932, and nothing that Franklin D. Roosevelt's government was planning to do would have had an appreciable impact on it—except for Roosevelt's increasing interest in stopping aggression in Europe and Asia. But however that may be, affluence enabled postwar liberals to be secure in their faith that the New Deal had made good on Harold Ickes' promise to "take control" and "develop a better system for the people."

Some observers on university faculties, especially in political science departments, did notice that the populist conception of grand designs for government control was a fantasy. They saw that private interests themselves were deeply involved in the "interior" processes of policy making in Congress and the new bureaucracy. Academic students of the American political system exhumed an old treatise written in 1908 by Arthur F. Bentley, *The Process of Government,* which extolled the dominance of "groups" in politics. In 1950 David Truman updated Bentley's analysis and rearranged his title in a widely influential survey called *The Governmental Process.* Truman contended that the old populist notion of the "public interest" was a myth, that politics in fact consisted of nothing but the conflict of vying "interest-groups," and that government merely reflected the underlying struggle of interests: "What a particular government is under these circumstances," said David Truman, "its 'form' and its 'methods,' depends upon the character of the groups and the purposes it serves." Harold Lasswell put the matter more bluntly: "Politics," he said, is "who gets what, why, and how."

This vision of the national political system as simply the sum of special interest pressures would have appalled Woodrow

Wilson. But the pluralist theorists held that it was not only a fact but a boon. They contended that in politics, as in Adam Smith's economic universe, exchange and interaction among groups were mechanisms that enabled them objectively to co-operate for the greater good of society. To illustrate this point in his book, Truman quoted a government pamphlet description of the political economy of oil, in a passage that reveals the pluralists' optimistic assessment of pressure group politics so nicely that it deserves to be quoted here in full:

> An oil operator brings oil to the surface of the ground; the local government prevents the theft of oil or destruction of equipment; a railroad corporation transports the oil; State and Federal Governments prevent interference with the transport of oil; a refining company maintains an organization of workers and chemical equipment to convert the oil into more useful forms; a retail distributor parcels out the resulting gasoline in small quantities to individuals requiring it; the Federal Government supplies a dependable medium of exchange which allows the oil operator, the railroad, the refining company, and the retailer to act easily . . . finally, government maintains a system of highways and byways which allows an ultimate consumer to combine the gasoline with other resources . . . in satisfying his desire for automobile travel.[4]

A present-day observer is astonished by this comforting picture of the oil production and distribution process. Neither the federal pamphlet nor Professor Truman bothered to note what many would now regard as the most critical functions of the state and federal governments. We do not learn here (did Professor Truman not know, or did he just not believe it important?) that the state governments of Louisiana and Texas prescribe and enforce limits on the amount of oil that may be drawn from wells; nor are we told that the federal government complements this output-restricting scheme with the Connolly "hot oil" act of 1935, which forbids interstate transport of oil produced in violation of state production quotas. The purpose and effect of these regulatory measures is, of course, to decrease the amount of fuel available to "satisfy" the consumer's "desire for automobile travel," and to increase the profits enjoyed by oil producers. In other words, Truman admitted that government policy toward oil was largely shaped by the industry itself and tailored to the industry's needs. But he did not notice that oil producers—who in his view were simply one "group"—would use their power to exploit consumers—whom he considered not "the public" but just another "group." Indeed, Truman does not seem to have entertained even a hint of such suspicions, because he plainly felt no compunctions about taking at face value and displaying as an authoritative source a government pamphlet produced by the same industry-dominated complex of government institutions.

Pluralists like Truman believed that interest-group politics did not produce systematic exploitation or inequity, because they assumed that all significant interests would in time be recognized by the "groups" that shared them, who would then organize themselves for political action. The result was, happily, that governmental response to group pressures would approximate the importance of different group needs. The populist grand design of the New Deal had failed, it was true: "[Despite] the powerful efforts of many presidents and the somewhat utopian yearnings of many administrative reformers," Robert Dahl observed, "the vast apparatus that grew up to administer the affairs of the American welfare state is a decentralized bargaining bureaucracy." But this was no cause for concern, since it meant merely that "bureaucracy has become a part of . . . the 'normal' American political process." And in Dahl's view such a result could be regarded with equanimity, since in the "normal" American political process, ". . . there is a high probability that an active and legitimate group in the population can make itself heard effectively at some crucial state in the process of decision."[5]

Thus, the pluralists provided a rationale for jettisoning the old populist fear of a government run by constituent interest groups. What Woodrow Wilson had identified as a single tyrannical "group"—the "big business interests"—had become in the hands of David Truman, Robert Dahl, and their colleagues, a galaxy of relatively particular interests, economic, ideological, religious, and civic. In politics big business did not seem to be either a monolithic or, on the whole, an exceptionally more potent amalgam of specific interests than other groups.

In the economy—which was in both political and economic theory, sharply differentiated from the political governmental sphere—the power of the great corporations could not be gainsaid. This presented an admitted difficulty. But even this, the old populist bugaboo of monopoly, was soon solved, thanks to a pluralistic concept devised by Professor Galbraith. "[P]rivate economic power," he assured liberals in 1952, "is held in check by the *countervailing power* of those who are subject to it. The first begets the second."[6] Galbraith's theory meant that, although the New Deal had not in fact managed to impose meaningful regulatory constraints on the great corporations, there was little need for concern; their power was offset by countervailing centers of power held by equally well-organized customers and suppliers, whether the latter were unionized workers, agricultural cooperatives, or simply other monopolistic corporations. Because of this countervailing power, each industry's monopoly profits would be bargained away while goods were in the process of being produced and distributed and before they reached the consumer.

Theodore Lowi has observed that the pluralists had simply transferred to politics Adam Smith's conception of the economy as a domain where "the invisible hand"—natural competitive forces—produced a just distribution of benefits and burdens, with no need for central direction from above. Galbraith's countervailing power theory turned this process of interdisciplinary larceny around. He picked up the pluralists' notion of competing power blocs, and took it back to economics, replacing Smith's original invisible hand of free competition with a new self-regulatory force, more plausible in a modern corporate setting. His ingenious proposal served the times well (although on the merits it suffered fatally from the fact that Galbraith never explained why "countervailing" corporations would want to pass on to consumers the fruit of their power, instead of just keeping it for themselves in higher profits, salaries, and wages). It removed the last obstacle in the way of a generation that mainly wanted to look upon the mid-century political economy of the United States and see that it was good. Previously, Joseph Schumpeter, Adolph Berle, and Frederick Lewis Allen had said that monopoly power was essential for technical progress;[7] Galbraith showed that monopoly was not a spur to corporate exploitation.

The Attack on Populism

In this world of ubiquitous bargaining among interest groups, the old populist anxiety about control by the public or the majority seemed unnecessary. And indeed popular control over elites soon came to seem positively dangerous to many liberals. The reason for this was Senator Joe McCarthy. McCarthy shocked the postwar liberal generation in a manner from which it has never completely recovered. For many months polls showed that an astonishing 50 percent or more of the electorate approved of McCarthy's crusade against radicals, bureaucrats, generals, and especially intellectuals. This seemed to be proof positive that the masses were not a reliable ally of progressive and rational public policies. Politics dominated by interest groups might not work by the rules taught in civics class; but at least the issues that its constituents struggled over were sensible, limited, negotiable. Far better to have peaceful conflict about "real" needs that can be managed by shrewd political professionals or sophisticated bureaucrats, than to look toward the populist ideal for guidance. That way lies the madness and demagoguery that McCarthy represented. "As geologists cover the earth prospecting for oil," David Riesman and Nathan Glazer observed caustically in 1955, "so politicians cover the electorate prospecting for hidden hatreds and identities."[8]

Having thus soured on populist politics, intellectuals were greatly attracted to Richard Hofstadter's brilliant and sweeping reinterpretation of the entire history of twentieth-century American reform. The thesis he presented in *The Age of Reform* argued that it was *not* anomalous that Wisconsin's distinguished liberal Senator Robert LaFollette, Jr. was replaced by McCarthy, the most effective reactionary demagogue of the century. Hofstadter pointed out that when LaFollette's father, the great Progressive governor and senator, attacked the New York "money trust," he sounded remarkably like McCarthy when he attacked Harvard intellectuals, who were, after all, simply another kind of eastern elite. He concluded that both the Progressives (and Populists) and the anticommunist zealots of the 1950s based their careers on the exploitation of the same popular "impulse"—in Riesman's terms, the same complex "of hidden hatreds and identities." "Populist thinking," Hofstadter said,

has survived in our own time, partly as an undercurrent of provincial resentments, popular and "democratic" rebelliousness and suspiciousness, and nativism. . . . The impulses behind yesterday's reform may be put in the service of reform today, but they may also be enlisted in the service of reaction.[9]

The liberals' contempt was not limited to the populist political style. They took a condescending view of turn-of-the-century ideology as well. Hofstadter described the general theme of the period as a sentimental and even reactionary effort to revive a "type of economic individualism and political democracy that was widely believed . . . to have been destroyed by the great corporation and the corrupt political machine . . . to bring back a kind of morality and civic purity. . . ."[10]

Hofstadter and the generation for which he spoke did not repudiate the idea of reform *per se*. They embraced what they took to be the distinctive and far more sophisticated reform tradition established by the New Deal. "With its pragmatic spirit and its relentless emphasis upon results,"[11] the New Deal in their view repudiated the populist-progressive tradition; it represented the final triumph of bureaucracy, organization, and machine politics (and the final demise of WASP hegemony in national elections) which the older generation of reformers had struggled to forestall.

Given this dim view of mass politics, it is not surprising that social theorists of the 1950s and 1960s denigrated the institution of popular elections. Not that they actually proposed the elimination of this most sacrosanct element in the populist conception of democratic government (though they did oppose *extending* the role of elections any further, and often criticized the establishment of direct primaries that occurred during the Populist and Progressive period). The pluralists contended that the impact of elections on policy was relatively slight, or at least far less pronounced than was generally imagined; interest groups managed the behavior of Congress and the bureaucracies almost without regard to the quadrennial ceremony of democracy. Furthermore, and most important, even in regard to the particular decisions governed directly by elections, namely the choice of candidates, they showed that spontaneous popular sentiment was far less decisive than the manipulations of party professionals. And they felt that the dominance of the "bosses" over the nomination and election processes was, on the whole, a good thing. What prescriptions for electoral reform they approved were mainly designed to constrict the scope of direct popular control and reinforce the power of the professionals.

A variety of theories were propounded to support these antipopulist conclusions. Some argued that boss control was actually *more* democratic than systems emphasizing direct democracy. James MacGregor Burns, for example, urged that the most secure way to achieve representation of all sectors of the electorate is a regime in which there is little or no effective democracy *within* political parties but vigorous competition *between* the parties for votes in the general election.[12] Related to Burns' position was that of Professors E. E. Schattschneider and V. O. Key;[13] they alleged that the vagaries of opinion and the low level of popular interest in primary elections meant that party cadres would represent the party membership more accurately than the often narrow constituency that controlled the outcome of primaries. Still a third variation of this theme acknowledged the value, in presidential elections, of just a few primaries; they provided a relatively cheap index of the candidates' popular appeal and their ability to campaign, criteria the convention managers would want to evaluate along with other factors such as the candidates' support among all elements of the party coalition, their appeal to independent voters outside the party, and their relative access to financing.[14]

Advocates of this limited antipopulist position—the position that democracy is better served by back-room deals off the convention floor than by open confrontations in primaries—could (and can) point to many specific cases for support. Whenever a relatively extreme candidate—like George McGovern or Max Rafferty—captures a party nomination, his party seems to lose the general election by an overwhelming margin, often in a manner that inhibits debate and denies the electorate a meaningful choice about the issues of concern to most voters. The "bosses" can sometimes pick a more representative candidate than a primary election can produce (though often this argument is specious since the party organization, if it has any cohesion and force, ought in normal circumstances to control the outcome of primaries).

On the other hand, the limited antipopulist argument depended on two crucial assumptions never acknowledged by its proponents. These were that the John Baileys and Richard Daleys actually wanted to *win* elections, and that they neither harbored any ideological differences from the membership, nor identified strongly with the preferences of one internal party faction against the other. As long as all was harmony within the ranks of the New Deal coalition, these assumptions corresponded to political fact. But in the late 1960s, as internal friction among Democrats flared into bitter antagonism, the power of the professionals to dictate the choice of party candidates became both more flagrant and less compatible with democratic principle.

However, to a second group of antipopulist theorists, it did not seem in itself disturbing that in 1968 internal antagonism broke out between the Democratic organization and the unorganized but relatively numerous (and extremely vocal) anti-Vietnam constituency. These theorists were more or less frankly antidemocratic, or at least favorable to social values other than democracy. A number of theorists simply trusted the bosses more than the people; if competent interest brokers did not restrict the menu of candidates from which the public could choose in the general election, the result might be (as it was in the 1946 Wisconsin primary) a demagogue or a fanatic.[15] Another similar argument, not quite so overtly antidemocratic, was that managed nomination systems produce a relatively low-key kind of politics, in which divisive issues are not articulated, or are blurred when they are mentioned by the candidates. If the people do not understand the issues too well, they won't fight about them too much. Finally, a more subtle variant of this theme, propounded by Yale Law Professor Alexander Bickel, emphasized that by muting conflict and pushing both parties to the center, the present electoral system, though it may diminish direct popular control and majority rule, nevertheless promotes social stability and, most important, ensures that candidates and administrations seek to acquire for their policies the "consent of the governed"—*all* the governed, losers as well as winners.[16]

During the turbulence of 1968, Bickel was actually an advocate of internal party democratization, as a leading member of the private commission chaired by Iowa Governor (now Senator) Harold Hughes, which engineered the decision of the 1968 Democratic National Convention to commit the party to reform nomination procedures. His antipopulist arguments were offered in support of retaining the electoral college; they were based on his fear that the direct popular election scheme for electing presidents, which nearly passed Congress in 1969 and 1970, would end the two-party system.

The Paralysis of Ideology

But Bickel's interest in party reform was unusual, if not unique, among important academic enthusiasts of a managed electoral process. They were uniformly silent, perhaps baffled, when the nation's electoral system reached the dreadful impasse that paralyzed politics between the March on the Pentagon in October, 1967, and Eugene McCarthy's triumph in the New Hampshire primary five months later. All who were experienced in the workings of the system—the press and politicians as well as the academic theorists—could see no way out. The system was understood to offer no reasonable possibility of a revolt from within the Democratic Party; the power of an incumbent president and party leaders was too great to permit that. So there was no way within the system to raise the Vietnam issue in a meaningful way.

Clearly, this was wrong. Not only did it violate populist democratic principles, but it also threatened conservative norms such as legitimacy, consensus, and stability as well. Yet the antipopulist academics were no more able than was Mayor Daley to imagine any alternatives to the system, or even to consider the possibility of significant internal reform. Though largely intellectual, their stake in an environment in which the people's choices were restricted tightly by professionals' judgment was little less than that of the professionals themselves. They were immobile. They couldn't contemplate change, even to save themselves. It remained for the idealists who went to New Hampshire in 1967 for Eugene McCarthy to tap the widespread yearning for relief from the status quo, to salvage what chances for change remained within the system, and thereby perhaps to save the system itself.

Social scientists were silent in the face of the strains of Lyndon

Johnson's second term because they had concluded that political thought had reached an "end of ideology." In their view, all conflicts were about means and not ends, and even traditional battles over the division of society's resources were rendered unimportant by permanent economic growth. This end of ideology turned Marx on his head, just as Marx was often said to have turned Hegel on *his* head a century before. History had come to a stop. All contradictions had disappeared. Basic harmony about values prevailed among all groups within society.

Despite this end of fundamental conflict, the state did not wither away. Clearly, the state grew larger and larger. This was not, however, a cause for alarm, even though government itself was perceived to be heavily influenced by private interests. Some observers managed to keep on believing that a mysterious —and unidentified—dynamic principle assured that government programs, especially when they were dominated by the federal executive branch, were *inherently* progressive, inherently favorable to the weak and the poor. Frederick Lewis Allen, for example, boasted that

> patchwork revisions of the system—tax laws, minimum wage laws, subsidies and guarantees and regulations of various sorts, plus labor union pressures and new management attitudes . . . had brought about a virtually automatic redistribution of income from the well-to-do to the less well-to-do.[17]

Others believed that the pressure groups themselves were not, on the whole, pernicious, nor that their overall impact was unrepresentative.

But, mainly, the theorists believed in high government *officials,* in the new breed of politically sophisticated technocrats who were thought to manage the exercise of government power. These bureaucratic leaders had to be expert enough to know the "right answer" from a technical point of view, and shrewd enough to broker the relevant interests as well. Even if all one

of these technocrats did was to negotiate the terms of a compromise between contending interests, his proficiency assured
that precisely the *right* compromise had been struck; the gains
of all participants had been maximized, their respective losses
minimized, and affected interests not so well represented in the
political process had at least been given some recognition.

In effect, this admiring image of the technocrat superimposed
a New Dealish kind of statism over the Hobbesian "war of all
against all" that the first round of pluralist theories had constructed after World War II. Without coming right out and
saying so, the end of ideology theorists had fabricated a grand
synthesis in which government once again was assigned its
populist role as a politically autonomous source of support for
"the public interest." This emphasis was never clearly articulated, much less explicitly defended. But its presence was critical to the confidence liberal academics manufactured about the
state of the polity in the Kennedy and early Johnson years. When
Paul Samuelson told freshman economists in his first-year
economics text that America has a "mixed" private and public
economy, he took this to be a reassuring message; ultimate control, he assumed, rested with the public, which had in its wisdom
chosen to leave much of the economy in "private" hands, while
subjecting other portions to greater or lesser measures of government *diktat*.

In other words, Samuelson did *not* mean that the "mixed"
public and private character of the economy merely reflected
different strategies pursued for reasons of their own by individual groupings of private, predominantly corporate, interests
—that airlines were regulated because the major companies believed that this was the most secure way to stabilize their market
shares and profit levels, whereas steel was unregulated (except
for tariff protections) because the steel companies found
oligopolistic pricing policies an adequate route to the same result. Similarly, Professor Galbraith used government intervention as the fudge factor in his description of the healing role of

countervailing power; where public constituencies such as consumers failed to organize for their own protection, Galbraith said, the government became the instrument of countervailing power on their behalf, through regulatory agencies.

There was nothing in the logic of Galbraith's conception of economic power blocs that could satisfactorily explain how the unorganized public could defend itself against the focused energy of a major industry—whether or not the public was "represented" by a frail entity like the FTC or the FDA. Similarly, there was nothing in David Truman's pluralist conception of politics to encourage his evident faith in the beneficence of government involvement in the oil production and distribution process. Yet, however muted, the idea of the state as agent of the public interest nevertheless retained a critical role. Indeed, in many political science departments, professors evidently became so impressed with the importance and the value of bureaucracy that their scholarship itself came to resemble a kind of rigorous and theoretically sophisticated management consulting service for various federal executive agencies.

The New Statism
The postwar liberal theorists refurbished the old Populist ideal of the public interest state—even as they debunked the "moralism" of the Progressives and the overblown rhetoric (if not the pluralistic programs) of the New Dealers—because they were obliged to. They were unwilling to face up to the harsh implications of reasoning in strict conformance with pluralist theory. There was simply no way in which an active state like the U.S. government in a purely pluralist polity could yield the "good society." If a government agency held full legal control over relations between consumers and the transportation industry, then strict pluralist logic would require the conclusion that policy would be biased heavily in favor of the industry. Only some notion that the state had—or ought to have—an independent ability to determine and enforce a "fair" balance be-

tween consumers and the industry could keep political theory from envisaging *and approving* an apparently exploitative result.

The problem with such a theory was that it could not confer legitimacy on a political system with which liberals in and out of the academy were (again, through the middle 1960s) manifestly well-satisfied. Social scientists did not often deal with this point in their writings, because "legitimacy" was the kind of moralistic concern that, with their emphasis on pragmatism and results, they found painful and irritating to notice. But the point was nevertheless clear enough. A strict pluralist view of politics had to lead to the conclusion that only a limited government was a legitimate government. Such in fact was the strong conviction of the original pluralists, the founding fathers who followed James Madison.

Hence, in order to keep big government from seeming illegitimate, the liberal social scientists had to invest government with at least some ability to rise above the pluralist struggle. Unlike the old Progressives and Populists, and even the New Dealers, they did not choose to rely on the institution of popular elections, or on the government's political responsiveness to the popular will. Their general contempt for the political efficiency and social value of direct democratic devices caused them to look elsewhere for an explanation of why the government could be itself an independent source of support for the public interest (or for paths to reform). Instead, their explanation emphasized the value of the government expert. They even welcomed the relative apathy of the general public, for that seemed to give greater discretionary power to bureaucratic leaders—and, to a lesser extent, to professional politicians.

Their expertise justified their authority in the early days of the New Frontier. Not since the first years of the New Deal had Americans placed such store by the idea that brilliance and good intentions would vindicate the public interest. But a few years later that myth was battered and reeling, sunk perhaps to its lowest state in the public's esteem in recent history. What Tom

Wicker called "the most corrosive internal disunity of modern times" was occasioned precisely because so many Americans believed that they had been betrayed by the foreign and military affairs experts from whom Lyndon Johnson sought counsel in taking the nation "almost secretively into a war he had pledged not to enter and whose validity and goals were deeply questioned by many of those who elected him."[18]

The 1968 election deepened the crisis of legitimacy. Because presidential control over the Democrats' nomination machinery deterred a serious antiwar candidate like Robert Kennedy from challenging Johnson, the system seemed rigged to prevent even an *ex post* electoral test of the war policy; this impression was not altered by the ease with which Hubert Humphrey eventually locked up the nomination without winning a single primary confrontation with antiwar forces. Finally, faith in expert leadership as the salvation of government was dashed by Ralph Nader. If, as he alleged, the federal regulatory apparatus had been captured by private industry, such expertise as may once have inhabited the agencies had either disappeared or lost its value to the people.

Dissenters Left and Right

The U.S. government was suddenly seen by a substantial and vocal body of citizens to be exercising power on illegitimate terms. This perception of illegitimacy launched the new populist crusade. But before this new generation of reformers were able to put traditional liberal policies at issue on the national political agenda, much philosophical groundwork had been laid for them by left- and right-wing dissenting movements within the academy.

The New Left had ridiculed the assumption that American pluralism was really representative of all legitimate interests in the nation; it was heavily biased, they said, in favor of the powerful. On close examination, supposedly redistributive liberal programs—the graduated income tax, urban renewal, support for higher education—turned out to be regressive in their actual operation. In general, the academic and student left decried the liberals' too-easy acceptance of bureaucratic giant-ism. They revived the participationist side of the populist ideal that the New Deal version of populism and the pluralists had neglected. It was not enough, the New Left said, for government to act in the name of the people. The people must be able to participate, as actively and directly as possible, in government decisions—indeed, in all decisions, whether formally public or formally private, that "affect their lives." Community control and decentralization came into vogue, because reducing the scope of government seemed to be the only way in which the radical participationism of the New Left might be implemented.

Much less adept at insinuating their slogans into the political talk of the times, but nevertheless far more penetrating in their critique of postwar liberalism, was another academic splinter group, the right-wing economists and lawyers centered at the University of Chicago. Over more than two decades and in innumerable journal articles and books, the Chicago economists produced rigorous demonstrations that economic theory—to which "liberal" as well as "conservative" economists subscribed —yielded no justification for many of the regulatory ventures Congress had approved during the first half of the century. Prices would be lower, service better, innovation faster, they attempted to prove, if regulation were lightened or eliminated outright from much of transportation, finance, communications, securities exchange, and power generation and distribution. They dismissed the liberals' image of bureaucratic expertise by show-ing how foolish decisions at agencies like the FCC actually were, and further by pointing out how absurd and even antidemocratic it was to establish regulatory schemes in which matters as sub-jective as entertainment television programming would be evalu-ated by a panel of lawyers and politicians. The marketplace would satisfy the wants of the people more effectively, they con-tended, and in a manner more commensurate with national con-ventions about fairness than the clumsy regulatory machinery created by the New Deal.[19]

However, the Chicago economists did not deal with *how*—and whether—their economic reforms might actually be brought about.

More attuned to the role of politics, both in theory and practice, was a third group of dissenters that also formed, perhaps not by accident, at the University of Chicago. These were political scientists who produced a still-expanding body of anti-pluralist writings, beginning in the middle 1950s and culminating in three general tracts, *The Decline of American Pluralism* by H. R. Kariel, *Private Power and American Democracy* by Grant McConnell, and *The End of Liberalism* by Theodore J. Lowi. The Chicago political scientists admitted the pluralists' premise —that "interest groups" dominate American politics. Indeed, they often showed that the power of interest groups was more pervasive than even the pluralists had imagined. The public battle between liberals and conservatives, between Democrats and Republicans, in terms of which the press and even scholars understood much of politics, was irrelevant; the only thing that actually determined the behavior of the parties was the question of which interest groups they chose to serve. Every effort of well-intentioned liberals to plan the development of one or another regulated sector had been quickly smashed by the regulatees. All these observations would neither have surprised nor disturbed conventional liberal pluralists. What set Chicagoans H. S. Kariel, McConnell, and Lowi apart was their insistence that pluralist government was one-sided. In general, interest groups did not "bargain" with one another, thus moderating one another's aggressive designs. Instead, each group quietly carved out its own piece of the action, creating or subverting specific governmental institutions wherever convenient. The objective in each case, successfully attained in many, was to establish an essentially autonomous subsystem—what the perceptive Washington journalist Douglas Cater called a "subgovernment."

David Riesman and V. O. Key, two eminent pluralists, had used the term "veto groups" to describe the behavior of organized interests in American politics. They maintained that interest groups could not really initiate important actions or acquire majority support for their designs; all they could do was "veto" proposals that appeared injurious to their welfare. The Chicago political scientists argued that this negative conception of the power of organized interests sold them short; in fact, they frequently originated plans for government policy, and carried them to fruition. Their creativity was manifest throughout the government, in the architecture of arrangements for officially sanctioned cartels, subsidies, tax loopholes, tariffs, import quotas, patent restrictions, franchises, contracts, and the entire cornucopia of largesse made available by government to those clever enough to claim it.

The Chicago political scientists did not draw a portrait of a monolith like Charles Reich's corporate state or Professor Galbraith's (the new Professor Galbraith) new industrial state. On the contrary, the essence of the system was its Balkanization. The power of a particular interest group was strictly or largely limited to a discrete domain. But within that domain, it was omnipotent. It was precisely because of the decentralized character of the system—the "derangement of powers" abhorred by Lippmann—that neither Madisonian nor populist checks would work. That was why liberal government had become unaccountable and illegitimate.

The Chicago political scientists defined their enemy as "interest-group liberalism." They tried to show that this pluralist mentality had been solely responsible for the evils of the system as it stands, establishments organized by and for particular private interests but graced with sweeping statutory mandates to identify and enforce "the public interest." In fact, the analysis of the Chicago political scientists makes a somewhat different point: the cause of the present crisis of legitimacy does not lie solely in the Hobbesian logic of pluralism; nor does the difficulty lie wholly in the statist heritage of traditional populism, which flowered during the New Deal. The problem is that postwar liberals embraced *both* pluralism and statism, *unaware* of the antithetical features of these two visions of politics, and without perceiving any need to impose limits on the logic of either. They did not see, as the founding fathers did, that if one really believes politics consists of the self-seeking strategies of discrete factions or groups, one has to conclude that the power of the state must be controlled strictly. How else could the capacity of these selfish factions to injure the public, and to impair the liberty of individuals be kept within bounds? If the state is going to be essentially unlimited in its power—like the post-New Deal U.S. government in respect to the substantive ends for which it may legislate—that power must be anchored to some reasonably effective machinery for public accountability; otherwise, what is left is merely an empty statism.

The postwar liberals made the mistake of trying to eulogize pluralism without the saving instinct for constraint manifested by the founding fathers. They praised New Deal statism while demeaning and even diminishing its roots in the populist ideal.

9

Halfway up from Liberalism: The New Populism and the State

One of the most perverse habits of the postwar liberals was their inclination to revere the New Dealers, while scorning the Progressives and Populists. Inspired by Richard Hofstadter, many liberals still understand "populism" as an epithet, connoting the naive moralism which they believe stymied early twentieth-century reformers. Yet New Deal ideology was itself a variant of the populist tradition, rather than a departure from it. Furthermore, the New Deal version of the populist ideal was, if anything, *more* naive than the version nurtured by the old Populists and Progressives. Glib New Deal promises of a new regime conjured a moratorium on politics, during which well-intentioned reformers could actually work out new social arrangements in tune with expert definitions of the public interest.

The first generation of twentieth-century reformers did not share the New Dealers' hubris about "taking control" of things. They believed that it was, as Woodrow Wilson said during the 1912 campaign, "an open question" whether government was "strong enough to overcome and rule" the private interests that dominated politics and the economy. The Progressives had a tragic sense about democracy, a sense that some inherent fault might make it impossible for democratic government to fulfill itself.

It is true, of course, that the Progressives often chose ineffectual strategies to cope with this mysterious and disheartening flaw in democracy. They were wrong to think that once the people had the power to initiate legislation directly, or to recall elected officials, they would themselves be able frequently to intervene, bring government to a halt, and thus remedy special interest abuse. But the Progressives were clearly right to feel that government could not safely be left to run itself. They saw that regular elections were not enough of a check. They were too predictable, sometimes too infrequent, and certainly too little adapted to focusing public interest on specific issues and official transgressions. Without some additional agency of review, some mechanism for intervention by guardians of the public weal, the integrity of government could not be assured. Democracy, the Progressives perceived, was not self-regulating.

This central insight of the Progressives and the original Populists has now been rediscovered. The most attractive feature of the current recrudescence of populist thought is precisely this skepticism about government, this sense that American democracy is flawed. The new populists want to structure the American political economy in a way that will minimize its vulnerability to special-interest domination. In particular, they want "fail-safe" mechanisms that, like the initiative and recall, will permit outside forces to interrupt the routine of government and set it back on a course faithful to public interest. In short, the new populism has brought back to left-of-center politics a profound distrust of government—not just as prosecutor or censor, not just as a threat to minorities or individuals, but as a foe of the majority, of the public itself.

But the new populists have not gone so far as to renounce the statist side of the populist ideological tradition. Nor indeed have they managed in any systematic way to reexamine regulation as a technique of reform. Like the Progressives, the new

Populists are schizophrenic about government. They distrust it and at the same time they feel obliged to rely on it. In the end, the new populists have kept faith with the affirmative ideal of democracy, with the notion that reform measures should be premised on the hope that the public will be able, through government, to seize and maintain affirmative control over powerful special interests. Like their forebears, they have invested much of their time, energy, and prestige in championing grand regulatory designs to subject private interests to affirmative public control.

Tinkering with the Regulatory Establishment

Enthusiasm for regulation is evident on several fronts of the new populist campaign. In the first place, it is reflected in a host of relatively modest suggestions for improving the existing system, which I would call, not in any derisive sense, "tinkering" reforms. Most of these are aimed at curing common symptoms of the political malaise which has hamstrung regulatory institutions. They include proposals to give greater emphasis to criminal sanctions and suspension of officials; to expand legal rights of access to information controlled by public and private bureaucracies, and to create wider disclosure obligations; to require all meetings between regulators and industry representatives to be a matter of record; and to make it more difficult for regulatory officials to obtain jobs with regulated interests, and vice versa.

None of these proposals has much potential for harm. On the other hand, none of them seems likely to trigger dramatic changes in the agencies' performance, at least not by itself. Virtually every Nader's Raiders report demands new criminal or other penalties for violators, especially for officials who refuse to enforce pollution, health, and safety standards, and the like. But drastic personal sanctions for official misdeeds will not apply to many instances where existing anti-corruption statutes do not already apply. Bureaucratic decisions that favor industry may seem deplorable, but they cannot—except where money changes hands, as in the Vesco affair, or perhaps where a public official sets out systematically to subvert a program he is charged with enforcing, as with Howard J. Phillips' acting directorship of OEO in 1973—be made occasions for Draconian reprisal. Such decisions are usually too complex to make it fair to jail someone who agrees with the industry's position.

There are, no doubt, a few instances, this side of bribery, where private businessmen or officials commit their enterprises to strategies which they know are illegal. For most of these offenses, we already have criminal sanctions. For those that we do not, we should adopt them, but not on the mistaken theory that dramatic behavioral changes will follow. The more difficult question, which new legislation will not solve, is how to ensure *enforcement* of criminal sanctions for regulatory offenses. Not only prosecutors, but judges and even juries are reluctant to treat conspiracies to restrain trade in the same way they would treat conspiracies to burglarize homes. Statistics produced by the Nader Study Group on Antitrust Enforcement confirm this aspect of our social psychology.

Information-access requirements, another tinkering reform, will be very useful, but only if their enactment coincides with the development of an active elite of public-interest lawyers and other professionals who would obtain and disseminate the data made available—and then put it to use. On this point, the precedent of the securities laws of 1933 and 1934 is instructive. Disclosure provisions in those reform statutes have succeeded in transforming the climate in which the securities industry operates —but mainly because there is an active constituency of securities firms, lawyers, and investors ready to make use of the laws and the data.

New Populist Reforms: The First Generation
In addition to generalized tinkering with existing regulatory techniques, contemporary reformers have proposed a variety of new regulatory laws and whole agencies to remedy abuses in specific areas of the economy. One of these, the National High-

way and Traffic Safety Administration, has been impressively successful in forcing safety innovations on the auto industry. By 1970, the auto safety program appeared to have reversed the upward trend of annual automobile accident fatalities, a remarkable achievement for an agency barely four years old. Prodded by Lowell Dodge, the Director of Nader's Center for Auto Safety, the Traffic Safety Administration has overseen the development of airbags despite bitter resistance by the auto industry. It is expected that the airbag will prevent 9,000 highway deaths and 700,000 disabling injuries per year; as the agency gradually stiffens its standards, these figures will soar to 20,000 deaths and over 2,000,000 injuries prevented. Needless to say, this achievement will make the National Traffic and Motor Vehicle Safety Act, which Nader single-handedly persuaded Congress to enact in 1966, the most dramatic and surely one of the most useful consumer protection reforms ever adopted.

Two other new residents of Washington's regulatory establishment, the EPA and the CEQ, have pursued their tasks with zeal and relative effectiveness. The CEQ has been confined merely to issuing reports and to advising operational government agencies of their responsibilities to consider environmental issues in carrying out programs. But despite undernourishment from Congress's appropriations committees, and despite the uncertainty of White House support, the CEQ has generally managed to live up to its mandate. Senator Muskie's leadership in Congress has provided EPA with a burgeoning array of antipollution legislation to enforce. EPA Administrator William Ruckelshaus resisted industry and political pressures to stray from the course marked out for his new agency by these important regulatory statutes.

In addition to these three new agencies, and several others which are certain to be created by Congress in the near future, the new populism has made an impact on most important existing regulatory bureaucracies, either through the enactment of new legislative authority or simply through stepped-up enforcement of once dormant programs. As a result of Ralph Nader's prodigious lobbying efforts, the Department of Transportation has responsibility for administering the Natural Gas Pipeline Safety Act (1968); HEW has gained the Radiation Control for Health and Safety Act (1968); USDA has obtained the Wholesome Meat Act (1967), and the Wholesome Poultry Products Act (1968); Interior has acquired the Federal Coal Mine Health and Safety Act (1969); and Labor has acquired the comprehensive Occupational Health and Safety Act (1970). Without new legislation, Nader's muckraking turned the FTC from one of the least zealous enterprises in Washington into one of the most zealous; the same technique revitalized the FDA, though less dramatically.

In short, the legislative and administrative achievements of the current reform movement already approach the records established in Woodrow Wilson's first term and Franklin Roosevelt's first two terms. The movement has barely passed its adolescence and the 1970s could prove to be the century's most productive decade, a triumph of the populist spirit, at least from the standpoint of the number of legislative victories won.

With respect to a more fundamental issue, however, the outlook is not necessarily so bright. It is far from clear that the artifacts of this reform period will show more durability than their predecessors. There is nothing in the legal or political structure of EPA or NHTSA which encourages confidence that their zeal will long survive the passing of the popular passions that now support them. Other new programs appear never to have gotten much beyond the starting gate at all. According to reformist New York State Public Service Commission Chairman (and President Kennedy's FPC Chairman) Joseph Swidler, the pipeline safety law has preempted effective state safety standards with dangerously weak new federal standards—standards which, moreover, are left substantially unenforced. There are similar unhappy cases, such as the strangulation of the coal mine safety law. In *Sowing the Wind,* a brilliant exercise in self-criticism— unique among the *oeuvre* of Nader's Raiders—one of Nader's top aides, Harrison Wellford, has shown that the 1967 and 1968 Wholesome Meat and Wholesome Poultry Products laws have not significantly improved—and may eventually degrade—the quality of inspection. Influential elements in the USDA see the new laws as a possible excuse for dismantling federal meat inspection facilities altogether and turning the responsibility entirely over to the states.

Nader and his colleagues should not be overly faulted for the afflictions which have beset this first generation of new populist reforms. Each of these measures was aimed at an important and relatively concrete problem. Where this first set of reforms has failed, the cause has mainly been the simple fact that they were entrusted to hostile, producer-oriented agencies to enforce. This difficulty can be corrected, at least temporarily, by putting the laws in the hands of more sympathetic administrators. Senator Ribicoff has already proposed that the meat and poultry inspection legislation be taken away from USDA and given to a new federal consumer safety agency, which new populist forces on Capitol Hill are in the process of trying to have set up.

However, the reformers deserve more blame for the flaws in their next series of regulatory innovations. They are championing two ambitious new agencies, an "independent consumer protection agency" and a special federal corporation agency which would replace individual state governments as the issuer of legal charters to all major corporations. Both of these schemes display all the worst features of the old grand design mentality, and therefore seem fated to come to the same dismal end as the early FTC and the National Industrial Recovery Act. Ralph Nader has portrayed both these proposals as vital to his plans for building a more democratic America. Together, these two schemes for reform tell a great deal about the kind of America Nader wants to build.

Return of the Grand Design:
The "Independent" Consumer Protection Agency

The first of these new grand designs, the consumer protection agency, failed to become law in 1972 only because of a last-minute filibuster but as this book went to press, it seemed bound to pass in 1973 or 1974. Its main job will be to appear before other, older consumer regulatory agencies like the FCC or the FPC as a legal representative of consumer interests. The idea of a CPA has generated great excitement among consumer advocates; Nader himself has both privately and publicly called it "The most important consumer legislation *ever* considered by the Congress." With that kind of endorsement from Nader, of course, the bill should be expected to antagonize business. And it has. The Chamber of Commerce and other lobbies have fought it, or at least denounced it. And the Nixon Administration has fought with them, marching the president's pliant Special Consumer Affairs Assistant Mrs. Virginia Knauer up to Capitol Hill for hearings and conferences to explain why consumers don't really need whatever protection this new bureaucracy might afford.

But I suspect that, once the new agency is established, both reformers and conservatives will be surprised.[1] The public will wonder what the shouting was all about during the two years in which Nader and his allies struggled to maneuver the measure through Congress. The CPA is likely to serve as one more reminder that calling a government institution "independent" will not make it so, The agency will have very broad powers—which is to say, very vague responsibilities. But the administrator who will formally exercise these powers will be appointed by the president—the same president whose appointees to other regulatory posts are supposedly proving so spineless that this new CPA is needed to keep them honest. There is, once again, nothing in the bill to make this consumer protection agency any more "independent" of corporate and political pressure than its predecessors.

By itself, this might not be grounds for scuttling the idea of a consumer agency. After all, presidential appointees to regulatory agencies have *sometimes* turned in creditable performances, especially in times like the present, when public concern about consumer protection is relatively intense. Hence, we could probably count on at least a fair performance from the new agency, at least until the present wave of enthusiasm for reform fades.

Unfortunately, however, the dangers in entrusting the proposed CPA to the care of a presidential appointee are far greater than in the case of traditional regulatory agencies. For this institution is to have an ombudsman-like function which is quite unique. This fact will give the president an overriding incentive to clamp down on any activist ambitions the agency may entertain. Existing agencies like the Antitrust Division or the FDA threaten the interests of campaign contributors. That alone has been enough to induce most presidents to keep a rein on the agencies' operations. But the new CPA will directly threaten members of the president's own administration; therefore, it will threaten the president himself. He is, after all, responsible for the performance of the federal bureaucracy and the integrity of its programs. It will hardly suit his political convenience to put gadfly government lawyers in the business of revealing that one agency after another has turned out to be faithless to its statutory mandate. No president, "liberal" or "conservative," could afford to have one of his own appointees give and publicize damning evidence of his own misfeasance.

Let us imagine for a moment how this problem will arise in practice. The FPC might, for example, be entertaining an application for rate increase by an interstate gas pipeline company. The hearing has attracted literally no public or press attention, but the CPA staff recommends that the agency intervene to oppose the application. Does the administrator simply file his opposition? Does he issue along with it a press release, explaining in language clear and lively enough to be used by the media what stake consumers have in the outcome of the proceeding? Does he call a press conference? Or does he call up the FPC chairman, to see if something can be worked out, or to see how much the FPC "cares" about the case? Or does he first bring the matter up with an assistant to the president, who in the nature of things will be the same assistant who supervises ("coordinates") the FPC along with other consumer regulatory agencies?

In any event, the case is going to come before the presidential assistant, if it ever gets beyond the CPA administrator. It is unlikely that the White House aide will have to read about it first in the newspapers. If he does, he will still be able to establish substantial control over the outcome of the matter. And it will be the last time a similar issue—if it is a sensitive one— will be presented to him *after* the CPA has decided to act. Once the case does come before the presidential assistant, there is little question about how he will want to settle it. He will want it taken care of *quietly*. He will discourage or forbid press involvement. He will keep the lid on.

The issue of White House concern over consumer agency practices will be especially sensitive because of the fact that almost any decision to intervene before another agency will be interpreted publicly as an attack on the integrity of the other agency. It will not seem merely a routine precaution. It will appear to represent a judgment by the CPA administrator—and perhaps by the White House as well, since the CPA is not legally independent—that the agency in question cannot be trusted to protect consumers. This public impression will be especially strong, and hence White House surveillance of the CPA particularly close, if the CPA has the power to intervene in other agencies' investigations, as Nader and his allies desire, rather than just in formal open hearings, as the Nixon Administration and Representative Chet Holifield intend.

Unfortunately, an environment in which only quiet, internal solutions are encouraged is not likely to be favorable, in general, to the interests of any group so diffuse as consumers. Within administrations there is often, of course, bitter intramural conflict over issues of all kinds. But if one agency is backed by well-organized and well-financed private interests, and the other has no such outside support, it is not hard to predict which way the administration will decide, in most cases, to "tilt." To be sure, in the case we have posed, CPA staffers could leak their problem to the press or to Ralph Nader or to an antiadministration congressman—if it seems important enough to them to run the high attendant risk of injuring their careers. But even if they did leak the story, the resultant counter-pressure could only force the White House into allowing the case to be *filed*. It would not keep the president from modulating the vigor and especially the publicity with which the litigation is conducted. If the CPA administrator does not respect the president's overriding interest in public harmony among his official family, or if he cannot control his staff, then he will be replaced by an Eliot Richardson or a Don Rumsfeld or, for that matter, a Virginia Knauer, whose ultimate loyalty can be assured. The administrator will be no more likely than Mrs. Knauer to make a practice of public denunciations of other presidential appointees and the industries with whom they are, presumably, excessively friendly.

If this much-ballyhooed reform does turn out in practice to be a domesticated member of the president's official family, the new populist leaders who promoted it will deserve censure for something more serious than mere negligence or naivete. During the two-year legislative battle over the bill, ritual denunciations from the right no doubt reinforced the reformers' hopes that the measure they were backing would really deal a nasty thwack to the hide of big business. But there were also a few critics on the left who, while basically sympathetic, pointed out the fatal contradiction between the legal and political mandates that would handcuff the new CPA. Michigan Senator Philip Hart raised the issue cogently, when he complained on the Senate floor in December, 1970, just before the bill was approved by an overwhelming majority of seventy-four to four, that any administrator of the new agency would feel "his first obligation to be not so much to the consumers of America, but to the president who appointed him."

Two weeks after the Senate passed the bill, it died because the House Rules Committee refused—by one vote—to report it to the floor. This provided the reformers with a chance to try a new approach. They might have used the chance to embrace the suggestion of Senator Hart, who would have subordinated the consumer agency not simply to the president but to a board of directors chosen partly by the president, partly by the chief justice of the Supreme Court, and partly by Congress. Or they might have examined another variant: a board of directors having representatives from private institutions such as legal, consumer, and environmental organizations as well as the three branches of government. As a matter of fact, Office of Economic Opportunity (OEO) lawyers successfully maneuvered through both houses of Congress a proposal to create just such an independent corporation to shelter their work; however, it was then vetoed by President Nixon. But, even though a truly independent entity like the Hart or OEO proposals might require some additional years of public education before a president would become unable to prevent its enactment, new populist leaders might have embraced such a chance to create a climate for meaningful reform.

However the consumer advocates were of no mind to run that kind of risk. In January, 1971, when the ninety-second Congress opened, the original sponsors of the consumer agency bill, Representative Ben Rosenthal of New York and Senator Abe Ribicoff of Connecticut, introduced a proposal substantially identical to the old one. Incredibly, they had even stripped the measure of the only semblance of political independence it had originally enjoyed. In the 1970 version, the administrator was given fixed tenure coincident with the term of the president who appointed him; once hired, he could not be fired until the next presidential election. But the 1971 bill—the one which passed a year later—provides that the administrator shall serve merely at the pleasure of the president, which means that he will have no more protection against presidential *dis*pleasure than any other appointee. In other words, after winning an overwhelming victory in the Senate and losing in committee in the House only because of a fluke (liberal committee member Richard Bolling was vacationing in the Caribbean when the Rules Committee deadlocked over the bill), the reformers chose not to try for a proposal that might actually have worked.

They chose to play it safe. They wanted a victory, preceded to be sure by a dramatic public struggle. And that is just what they got.

The Birth of a Bureaucracy

The progress of this bill through the Congress shows how incentives inherent in populist politics make it attractive for reformers to promote unworkable grand designs like the CPA. The idea originated in a bill to create a "department" of consumer affairs, introduced by Ribicoff and Rosenthal in 1969, Nixon's first year in office. No one paid much attention to that bill. When I accompanied Bess Myerson to testify about the bill in March, 1969, the Ribicoff assistant who was responsible for it conceded that its backers were not seriously interested in having it passed at all; they only wanted to create an issue that might embarrass the president in a field where there was great potential voter appeal. "After all," the Ribicoff staffer laughed, "the last thing we would want to do is to create a brand new department of consumer affairs and then make its secretary answerable to Richard Nixon—and in addition staff the whole thing with Republicans who would get civil-serviced and could never be removed!"

The next year, however, this healthy cynicism had disappeared. Popular interest in consumerism was up. The reformers wanted something to show for their trouble. They wanted what liberals almost always seem to want, a new law—and a big one this time, not just a narrow measure confined to one field like safe vehicle design or deceptive packaging. They wanted something that could in some degree sound like a general answer to the whole problem of "consumer protection."

In this atmosphere, the notion of a whole new consumer affairs bureaucracy was irresistible, politically and psychologically. The concept fit snugly into ideological tradition, into familiar patterns of legislative form, and into the conventions of liberal oratory. (Indeed, the speeches practically wrote themselves—"Business has a department all its own! Labor has a department of its own! And even the farmer has a department of his own! What I want to know is why can't the 200 million consumers in this land have a department of their own, an agency which will fight for their interests at the highest levels of government, just the way all the special interests do?")

To achieve their objective, the reformers decided that it was premature to fight to establish a cabinet-level office. So the title of the 1969 agency was scaled down. In due course, I received a telephone call from Congressman Rosenthal. He asked me to put in a special plea to Bess Myerson, my boss, to come to Washington the next week for a press conference at which the bill would be announced. "What's in the bill?" I asked.

"Everything," Ben Rosenthal replied. "Ralph Nader and I just got together and designed a new agency and gave it all the powers we could think of." That was the independent CPA.

Nader, Ribicoff, and Rosenthal boasted of the scope of the powers they gave their new agency—on paper and they gloried in the ensuing battle to stop the administration from watering the measure down. The administration's counterproposal would have located the function of protecting consumer interests in regulatory proceedings in the Justice Department, rather than in a new and separate agency. The reformers denounced this alternative as one that would "render the whole bill meaningless." In truth, however, there was no particular reason to believe that either the Nixon bill or the reformers' bill would be markedly better (or worse) than the other. In both cases, the official in charge of intervention in the affairs of other federal bureaucracies would be answerable to the president.

Indeed, it could be argued that the reformers' new agency would provide a *less* secure setting for consumer advocacy than the Justice Department, for it would put the agency's top management closer to the White House. Possibly, an assistant attorney general would find himself more inclined toward interagency mischief than would a direct presidential appointee. As a matter of fact, the Justice Department's Antitrust Division has, under both Presidents Johnson and Nixon, frequently challenged the anticompetitive proclivities of other federal agencies. The most dramatic recent instance of this program was indeed Donald Turner's decision to take the FCC to court to abort the ABC-ITT merger. The division has on subsequent occasions attacked the SEC, the Department of Commerce, the CAB, and other agencies. In contrast, Mrs. Knauer, who reports directly to Nixon, has publicly engaged other members of the administration only very rarely and then very gently. Such encounters as she has dared, like her 1969 disputes with USDA over the percentage of fat and chicken permitted in hot dogs, seemed to have been staged and coordinated by the White House. It is not easy to imagine Mrs. Knauer intervening in a case like ABC-ITT.

When Nader, Rosenthal, and Ribicoff reintroduced the consumer agency bill in 1971, the administration at first chose not to introduce a countermeasure. Instead, the White House backed a modified version of the Rosenthal draft prepared by Government Operations Committee Chairman Chet Holifield. The Holifield bill, which ultimately passed the House over bitter public opposition from Rosenthal and Nader, limited the agency's right to intervene before other bureaucracies in cases which had already reached the stage of a formal hearing; the original proposal allowed intervention in matters even when they were in the prehearing, investigatory stages. Just as in the 1970 fight, much was made by the reformers of the differences between their "strong" bill and the administration's "weak" bill. In fact, the vigor and integrity with which the new consumer agency would perform its mission would have little to do with the extent of its formal powers—at least with the quite trivial question of whether they matched the Nader-Rosenthal concept or that of the administration and Holifield. Even under the relatively more limited version, the administrator would have his hands full just doing an adequate job in the open regulatory hearings which would merit his attention (especially since parsimonious Mississippi Representative Jamie Whitten would control his appropriations). The real question was how free, politically, the administrator would be to use his legal powers, whatever they were. Neither bill gave much cause for optimism on that score, since under either one the more vigorously and, especially, the more publicly the administrator used his powers, the more trouble he would make for his boss, the president.

Still, the consumer crusaders whipped up a considerable anxiety among their constituents in the press and the consumer movement over the differences between their bill and the rival Holifield-Nixon bill. After the House passed the Holifield proposal, the traditionally staid and nonpolitical *Consumer Reports* ran an angry *postmortem* feature entitled, "The Unmaking of a Consumer Advocate." Consumer Reports urged its readers to write to their senators to demand that the House vote be reversed in the Senate. Nader himself showed an uncharacteristic lack of composure, excoriating Holifield and his supporters, including AFL-CIO chief lobbyist Andrew Biemiller for "stripping the bill of its integrity and effectiveness."

No doubt, Nader's anger was at the time quite genuine. Nevertheless, it is hard not to conclude that in an objective sense he and his allies had staged a brouhaha over a technicality about the consumer agency's legal jurisdiction. They had done this even though, before the public fight got started, they had already stripped the agency of its only semblance of political independence—surely a far more fundamental question.

Of course, just because their product was not all that the promotional wrappings claimed, the reformers' deception was not necessarily willful. Nor is it necessarily true that they simply succumbed to the psychological temptation to believe in their own propaganda. Perhaps they were calculating, but calculating in order to serve what they considered to be the public's best interest as well as their own desire to show their populist zeal and their political muscle. They may have thought that a genuinely strong measure could not pass and, as Nader himself has been quoted, "Anything would be better than what we have now." After all, political leaders as sophisticated as he, Ben Rosenthal, and Abe Ribicoff know (as does any advertising executive) that "the most important consumer legislation ever considered by Congress" will go over better than the sort of appraisal a *Fortune* magazine researcher pried out of a Ribicoff aide: "[The new agency may] have its place in the sun, like the Peace Corps or OEO," the aide said; "then it will carve out a rather cautious domain of its own and become part of the bureaucracy."

To me, the aide's skepticism in fact seems not skeptical enough. After all, the Peace Corps and OEO enjoyed their "place in the sun" only because they were supported by Presidents Kennedy and Johnson. They did not die natural deaths. They were strangled by a hostile President, Richard Nixon. As I have argued at some length here, the CPA is going to face a fundamentally hostile White House from the date of its birth, whether or not the president is the same avowed conservative who killed the pet reforms of his liberal predecessors. But in any event, it is not that important whether the consumer agency dies in 1972 or 1977 or even 1981. What should be noted is that the struggle over the CPA is a most disquieting omen of the future of the new populism as well as a kind of shade of similar past episodes.

Inevitably, these truculent rhetorical antagonisms over legislative minutiae recall such reform struggles as the one between Wilson and Theodore Roosevelt, between Wilson's "New Freedom" and Theodore Roosevelt's "New Nationalism." When those two verbal creeds clashed, few bothered to notice that neither one could have actually functioned any differently or any more effectively than the other. While that populist debate took place in a grander arena than the battle over the consumer agency bill, the same "grand design" syndrome is evident in the present case. And though the CPA debate may seem less consequential than the 1912 question of who would be president and what his reform philosophy would be, the reappearance of this political syndrome seems nonetheless acutely distressing. Who but Ralph Nader should know best how critical it is to tailor legislative reforms to the political realities in which they will actually function? But still he and his associates have done just what their predecessors did. They have promoted and enacted an instrumentality which must by any lights seem politically unfit to serve its proclaimed function.

Return of the Grand Design: Federal Incorporation

As regulatory reformers, the Progressives too often struck bad bargains with their foes. By the terms of these deals, the reformers gained control of the verbal superstructure of government regulation. They manned the mechanisms that generate verbal descriptions of government programs and policies; and they dictated their content—the laws, speeches, news articles, and books that shape the external image of what the public's representatives have wrought in the public's name. At the same time, these changes in the superstructure were made amenable to the interests they affected. They did not threaten, and often actually reinforced, the infrastructures of political and economic power which the interests maintained for their own self-aggrandizement.

Of course, things did not always happen that way. Some regulatory reforms have worked more or less as their sponsors promised. And probably in no case did reformers and lobbyists actually get together over drinks and conspire to sell out the public interest. Rather, the circumstances of the political environment made the outcome seem reasonable and ultimately inevitable. The public's capacity to distinguish meaningful reform from counterfeit was—and is—not very refined. They have little ability to focus on the administration and enforcement of even carefully designed statutes. Hence, the pressures on democratic politicians point in one direction: satisfy both sides—the public with brave generalities, and the special interests with an enforcement mechanism they can stifle or subvert. The reformers may never have been conscious of how innocuous or pernicious were the measures they were putting across as grand designs for change. More likely, they just became so enveloped by the controversies in which they were engaged that they lost sight of the larger ends for which they had initiated them. The skills at stagecraft which first created public demand for reform were ultimately used to deceive the same public into believing that the reform had been achieved.

Unhappily, the perverse incentives that induce populist leaders to appease rather than to enforce popular yearning for change are built into the structure of democratic politics. They are as prevalent today as they were in 1914 or 1934. Reform elites need not—and do not—always succumb. But the temptation to do so is great, even though, or perhaps especially because, the urge is often only dimly apprehended.

If the new independent CPA seems to forecast a similar fate for the new populism, this portent can only be reinforced by the CPA's successor at the top of Ralph Nader's agenda for legislative action. This is the idea of "federal incorporation." Federal incorporation, or "federal chartering," means having the nation's 200 or so largest corporations obtain their certificates of incorporation, or legal charters, from the federal government. Until now, certificates of incorporation have been issued by the individual states. Most corporations obtain their charters from Delaware, whence they are lured by a corporation law tailored to the needs of corporate managements desirous of minimizing interference from obtrusive shareholders. If giant companies had to get their charters in Washington instead of Wilmington, Nader says, the requirement would cease to be a mere formality. The federal charter, he explains, would "make the grant of corporate status conditional on a responsiveness to well-defined *public* interests [not just private securities holders] and a *social* accounting of corporate performance." If the corporation ceased to be responsive to those "well-defined public interests," whatever they might be, then it would be punished or even perhaps lose its charter altogether.[2]

It is not clear what the practical significance of losing a charter would be to an institution like the General Electric Corporation. Obviously, its factories would not shut down. It would not seem likely or even constitutional to expropriate securities holders summarily. Perhaps top management could be suspended or replaced, though even that seems somewhat impractical, except in the cases where particular individuals were judged guilty of serious misconduct. But whatever the manner in which it would be applied, Nader plainly sees the concept as the appropriate legal focus for the nation's effort to cope with the entire general problem of corporate power. It is, he told an October, 1971, conference staged in Washington to launch his federal chartering campaign, "the most viable mechanism to achieve corporate accountability."

Nader's theory appears to be that, in creating a new FCA to issue corporate charters, Congress could be persuaded to impose a slew of restrictions on corporate behavior that it would not otherwise enact. At his Washington conference, he urged that federal chartering would mean "strict" antitrust standards to keep corporations from retaining more than 12 percent of their markets, "corporate democracy" provisions to "reduce the dominance of [management] oligarchies" over share-holders and bondholders, "disclosure" rules that would "end corporate secrecy," and a "constitutionalization" of the rights of corporate employees against their employers.[3] Morton Mintz and Jerry Cohen, both close associates of Nader, added to this list in their bestseller *America, Inc.* a ban on corporate conglomeration that would mean that "RCA could be compelled to get out of book publishing and CBS to free the New York Yankees."[4] They also suggested that some sort of general injunction against environmental offenses could be written into the charter.

Surely these are not all unworthy goals. But the mystery that remains to be unraveled is how Senator James B. Eastland will be hoodwinked into letting them pass his Judiciary Committee wrapped in a "federal incorporation" package when he would not do so if they were introduced separately as antitrust amendments or corporate freedom of information bills. More in line with the relevant precedents would be a scenario in which Senator Eastland and his populist opponents collaborated in hoodwinking the public. The reformers' gaudy label would be allowed to remain attached. But it would grace a legislative pastiche that, like the original Clayton and FTC acts of Woodrow Wilson's first term, would comprise mainly innocuous provisions. This would be handed over to a new bureaucracy which, like the old FTC, would inconspicuously and, if necessary, gradually eviscerate the new law.

Champions of the chartering idea acknowledge that it might turn out in practice to be as disappointing as its predecessors. But, they claim, there is a difference in this proposal which will radically reduce that risk. The public interests protected by the scheme will be "well-defined," and the standards defining violations will be "objective." Hence, the agency will have no discretion to abuse; enforcement will be automatic. But this claimed difference is simply a vain hope, even an undesirable one. Does Nader really believe that Congress will legislate a flat and arbitrary percentage limit on the market share that a corporation can attain for itself—whether it is 12 percent or 50 percent or 75 percent? Does he think that, if some such limit were adopted, there would not even be a provision permitting an offending company to rebut the presumption that it had effective market-power? Even if the *Fortune* 500 proved disinclined or unable to stop passage of the bill, even if Chairman Eastland embraced it—conditions I do not think we are likely to see met—would Nader himself or any other responsible person want such a meat ax blindly swung through the economy? And even if such a clumsy and arbitrary restriction found its way into a federal incorporation statute, it still would not begin to eliminate the FCA's discretion as to how and when to bring enforcement proceedings.

In any event, it is simply a delusion to expect objective standards or mechanical enforcement procedures in a scheme so general in its objectives and scope as this one is. Policy as well as politics would ensure that any federal chartering statute for the nation's biggest companies offer vague, not to say vacuous, principles for determining the requisites of getting and keeping a license. These standards would surely stop short of expressly requiring any major changes in existing corporate policies or structures. Instead the law would pass the buck to the new agency. Though this agency would in theory be permitted to invoke the new enforcement tool of revoking a company's charter, in practice this sanction would be an entirely empty threat. The FCA would be no more likely to revoke the charter of GM for monopolizing auto sales than the FCC recently proved willing to consider revoking the license of WNBC-TV for flouting commission standards for the broadcasting of anti-smoking spot commercials. There is no magic in the notion of a federal corporate charter that could lift the FCA above the constraints that inhibit other regulatory bureaucracies. It would soon find itself administering a highly general set of standards backed by conventional civil and criminal sanctions, doing its best (or its worst) to stretch its thin political and financial resources to meet exorbitant enforcement responsibilities.

The plain truth is that federal chartering can be seen as an inspiring cause only to those whose vision is impaired by the grand design mentality. And so it is that charter proponents are as enthusiastic as Harold Ickes once was in articulating the populist nostrum that the public through its government should (and can) "take control" of things. "A rational society," affirm Mintz and Cohen, "has long-term goals and priorities. The legitimate government should set these goals and priorities free from undue influence by the corporation."[5] Morton Mintz is one of the best investigative reporters in Washington. Jerry Cohen, as counsel to Senator Hart's Antitrust Subcommittee, spent five dramatic years exposing corporate political shenanigans in the federal bureaucracy. They are as familiar as any two men in the United States with just how free from "undue influence" regulatory agencies can be. Yet still they blithely predict that the FPC Federal Corporation Agency will write "goals and priorities" into the charters of the corporate giants, and that the corporations in their turn will instantly comply—from top management to division head to subsidiary to sales manager to union local. "Federal chartering," Mintz and Cohen quaintly conclude, "would allow the public government to regain its proper role as *quarterback* of the economy. . . ."[6]

Even in Progressive rhetoric it would be difficult to find a flight of populist fancy as unalloyed and unself-conscious as this athletic metaphor. But intriguingly enough, one does find in the political struggles of the Progressive era considerable attention devoted to the object of Mintz and Cohen's ardor. Indeed, federal chartering received its most sustained and serious political attention during the Republican administrations of Theodore Roosevelt and William Howard Taft. In fact, it was then the pet project of Wall Street leaders, because they believed that it would cement a cooperative relationship between the federal government and big business. Among its most influential boosters were Judge Elbert Gary of U.S. Steel (famous for "Judge Gary's dinners" at which all members of the steel industry gathered and cordially agreed on the price they would charge for their products), John D. Rockefeller of Standard Oil, and George Perkins, prime minister of J. P. Morgan's financial and industrial empire (which included the Steel Corporation).[7] Though their hopes for a legalized corporate state now seem somewhat overblown in view of the feckless career of the NRA in the early 1930s, their basic assumption seems as valid now as it seemed then. Instead of a functioning grand design for controlling "corporate America," federal chartering seems more likely to yield just one more captive federal regulatory agency.

Foothold for Reaction?

Yet the odds are high that the concept of the federal charter will soon become law. Even more than the CPA, this is a political "natural"—perfectly attuned to liberal ideological and rhetorical convention, and an apt vehicle for accommodating the political needs of all the affected interests and participants in the enactment process. When, at an assemblage in Boston in 1971, chief executive officers of major national corporations were asked whether they expected to be covered by a federal requirement to hold a federal corporate charter, over one-half replied that they expected such legislation to pass before 1980. The remarkable thing about that informal poll is that it was taken before any legislation was introduced, and indeed before much general publicity had been given to the federal chartering idea at all. It is almost superfluous to add that the executives at the conference did not profess special concern about the prospect that they regarded as politically inevitable. They understood well that "federal charter" was merely a label, and that what mattered was not the label of the package but the contents and, especially, how and by whom the law would be administered. Their understanding of those simple facts is perhaps ultimately the surest guarantee that the proposal will, in some form at least, become law.

Indeed, it is not at all inconceivable that, once loosed on Capitol Hill, the federal chartering concept could become an instrument for *weakening* extant protections against excessive corporate power, inadequate as they may seem. Mark Green and the rest of the team that produced the mammoth Nader Study Group report on antitrust are highly critical of the enforcement record of the Antitrust Division of the Justice Department. But are they confident that the division's job would be easier if it had to share authority over the nation's largest corporations with new FCA? Insofar as the new agency would have authority to promulgate or enforce any sort of antitrust standards, could we be sure that it would be more strict than the division? Might it not turn out to be less so? If so, would the federal courts follow precedent and hold that the new FCA had "primary jurisdiction" over questions where there was a conflict between its authority and that of the Antitrust Division (or the FTC for that matter)? This rule would mean, as it has in the case of cartel-managing agencies such as the Federal Maritime Commission (FMC) and the CAB, that the division would face much greater difficulties in prosecuting antitrust offenses than it did before corporate defendants secured the shield of a federal charter. Private parties bringing treble damage actions under the Sherman Act—which has become an increasingly potent

spur to antitrust enforcement because federal procedural rules
now permit multimillion dollar antitrust class suits—might effectively be barred altogether.

The threat that corporate chartering could end in degrading
such federal controls over corporate power as presently exist
is not just an abstract possibility. To the extent that precedents
are relevant, they are not a cause for optimism. In general, the
worst and most socially damaging offenses against free-market
principles are committed under the protective cover of regulatory statutes. Even where statutes do not confer express power
to the agency in question to grant antitrust immunity, the practical effects are sometimes the same. For example, according to
Northwestern Law Professor Robert W. Bennett, the FCC has
used its licensing power to approve many newspaper mergers
with television and radio stations in the same markets that
palpably violate Section 7 of the Clayton Act.[8] It is true that
since Assistant Attorney General Turner started the division's
program of scrutinizing the anticompetitive effects of regulatory
policies, the division has challenged FCC lassitude about multi-
media mergers and ended its practice of approving Clayton Act
violations. But who can tell whether the task would be so easy
at the FCA, when it comes into existence?

Certainly there are forces within the Nixon Administration,
at one time represented most articulately by former Commerce
Secretary Peter G. Peterson and former Treasury Secretary
John Connally, who favor "modernizing" the antitrust laws (a
euphemism which populist enthusiasts should easily recognize
as a cover for weakening antitrust). And perhaps not coinciden-
tally, former House Judiciary Committee Chairman Emanuel
Celler submitted in the fall of 1971 an antitrust revision bill
that would put the top 200 industrial corporations and the
top 100 financial organizations under a new cabinet-level administrative agency; at the same time, Celler's measure would
eliminate all private antitrust suits against these companies. It
takes little imagination to see how easily such conceptions of

reactionary change could fit into a bill for granting federal charters to the nation's corporate giants.

The most direct historical analogy to Nader's FCA is the old "Bureau of Corporations" created by Teddy Roosevelt in 1903 to appease popular antitrust sentiment. Friendly to the cause of corporate concentration from the outset, the bureau played field general in the unsuccessful campaign to enact a federal chartering statute under Progressive sponsorship. The bureau and its corporate allies then viewed federal chartering as a mechanism to "provide a method by which reasonable combination may be permitted." Small business and other anticorporate forces viewed the proposal in precisely the same light, and they therefore quashed it.[9] It would surely be the height of irony if this long-dead scheme to turn reform slogans to reactionary purposes would at last ride to victory on the idealism of Ralph Nader and his new populist legions.

Nader's Vision of the Future

Of course, Ralph Nader's hopes for the federal charter may not prove entirely misplaced. At least one of the sections he wants to include in the law—the one requiring extensive obligations of disclosure of corporate information to the public and the government—will be very valuable, at least if public-interest lawyers, journalists, and scholars are available to make use of it. Nader knows no contemporary peer as a master of political theatrics. His judgment thus deserves some deference when he estimates that he can most effectively sell such a proposal under the "federal charter" label. Perhaps, further, he will obtain advances like corporate disclosure without having to sacrifice advances won in the past, such as antitrust restraints now on the books. If Nader is able to handle all corporate America and a hostile administration as deftly as he handled the automobile industry in 1966, then at least the law itself will be a good one, however perversely it may be administered.

So one can wish Nader well on the federal chartering struggle, while at the same time remaining skeptical about his risking so much for a gain which, at least at this point, seems likely to be measured mainly in column inches. But one must regret the larger implications of the enterprise. To the extent that splashy legislative reforms like the consumer agency and federal chartering fire his enthusiasm, Nader appears to be an utterly traditional—and conventional—reformer. His goal—which even Richard Nixon could endorse if popular sentiment were to grow strong enough—is to achieve a kind of third New Deal. His strategy is to whip up public opinion to so intense—if ephemeral—a frenzy that Congress can only appease it by enacting his proposals as fast as his *pro bono publico* legislative draftsmen can turn them out.

Unfortunately, there is considerable evidence to support this conclusion in other facets of Nader's program and in his tactical *modus operandi*. His obsession with corporate bigness, itself an incident of the federal charter campaign, is one thing. Nader, and his new populist legions in general, ascribe quite marvelous qualities and effects to the prospect of a "tough" antitrust attack on big business. To be sure, wider enforcement against price-fixing (which is done by the corner druggist as much as by the steel oligopoly) would be a good thing. And even the heralded "deconcentration" lawsuits to break up "tight oligopolies" like autos and cereals and aluminum might improve economic efficiency in those (relatively few) markets.

But many new populist spokesmen would have us believe that waving a big antitrust stick would do much more. It would, they say, radically alter national patterns of economic and especially *political* power. They boast that it would hasten the millennium when Washington would no longer be what Nader has called a "bustling bazaar of accounts receivable for industry-commerce."[10] But the sad fact is that the structure of national power has roots rather too deep to be shaken by a few, or even a good many, suits under the Sherman Act. ITT, one of the two most prominent targets of Nader's efforts to expose and punish bigtime bribery in contemporary Washington, is a very large corporation. But Nader's second target, the national dairy lobby, is a confederation of very small entrepreneurs. Once they become as well-organized as these milk producers, small entrepreneurs appear to be just as ruthless and effective as an ITT. The auto industry will be no less powerful in Washington or Lansing if the variety of corporate labels on auto factory doors increase from three to six or eight (or eighty for that matter).

What a spate of antitrust lawsuits, whether or not spurred by a new antitrust statute, could produce, apart from some marginal improvements in the efficiency of certain selected industries, is high political drama. Accordingly, the striking aspect of the new populist antitrust campaign is not *that* the movement is promoting antitrust but the *way* it is promoting antitrust. The goal implicit in new populist propaganda tactics seems less the modification of routine administrative policy than the preparation of public opinion—not for enduring change but for the "big case." Whether they realize it or not, the new populists are investing most of their antitrust resources into building precisely the kind of popular mood that Teddy Roosevelt handily appeased with his "symbolic" victory over the House of Morgan in the *Northern Securities* prosecution of 1903. It is only too easy to imagine a Richard Nixon making the same gesture if public feelings begin to run higher than they run now about the dangers of corporate bigness.

Indeed, we have already had foretastes of how effective a few big symbolic cases might be in diverting contemporary populist opinion into innocuous channels. To counter the 1972 ITT scandal, Richard Kleindienst brought what the administration billed as a major antitrust initiative against the three television networks. The case generated front-page headlines for several days. It also drew applause from Nader's own antitrust experts, who encouraged reporters to pay serious attention to the case on the ground that it treated antitrust as a "structural" problem rather than just a series of isolated price-fixing plots. Yet the practical effects of the case, if the Justice Department is ultimately victorious, will be to reduce slightly the networks' role in the process of producing television programs, and to increase slightly the role of other potential sources of funds, mainly advertisers and advertising agencies. The impact of this step on the quality and diversity of programs themselves is unlikely to be either positive or significant.

A similar episode occurred earlier in the first term of the Nixon Justice Department, when antitrust chief Richard McClaren undertook to stop the spread of "conglomerate" mergers. Conglomerate mergers—mergers that join two non-competing enterprises—had never before been attacked under the Sherman and Clayton acts. At the time, much was made of the awesome power wielded by the new breed of corporate empire builders who were the prime targets of McClaren's lawsuits. But it has become clear that most of these supposed giants, like Jimmy Ling of Ling-Temco-Vought, were charismatic promoters who deserved to be feared mainly by the investors who relied on them. A few conglomerate kings, like Ben W. Heineman of Northwest Industries, were in fact able and innovative managers who, had they been permitted to complete their acquisition programs, might have provided sluggish old behemoths with effective direction for the first time in many decades. Indeed, many observers believed it to be more than coincidental that the Nixon administration discovered the conglomerate issue only after established corporate managements like those of B. F. Goodrich, Jones & Laughlin Steel, and the Chemical Bank New York Trust Company found themselves facing takeover threats from the new conglomerateurs. In any event, however reactionary its true motives, and however negligible its effects on the economic welfare of consumers, the Nixon anticonglomerate campaign was embraced by new populist enthusiasts of antitrust.

In other important respects, the tenor and scope of new populist operations—Nader's in particular—suggest a preoccupation with the same strategic psychology, the same overriding interest in triggering an apocalyptic instant of public radi-

calism. This attitude is especially evident in the Nader Reports
—"full of documented outrage," as Leonard Ross observed in
The New York Times Book Review, but "never attempt[ing] to
draw together the elements of an effective policy."[11] Nader in-
vented the term "public-interest lawyer," but most of the lawyers
on his growing staff function neither as litigators nor as political
organizers, but as propagandists and journalists. It would be too
flip to say that he wants quantity rather than quality, output
rather than impact—too flip but not entirely wrong. The private
institutions he has created to house his present activities are
more important as instruments of a strategy of public relations
than as vehicles to institutionalize the new populist cause. It is
hard to avoid the conclusion that most of Nader's work seems
directed at mobilizing for the moment, not organizing for the
long term.

Perhaps the best illustration of this preoccupation with turning mass fervor into sweeping legislative change came with the
extraordinary attention he lavished on Congress in the summer
of 1972. In a kind of parody of all the "raiding" parties of the
past, each of which had more or less modestly been directed at
single agencies or sectors of policy, literally hundreds of professionals, graduate and undergraduate students swarmed
through the corridors of the House and Senate office building
for three months. Their report documented at impressive length
what Nader himself had observed angrily in the *New Republic*
a year before, in August, 1971: "[The] federal legislature faithfully reflects the poor alignments in the society. Power goes to
those senior legislators who service powerful interests, while
isolation goes to those who merely represent powerless people."
Suitably indignant at this discovery, Nader went on to urge that
Congress take on the role prescribed by populist theory—
"democracy's great advocate."[12]

Congress can and does become "democracy's great advocate,"
in the populist, mass democracy sense intended by Nader—but
only for moments where there is some intense national passion,
such as school busing, or, if Nader is successful in his propa-

gandizing, the corporate menace. During such moments, the public mood is itself "the power alignment in society," and men who must run for reelection every two years will "reflect" it, perhaps even "faithfully" so. At other times, the popular passion fades away and only the enduring structures of wealth and organization are left standing; then they are the relevant "power alignments" and Congress "faithfully reflects" them too.

How can it ever be different? Congressmen, after all, are elected not by the nation but by the people of individual districts, most of whom are not very interested in who their representative shall be, or what he does while he represents them. Most seats are lifetime sinecures. Normally, only 10–15 percent change hands each election year, of which most are due to retirements rather than rejection by the electorate. Given these circumstances, how does Nader expect that Congress will *ever* represent anything other than those interests that deliberately organize to influence their members? Either by the strategic use of campaign aid, by simple face-to-face persuasion ("the machine-gun-like impact of industry representation," James Landis once called it), or by furnishing legislators with economic patronage for their constituencies, they are bound to prevail most of the time. "The public" has in general a difficult time controlling elected officials, but the barriers to populistic control of the national legislature are especially high. By and large, they are insuperable—except for the public's highest priority issues, and except for the relatively brief moments when the public is capable of focusing on them.

Whether or not Nader is consciously aware of it, Congress is inherently unsuited to playing the role of "democracy's advocate" over the long term. In trying to force Congress into the mold of his own populist preconceptions, he can only be aiming to use it as a vehicle for brief dramatic moments of popular triumph. Once again, in short, the logic of the grand design mentality shows up in the pattern of his work.

When demands are put to Nader to spell out his vision of the social order he wants to create, he often declines to say anything at all. But on some occasions he has given specific replies that border on fantasy. He has spoken of a future in which "50,000 public-interest lawyers" will do what he and his raiders are doing now on a smaller scale. Obviously, this is not a number that can be taken seriously. Certainly Nader himself does not take it seriously, or at least there is little operational evidence that he does. He has made little effort to mobilize the conscience of the American bar. And he and his associates have thus far contributed little more than rhetoric to the fundamental problem of designing a new structure of financial incentives for public-interest law practice. (The most important advance in this field, the legalization of class actions in antitrust and other cases in the federal courts, was effected not by a populist legislative campaign, but by the U.S. Supreme Court's Advisory Committee on Civil Rules; the chairman of the committee was Harvard Professor Benjamin Kaplan, who has no known links to the new populist movement other than the fact that many of its leaders learned civil procedure from his casebook.)

Recently, Nader convinced a *Fortune* investigator that he sees before us a "consumer democracy" dominated by local "consumer soviets," based at shopping centers, which would collectively bargain with local retailers. A probing *Washington Post* reporter, William Greider, stirred his imagination to focus on a different object, a "model society." Nader confided that it would be a system that gives power to victims.

> In a system where power accretes to the victims, you would not just have rights, which we have plenty of, you would have remedies, which we have fewer of. And you would have representation, which we have even less of.

Nader added that

> we've got to have systems in our society that will plan alternative futures . . . and allow the displacement of

existing technologies by superior ones. That is absolutely
critical because, if that isn't done we can destroy the
world.[13]

In prattling on about "consumer soviets" and "accreting
power to victims," Nader may simply be putting on the reporter
and his audience. But whatever his motivation in throwing up
these smokescreens, the fact remains that they are smokescreens.
Ralph Nader's vision of the future for which he is aiming, insofar as that vision is revealed through most of his current propaganda and legislative activities, is that which motivated his
Progressive and New Deal antecedents. It is the ideal of the
grand design for democracy, the notion that the public can,
through legislation and regulation, exercise affirmative sovereignty over corporate power.

A Concluding Note: Can Regulation Ever Work?

I have offered a harsh judgment on the value of regulation and
especially about the value of some of the schemes for regulation
proposed by contemporary populists. It seems, therefore, only
fair that I add something positive to this criticism. Legisla-
tively imposed regulation has, after all, traditionally been regarded as democracy's main hope for curbing dangerous concentrations of private power. Is this hope wholly naive? Can
regulation never work? Are there not at least some circumstances
under which it can succeed?

Of course, there have been occasions when regulation has
worked. Indeed, it is working in identifiable instances right now.
Impressive examples are the contemporary efforts to impose
safety and pollution controls on the auto industry; they appear
to be in full stride toward their important objectives. Another
example is the FTC; former Chairman Myles Kirkpatrick and
Consumer Protection Bureau Chief Robert Pitofsky breathed
life into that long moribund bureaucracy. If the advertising and
retail lobbies do not persuade President Nixon to throttle the

commission's advance with reactionary appointees during his second term, the FTC may at last realize the vast potential of the Progressives' old FTC Act. But in general, regulation of industry would have to be regarded as one of the least successful enterprises ever undertaken by American democracy. And it seems likely to remain so, whenever populist legislative schemes impose unrealistic political demands on enforcement agencies.

Hence, the first basic rule for designing regulatory enactments is that the more modest the political demands that will be made of an agency, the more likely it is to prove successful. In applying this general rule, it may be helpful to keep in mind another broad distinction between two types of regulatory institutions. On the one hand, there are those with "defensive" or policing tasks—such as the FTC or the FDA—and those with "offensive" or managerial responsibilities, like the CAB or the Federal Reserve Board. Agencies in the latter category represent far more ambitious undertakings. Their task is to structure all or part of an industry's operations and thereafter direct the industry's course in the public interest. In contrast, policing agencies are designed not to preempt the free market, but to enable consumers to make better use of its processes, by thwarting anticompetitive or deceptive or unsafe practices. In general, regulatory schemes in the second category are more dangerous than the first. Policing agencies, if they are neutralized by industry pressures—always a substantial risk—will usually not produce more social harm than would have obtained if the agency had never been created in the first place. But, through agencies with managerial responsibilities over price, entry, and so on, industries can end up with far more power to serve their interests at the expense of the public than they held before the agency came into existence. Furthermore, the functions performed by many policing agencies—like the banning or labeling of unsafe products—are so important they should be created simply because their presence may add some slight measure of concern by affected industries over these vital matters (even if the chances are slim that politics will ever permit the agency to become the vigorous regulator that it ought to be). In general, experience seems to teach that regulation of the "offensive" or managerial genre should never be instituted, at least on a permanent basis, unless public-interest objectives are supported by the regulated interests affected by the scheme.

In each case, one has to compare the objectives which the agency is supposed to serve—in the eyes of public and private interests—with its prospective capacity to fulfill those aims in its political environment. If the public-oriented objectives are reasonably concrete (as in the case of the National Highway Traffic Safety Administration's mandate to force auto companies to protect the internal passenger compartment of automobiles); if private interests affected by the measure support its public interest objectives (as in the case of support by the banking community for the Federal Reserve Board's responsibility for maintaining a flexible currency); if public support for the objectives of the scheme is strong, informed, and deeply rooted enough to last over the time period it will take the agency to achieve the mission in question; then one can be relatively confident that a particular regulatory scheme will "work." To the extent that these conditions are absent, then one has to expect that the impact of regulation will probably be minimal or pernicious.

Obviously, these guidelines impose severe constraints on the utility of regulation as a device for democratic control of private power. The sad truth about the new populist movement is that its leaders have often ignored these cautionary limits. To that extent, their brilliance as legislators and opinion leaders is likely to go for naught in the long run.

This does not mean that the new populism can be dismissed as simply a futile echo of an archaic democratic faith. The enhanced performance of the FTC, the FDA, the FCC, and other agencies, and the addition of such vigorous new agencies as the EPA and the National Highway and Safety Administration are great and valuable achievements. Moreover, there is another, more creative and more promising side to the movement. This, the concept of "public-interest law," will be the focus of the next chapter of this book.

10
Populism in the Courts: The Concept of Public-Interest Law

Though most of American business was booming during the summer of 1969, the airline industry found itself embarrassed by one of its recurrent profit squeezes. Revenues had grown spectacularly throughout the 1960s. But costs had risen even faster, because the individual airlines had, as is their custom, been on a massive competitive binge, trying to outspend each other on new jumbo airliners, more frequently scheduled flights, fancier meals, more chicly clad stewardesses, and more television advertising. Of course, each individual airline saw these expenditures as a device to lure more customers to its planes, and hence to make a bigger profit for itself. But since every individual spending initiative was matched by the competitors, the net impact was simply to raise costs for everyone in the industry. Ultimately the spending wars would threaten to put all the firms in the red. Therefore, the airlines had petitioned the CAB to allow them to raise their rates.

The Public Versus the CAB

Congressman John Moss of California, author of the Freedom of Information Act, was puzzled when he read of the airlines' petition. He wondered why they needed to raise the price of an airline ticket at a time when their revenues were climbing steadily. So he decided to attend the meetings scheduled by the CAB at which the airlines were to present their cases. Moss wrote to the board to say that he expected to appear at the agency's meeting with the industry as a representative of the public, adding that the tradition of "rate-making by treaty must come to an end."

This would seem to be a modest enough step for a congressman to take as part of his legislative responsibilities. But to the CAB Moss was an unwonted—and unwanted—presence. Airline rate regulation had always been conducted in private, as a bilateral negotiation between the board and the industry. The board was not of a mind to end this tradition of secret decisions, even for a congressman. So Moss was officially informed that, though he could present his views in a perfunctory hearing, the key decision-making meetings would be closed. Only airline representatives and CAB officials would be invited. No member of the public, not even Moss, could attend.

Predictably, Moss was not happy with this rebuff, particularly after the CAB proceeded to approve a fare increase following the agency-industry meetings. Along with thirty-one other congressmen, he took an appeal to the Court of Appeals for the District of Columbia Circuit, just as the black community of Jackson, Mississippi, had done when the FCC tried to shut them out of license renewal proceedings for station WLBT. The Court of Appeals was also unhappy, just as it had been in the WLBT affair. "This appeal," Judge J. Skelly Wright began his opinion,

> presents the recurring question which has plagued public regulation of industry: whether the regulatory agency is

unduly oriented toward the interests of the industry it is designed to regulate, rather than the public interest it is designed to protect.[1]

Judge Wright's answer was unfavorable to the board. He reversed the board's decision and ordered the case returned for a hearing in which Congressman Moss and his colleagues could participate.

Wright's decision came down in July, 1970. Now, three and one-half years later, the case drags on at the CAB. But Moss, his staff economist Richard Klabzuba, and his lawyers at the Washington firm of Caplin & Drysdale have persevered. They continue to assert the consumer's interest in obtaining independent representation in airline regulation.

Unlike the similar challenge to FCC policies in the *WLBT* case, the *Moss* case has received little coverage from the general press. The CAB has no Nicholas Johnson to bring drama and draw attention to the routine of the board's decision making. But despite its obscurity, this litigation is one of the most crucial struggles now being waged by the new populist movement. It provides a particularly revealing test of whether litigation can become an effective mechanism for making corporate and bureaucratic power accountable. In the protracted trial that has followed Judge Wright's remand, light will be thrown on the issue of whether the courts can discipline a political infrastructure such as the CAB and the airline industry.

Moss's lawyers are making three requests, each of which embodies vital objectives of the movement to represent unorganized "public" interests through litigation. First, they are asking for consumer refunds. They claim that, since the initial rate hike was illegal, the new fares are unlawful and consumers are entitled to $250 million in excess fares paid out to the airlines. This is an important claim not because of the relatively trivial amount that any individual customer might win if it were upheld, but because industry-oriented agencies cannot be deterred from granting unlawful rates, unless they know that client firms will not be able to keep unlawful proceeds. If they are permitted to hold on to all the revenues, what difference will it make if some judge one day finds that the rate was illegal all along?

Second, the lawyers are asking for compensation for themselves from the airlines. They took the first appeal on a *pro bono publico* basis. But now the burden of representation has consumed well over $100,000 of the firm's resources. Such an effort cannot be maintained forever as a contribution to the public weal. American law has traditionally not required losing defendants to pay the victorious plaintiff's attorney fees. But unless this tradition is changed, public representatives will only rarely be able to engage in serious litigation before courts or regulatory agencies.

Third, and more important, the lawyers are demanding that the board strictly interpret standards written into the Federal Aviation Act, such as its command that rate increases be granted only when and to the extent that they are justified by "the need . . . for revenue sufficient . . . under *honest, economical* and *efficient management,* to provide adequate and efficient air carrier service."[2] Traditionally, the board has fixed rates simply by accepting the industry's figures on what their costs are, then adding a certain percentage to permit them to earn an appropriate return on capital. By this kind of "cost-plus" regulation, the CAB in effect looks the other way at the airlines' costly merchandising tactics. It does nothing to control the spiral of fare increase–cost increase–fare increase.

The standards written into the Federal Aviation Act are general and vague, as is characteristic of regulatory statutes inspired by the model of the grand design. But they are not so vague that they could not be refined into a set of rules of law, sufficiently meaningful to assure consumers of "adequate, economical, and efficient service by air carriers at reasonable charges," as the act requires. Either the agency, or if it refuses

—as it has for thirty-five years—the Court of Appeals could set those standards. Congressman Moss's lawyers have accepted the challenge of getting that task done.[3]

It would seem that this is a rather elementary objective—to see that a major federal enactment is, at least in a rough and general way, obeyed by the agency established to enforce it. But, in practice it has proven too difficult for our system of government to achieve over the thirty-five years since the Federal Aviation Act was passed. Nothing could more eloquently testify to the impotence of the system to live up to its own commitments to the public than the bizarre spectacle of a congressman going to court to enforce a law that Congress itself had enacted. At this point, the movement represented by Congressman Moss's lawyers is by no means certain to succeed where previous generations have failed.

Prerequisites for Progress

In order for the system to vindicate Moss and other litigants like him, two things have to happen. First, the federal courts have to assume a more decisive role in regulatory affairs than they have traditionally played. Second, methods have to be found to finance legal representation for heretofore neglected public interests before agencies and courts. Both of these simple-seeming changes will be complex and difficult to achieve, even if the proper political commitment is made to the principle of change.

To move toward the first of these two goals, the federal courts have to move beyond platitudes such as Judge Wright's condemnation of the board for being "oriented toward the industry it is supposed to regulate." They cannot be content to reverse agency decisions only when the agency's *procedures* have been unfair, as Judge Wright did. They have to begin to assume a greater share of responsibility for interpreting and enforcing the substance of regulatory statutes.

A variety of strategies is available to the federal courts to accomplish this step. One is to try to pump some life into the populist platitudes written into laws like the Federal Aviation Act and thereafter ignored; in cases like that of *Moss* v. *CAB,* where such an interpretation is appropriate, they must insist that "the public interest" should be construed as "the consumer interest," or that terms like "economical" or "efficient" be given meaningful content and be applied vigorously by the agency to evaluate the operations of regulated interests.

A second way courts can assume a more vital substantive role is to uphold the right of private parties to enforce regulatory laws in civil court actions, wherever private lawsuits could usefully supplement agency enforcement. An excellent example of this technique—in which its great potential impact can be seen—is provided by the evolution of the securities laws since they were enacted by F.D.R. in 1933 and 1934. The federal courts have taken the initiative in creating and expanding opportunities for private parties damaged by securities fraud to seek a remedy in court, rather than at the SEC. Hence, a corporation putting out a prospectus about a new issue of convertible debentures has to be far more careful to disclose the truth than a corporation putting out an advertising campaign about a new product. Even if the SEC lacks the resources or the inclination to act, the corporation and its lawyers have no way of knowing whether a private lawyer and his client will some day decide to sue. This is one important reason why the federal laws against securities fraud are generally believed to "work," while the federal laws against consumer fraud are acknowledged to be an abysmal failure.

Finally, there is a third strategy courts can use in moving toward a more active regulatory role. They can demonstrate that, when the agency strongly resists carrying out legal responsibilities, the court will simply take those responsibilities away and decide a case itself *on the merits.* In other words, it cannot be content merely to send a bad decision back to an administrative agency with instructions to follow the correct procedures next time around. Courts have traditionally been very reluctant to take this step, even in the most outrageous instances of bureaucratic abuse. For example, in the WLBT case, Commissioners Johnson and Cox, the dissenters, were convinced that Judge Burger would find procedural reasons to reverse the FCC when a majority of their colleagues voted to renew WLBT's license despite its racist programming. But they doubted that Burger would decide the case on the merits and order the commission to take the station's license away. Furthermore, they knew only too well that, unless Burger did go that far, the entire litigation would have no impact whatsoever either on the agency or on the degree to which broadcast licensees would feel obliged to respect legal standards of broadcast fairness. If Burger simply remanded the case a second time to the commission (with orders to hear it again), the agency would pay no more attention to the challengers than it had the first two times. Attempting to emphasize to Burger how vital it was that he decide the case for himself, Commissioners Cox and Johnson concluded their dissenting opinion:

> [It] would appear that the only way in which members of the public can prevent renewal of an unworthy station's license is to steal the document from the wall of the station's studio in the dead of night, or hope that the courts will do more than merely review and remand cases to the FCC with instructions that may be ignored.[4]

Judge Burger did ultimately decide to order the commission to refuse renewal to WLBT's license, declaring that "this administrative record is beyond repair." And since Burger's landmark ruling, the law has moved dramatically forward toward measurably greater accountability for wayward regulatory agencies. But the movement forward has been erratic, often hesitant, and everywhere full of indications that the advance may be summarily halted at any time, before it achieves anything more than the kind of symbolic triumph won in the first round of *Moss* v. *CAB*. The courts' ambivalence toward this revolutionary new trend in the law can be gauged by the fact that, although the chief justice wrote the landmark *WLBT* decision, he is also the author of well-publicized warnings to young lawyers not to look forward to using the courts for "reform," and of warnings to Congress not to overload the courts with too much environmental and consumer legislation.

But even if the courts embrace activism in regulatory controversies, the CAB and other such agencies will not become accountable unless lawyers are made available to bring bureaucratic mischief before them. This will not happen unless and until means are provided to assure that they will be compensated, as Moss's lawyers are demanding.

This is an exceedingly complex problem. Some of the major difficulties are suggested by the Moss case itself. First, there is the sheer magnitude of the costs. Even if some public-interest lawyers might be willing to work for lower salaries than private law firms normally pay, how and by whom can such sums be provided on a routine basis? Of course, if the lawyers eventually succeed in winning millions of dollars in refunds for the consumer public, the problem of how to compensate them for their efforts would become simple. They could be paid a percentage of the funds recovered, just as ordinary trial lawyers are paid a percentage when they win a negligence case for a client injured in an auto accident. But what if they only win the other parts of their case and fail to persuade the board or the courts that refunds should be awarded? Then where should the money come from? And what if, after years of litigation, they should lose altogether? Should they receive nothing for their years of effort? Or what if, at some point before the case is over, they find themselves unable to go any further without an infusion of cash? Should they receive progress payments?

These questions may seem simple, but in fact they pose a perplexing, perhaps an insoluble, problem. The stiffer the criteria for ordering compensation in cases like *Moss* v. *CAB,* the less likely it is that such cases will be brought at all. But if the standards are relaxed, the more likely it will be that not only good cases but also frivolous cases will be brought, by self-seeking lawyers interested only in recovery for themselves rather than in vindicating the interests of the consumer public. And however we set the criteria for obtaining compensation, the litigation process will be skewed in unexpected and probably undesirable ways. If compensation is permitted only in the event of victory, then cases will be brought only in instances where the agency's behavior is flagrantly illegal—so that ultimate victory, and a payoff, can be assured. If no progress payments are allowed, then lawyers will choose cases that pose no complex problems of proof, or they will settle early in the proceedings—long before issues of principle important to the public can be decided.

And even if we do manage to devise a system that calls forth a new class of lawyers who make their living by vindicating heretofore unrepresented interests of the public, we may not be pleased with the result. After all, that is essentially the system that governs auto accident litigation—and that consumerists currently wish to destroy, on the ground that litigating the issues of legal principle involved in accident cases costs more than it is worth to decide them. The same result may occur in the field of litigation over airline rate regulation, or in other, similar fields where the interests of the public are neglected by the political branches of government.

Inaction, however, carries greater risks than experiment. We cannot tolerate blanket acceptance of the status quo—a system incapable of keeping faith with legislative commitments and biased against the public interests it purports to serve. So ways must be found to compensate lawyers like those representing Congressman Moss at the CAB. No doubt it will be necessary to move forward cautiously, on a case-by-case basis, dealing with the problems as they come up, identifying the points at which the dangers of inspiring excessive and counterproductive litigation offset the possible gains in the consistency of law enforcement. In any event, the effort has to be made. And at this point, it is by no means clear that any of the necessary forces is ready to launch this large experiment in social engineering.

Hands Off the Bureaucracy

The main reason the future of public-interest law is in doubt
is that the legal profession and legal doctrine are themselves
deeply ambivalent about expanding the power of courts and
lawyers over important matters of public policy. Despite the
critical role that the federal judiciary has played in shaping the
national policies of postwar America, the belief persists that
courts are inherently undemocratic institutions and that activism to counter the practices of the "political" branches must
necessarily be "countermajoritarian." Ironically, this conservative attitude, the principal impediment to new populist litigants
like Congressman Moss, itself stemmed from branches of the
populist tradition—from the doctrinaire majoritarianism of the
Progressives and the liberal statism fostered by the New Deal.

Since the New Deal the courts have been troubled by their
status as an elite. They believe in the democratic principle that
the people, the majority, the public should rule. The law has
been haunted since that period by the image of the nine old
men of the anti-New Deal court who throughout the first third
of the twentieth century overruled legislative and executive decisions which appeared to reflect the popular will. Ever since,
courts have feared that judicial activism was inherently undemocratic and "countermajoritarian."

Led by Felix Frankfurter and then by Learned Hand on the
bench and, in the academy, by Herbert Wechsler of Columbia
University and Alexander Bickel of Yale, lawyers constructed
an elaborate set of strictures against judicial activism. The
philosophical basis of this jurisprudence was the simplistic old-
style populist majoritarianism that Walter Lippmann had dis-
patched in the 1920s. Hence, it resembled the teachings of
civics lessons more closely than it did the realities of American
government. Nor did it describe the behavior of the courts, or
even the positions of leading judicial conservatives themselves.
The logic of this majoritarian jurisprudence would, if taken
seriously, clearly bar the courts from deciding the most impor-

tant social issues before public sentiment had even been allowed to form, much less from pressing their views on such issues against the will of a popular majority. Yet that is precisely what the Supreme Court did when it decided to require the desegregation of American public education in *Brown* v. *Board of Education of Topeka*. Frankfurter concurred in that decision, and neither Wechsler nor Bickel has been willing to state flatly that he disapproves of it (though Wechsler was on the verge of taking such a position in 1960 and Bickel has been moving toward condemnation of *Brown* more recently, in the light of the popular reaction against court-ordered busing.)[5]

But even though the law has often departed in practice from the simplistic majoritarian principles of post-New Deal jurisprudence, the point of view fathered by Frankfurter has not been uninfluential. The same ideas still shape the way lawyers and judges think and talk and write about the role played by the law and the courts in shaping policy.

The best measure of how influential Frankfurter's majoritarianism has been on the law is that even those who opposed him and espoused the idea that the courts should be active champions of civil rights and civil liberties did not question his premise—that the executive and legislative branches were to be regarded as voices of the majority. They merely argued that the courts could legitimately take an activist position on behalf of the interests of *minorities,* since minorities were systematically short-changed by the (presumably majoritarian) political branches. If the courts did not stand up for blacks and dissenters, this theory ran, who would?

That seemed sensible enough to at least a good number of judges and lawyers. So on that basis they embraced activism in defense of minority interests. But deference remained the general rule, a rule, moreover, that was thought to be a fundamental safeguard of democracy.

This doctrinal barrier was considered especially important in the field known as "administrative law," the body of doctrine created to deal with the new regulatory establishment. Here the strictures against judicial meddling were especially rigid. And they were enforced with special zeal by the proponents of the new jurisprudence and by Justice Frankfurter in particular.[6] The administrative agencies were looked upon as the repositories of most of the great hopes for transforming the social order fostered by the New Deal. Moreover, judicial interference by laissez-faire zealots on the bench had crippled—or so it was thought—reformist administrative agencies before Franklin D. Roosevelt's appointees changed the ideological complexion of the federal judiciary. So new rules were handed down. And the new rules added up to a simple maxim: Hands off the administrative agencies.

The Basis of Statism
The key doctrine of the new movement to vest untrammeled authority in the hands of administrative leaders was the concept of "adminstrative discretion." Regardless of whether or not administrators' interpretations of governing statutes seemed somewhat out of line with congressional intent, regardless of whether their disposition of particular cases seemed somewhat out of line with the facts themselves, the courts were nevertheless supposed to defer except in the most outrageous cases of bureaucratic abuse. It was said that administrative heads had to have discretion in order to run their enterprises freely. And they were believed to deserve discretion because of the great expertise they were presumed to possess in the areas subject to their jurisdiction.

It was assumed that the agencies were responsible for complex questions of science and technology. In fact, however, the questions with which most agencies actually deal, even in technologically advanced industries such as air travel, are, at least in principle, straightforward simple economic issues—little more arcane than the types of questions that centuries before had induced common law courts to develop rules governing toll roads and ferry boats. Anyone who has had much contact with the routine operations of regulatory bureaucracies knows that their managers themselves often have but a superficial grasp of technological and even economic issues. In reality, they are often mainly expert in the intricacies of their agency's own *procedures,* a subject which is hardly technical at all, especially for judges.

But legal doctrine kept up the pretense that bureaucrats were *ipso facto* experts long after the rest of society had discarded it. Administrative expertise, as the courts knew it, was a mysterious faculty of intuitive understanding that made it unnecessary for them even to *explain* their decisions by giving a rational argument in their behalf. "The administrative decision," as Professor John Griffiths of New York University Law School wrote,

> was conceived of as that right decision which will be clear to an "expert" if, without the help (they would have said, the hindrance) of criteria, standards, rules, etc., he confronts a vast array of raw data.[7]

To be sure, Frankfurter and his followers did not go so far as to say that the agencies need give no reason at all for their decisions. They did require that agencies cite the statutory provision or other authority on which they supposedly based their determinations. But this proved to be a matter merely of going through the motions of justification. The agency could be content—and its decisions largely beyond appeal—if it merely stated that it found the result it wished to reach to be in "the public interest" in accordance with the grand design legislation from which it derived its authority.

In effect, the new administrative jurisprudence amounted to a kind of statism, sprung from precisely the same philosophical and political sources as the apotheosis of bureaucracy reflected in the academic writings on social structure by social scientists such as Daniel Bell. The *diktats* of the regulatory state were presumed to be beyond any need for reasoned justification. Within the area of their expertise, the bureaucrats' discretion held exclusive sway. They were above the law.

Of course, the courts, and especially the Supreme Court, conveniently ignored this "hands-off" approach in particular cases where, for one reason or another, it was outraged by what it regarded as shenanigans aimed at undermining the public interest. The court was often disinclined to defer to administrative judgment when some regulatory practice violated antitrust policy.[8] Indeed, for nearly a century, the court has made itself a bastion of protection for consumers against the zeal of the U.S. Patent Office to confer lucrative patent rights on corporate applicants, and against the inability of Congress to put a stop to the agency's lax patent policy.[9] In another judicial initiative in regulatory matters, the federal courts began to carve out potent private remedies for violations of the securities laws during the 1950s and 1960s. The impact of these was to create a system of judicial enforcement parallel to—but independent of—SEC enforcement. This greatly augmented the deterrent power of the regulatory scheme. But such forays were fitful and rare. The general rule was "hands off" no matter what.

Under the cover of this supposedly prodemocratic safeguard, the agencies went their merry way, which was often the way they were being pushed by the interests they were supposed to regulate. The ICC kept rail and water carrier prices high enough to ensure that the truckers would not lose any business to these lower-cost modes of transport. The FCC stopped the growth of cable television dead in its tracks to ensure that broadcasters would not have any inconvenient competition. The CAB kept on forcing air travelers to underwrite the airline industry's spending sprees.

Despite their inimical impact on the public, none of these policies could be challenged in court. Until Justice Burger ruled in favor of the Jackson black community's representatives in the *WLBT* case, no representative of the public was even allowed to intervene to argue in favor of the public's interest before the bureaucracies. And even with that procedural right established, the rule of deference required that the administrator's substantive judgment remain final, as long as it was within the broad area of discretion marked out by the "hands-off" requirements of post-New Deal jurisprudence.

Some Fallacies of Majoritarian Jurisprudence

Despite its broad acceptance, this doctrine of deference deserves no more respect than its premises. And the simplistic majoritarianism that rests at its foundation makes no more sense when it appears in a judicial opinion by Justice Frankfurter, than when it appeared in a speech by William Jennings Bryan. It is sheer romanticism to presume that most legislative and especially administrative decisions represent the considered judgment of anything like a majority of the public, or that such decisions are necessarily designed to promote the interests of the public. Precisely because the elective branches of government are formally open to public participation, they are vulnerable to domination by organized interests. This is especially true regarding populist issues.

Furthermore, through the appointment process, the electorate can exert more effective control over the federal courts than is often supposed. President Nixon's reconstitution of the Supreme Court provides only the most recent and dramatic example. Even the lower federal courts are staffed through a process which is no less visible or subject to public check than the process of appointing members of most administrative agencies.

Recently Professor Bickel has backed away from the simplistic majoritarian argument against an active judiciary, and searched for more sophisticated premises. He has attacked the notion that groups claiming the protection of the courts can realistically be classified as "minorities":

> Actually, a group of indeterminate size and momentarily insufficient political power or energy was appealing to the Court, and that is what always happens. In apportionment and free-speech cases as elsewhere, if such a group,

*which may handily be called a minority in the sense that
it did not prevail politically,* is to win its lawsuit, it must
do so by getting the Court to revise a decision arrived at
by the democratic process. . . .

In the political process, groups sometimes lose out, but
so long as the process is operational and both diffuses
power and allows majorities ultimately to work their will,
no group that is prepared to enter into the process and
combine with others need remain permanently or completely out of power.[10]

In this passage, which formed the philosophical core of his
1969 Oliver Wendell Holmes Lectures to the Harvard Law
School, Bickel embraces the pluralist orthodoxy popular among
political scientists in the 1950s and early 1960s. But this rather
pollyannaish version of pluralist theory is as bad a basis for
jurisprudence as political scientists had by 1969 generally
acknowledged it was for political science.[11]

The first problem with Bickel's pluralism is that it requires
(though he does not concede it) that he dispense outright with
the populist majoritarian premises that traditionally Frankfurter
and his followers had relied on as the foundation of their antagonism to judicial activism. For, if minorities have no special
status, but are merely ephemeral partners in coalitions that
drift together one day, then apart the next, gaining and losing
power in an endless flux, then it must also be true that the
concept of the majority is equally empty—and equally unde-
serving of respect.

In other words, the very argument Bickel uses to destroy the
idea that political minorities deserve special protection at the
hands of the judiciary destroys, at the same time, his own bed-
rock assumption that political majorities, as represented in the
executive and legislative branches, deserve special deference
from the courts. If majorities are merely temporary, shifting
coalitions, then decisions by the elective branches may well *not*
represent the work of a majority, since logrolling may result in
rewards to a number of minorities but injury to the interests of

everyone else. Moreover, if majorities form but then disappear, it may often be the case that policies once adopted by a temporary majority—as in a piece of regulatory legislation—may be forgotten or subverted later on. Should that process be ascribed to the "will" of the former majority? Should it be looked upon as a "decision" by the now defunct majority to be respected by reviewing courts—to forget about the problem that originally induced it to secure passage of the statute? If "minorities" can be defined only as groups that happen to be (temporary) losers on a given issue, and "majorities" can be defined only as (temporary) victors, then there is no reason why the victories (or the losses) of either should be accorded particular sympathy or respect.

In other words, once Bickel has forsworn the majoritarian premise from which he and his colleagues attacked the concept of an active judiciary, he is thrown back on the fairness *vel non* of the pluralist processes of group conflict as a moral basis for deferring to the political branches. His only defense for the ideal of a passive judiciary is the assumption that the political process that determines outcomes in the executive and legislative branches will produce results that are fair to all groups, if judges would just leave well enough alone. Though few political scientists would any longer be willing to embrace so seemingly naive a thesis, Bickel brandishes it like a banner: "groups sometimes lose out," he says, but "no group that is prepared to enter into the process and combine with others need remain permanently and completely out of power."

Unfortunately, this concept of pluralist theory is at least as naive as the majoritarian literalism originally employed as the basis for the notion that courts are inherently undemocratic. There is no more reason to believe that deserving interests will coalesce into "groups," or that each group will win a share of political success proportionate to its just needs, than there is to believe that the public or the majority will successfully control the actions of the legislative and executive branches. If anything, there is less reason to endorse the new pluralist premise than there was to endorse the old populist premise. For we can at least admit that, regarding issues where a majority is well-defined and intensely interested, the elective branches are very likely to be responsive to the majority will. Busing is, of course, one example (and Bickel is therefore obviously correct to say that, in that particular case, the courts' efforts to promote desegregation are countermajoritarian). But there is no reason to expect that the results of unregulated group competition for influence over the elective branches will produce fair results. As Judge J. Skelly Wright, author of the opinion in *Moss* v. *CAB*, wrote recently in the *Harvard Law Review*, in response to Bickel's lectures:

> The Professor would have us believe that . . . those groups with the most "intense" interests will be the most active in the process, and it is proper that the more "intense" interests be more richly rewarded. This is nonsense. The big winners in the pluralistic system are the highly organized, wealthy, and motivated groups skilled in the art of insider politics. . . . Perhaps the interest of a great corporation in a tax break is more "intense" than that of a political minority in its first amendment rights—that is, if intensity is defined by how conscious of their interests they are, how articulate and persistent they are in presenting them, and how much political muscle they bring to bear. . . . Unorganized, poor, unskilled minorities simply do not have the sort of "intense" interests in their rights which the pluralistic system regularly rewards.[12]

Once legal theory admits that the elective branches of government are primarily responsive to a pluralistic process of organized pressures (rather than the formal electoral mechanisms for guaranteeing majority rule), the case collapses for deferring to that process on an across-the-board basis. This is especially true in the case of issues involving direct conflicts between unorganized public interests and tightly organized and powerful minorities. In Chapter 8 I criticized post-World War II social scientists for embracing a Hobbesian pluralism without rejecting the statism they had inherited from the New Deal. Democratic government was in their view merely a grab bag for interest groups. This pork-barrel state lacked legitimacy. Legal theory—not just in the academy but in judges' opinions and lawyers' briefs—has been victimized by precisely the same error. Harvard Professor Louis Jaffe, one of the most influential students of administrative law of the postwar era, wrote an important article during the mid-1950s called "The Effective Limits of the Administrative Process: A Reevaluation," in which he noted various reasons why it had proven sadly necessary to revise the extravagant hopes vested by New Dealers in their grand designs for regulatory reform. Jaffe emphasized that it had turned out that "the regulated and client groups exert an effective pressure on the administrative agency in proportion to the importance of their economic function and to their organizational cohesion."[13] But he did not find anything especially disturbing in this fact. He did not conclude that, since the populist premises on which the agencies had supposedly been constructed had been proven false, the agencies should perhaps be abolished or subjected at least to much stronger judicial curbs than ever before.

Jaffe, and in this respect he has been altogether typical, did not perceive that, once the original populist foundations of an active and legally unchecked state were destroyed, the arms of the state lost their claims to legitimacy. They had become mere tools for the pursuit of private gain at the expense of the public they were originally thought to protect. As long as these agencies were left standing, they could only be legitimized by controls imposed on their power. Without such controls, they did more than defy the populist ideal of the sovereignty of the public. They also were shown to lack any justification whatsoever as instruments of social justice.

Thus, it is entirely consistent with democratic principle for courts to play an active role in checking bureaucratic and corporate abuse. And from a pragmatic standpoint, courts should be relatively effective in this role.

The Uses of Judicial Independence

Their "independence" is the first resource the federal courts can use to aid public and majority interests systematically neglected by the elective branches. This is a direct result of the constitutional guarantee of life tenure to federal judges, though the impact of the constitutional provision is often exaggerated. The average tenure of members of the federal bench is only thirteen and one-half years, which ensures that at any given time many judges will not be far out of line with society's dominant ideological and political forces. But the fact that judges need not be preoccupied with being reappointed helps them pursue an independent course—independent, that is, of the wishes of the politicians who appointed them and, more important, independent of the pressures to which elected officials are subject. If courts can oppose a majority bent on destroying a black child's constitutional right to desegregated education, then it can also oppose the drug industry and the FDA should they seek to erode the majority's statutory right to have useless drugs taken off the market.

But why, one might ask, cannot an interest like the drug industry deny appointment to a federal judge as it can to an FDA commissioner? Why can't the industry, once its agents see that they have reason to be concerned about the ideological sympathies of federal judges, use its influence to make sure that unsympathetic individuals are never appointed to the bench in the first place? What is to keep the federal courts from becoming industry captives just as the agencies are?

There is, of course, nothing to bar the drug industry from trying to keep populist-oriented lawyers from sitting on the federal bench. Indeed, the more populist issues come before the courts, the more likely it is that various industries will contrive to have some influence on federal judicial appointments. But there are good reasons to believe that they won't try very hard, and that, if they do, they probably will be less successful than they are in controlling appointments to regulatory agencies.

Unlike the ICC or the FDA, courts are general purpose institutions. They hear cases involving the entire range of legal problems, not just those that affect a particular industry. The chances that a particular judge—with the possible exception of a member of the Supreme Court or the U.S. Court of Appeals in Washington, D.C.—will have a decisive impact on a particular industry are very low. Furthermore, if an industry did wish to have a hand in the judicial appointment process, it would find that a good many other interests and issues were involved, from the standpoint of the Senate and the White House, which share the power to appoint, than are involved in appointing people to a regulatory agency. Those social forces which have traditionally perceived a substantial stake in the process of appointing judges—civil-rights and civil-liberties groups, segregationist representatives, even groups with strong sentiments on issues like obscenity or crime—will figure as prominently as or more prominently than will the American Retail Federation in the calculations of senators or the president. In addition, the tradition that appointments to the district and appellate benches go to the personal choice of the senators of the president's party would generally tend to make it difficult for special interests of any stripe to control the selection process. A senator's choices are likely to reflect his own personal contacts and convictions, and the preferences of the local legal establishment. Suggesting the name of a prominent local lawyer to the president as his next appointee to a vacancy on the district court is not likely to be the sort of decision which will get a senator into trouble when he runs for reelection. No one, including most national lobbies, could discipline him.

All this does not mean that appointees are likely to approve every lawsuit brought in the name of Ralph Nader, nor even that all federal judges will turn out to be men of great distinction. But it does make it implausible that federal judges would be the "railroad-minded" hacks Richard Olney predicted ICC commissioners would be, and that they would probably be even if they were given life tenure.

Of course, even though special interests are unlikely to create a captive judiciary by influencing the judicial appointment process, it is possible that they could in some instances create excessively cordial relationships with judges after they have been appointed, in the same way they create such relationships with regulatory bureaucrats. Industry executives and lobbyists could pay courtesy calls on judges. Judges could be invited to speak at industry affairs for large lecture fees. Judges could be bombarded with industry propaganda.

But this prospect is also implausible. It would be shocking if members of the federal judiciary were to allow themselves to accept any favor or make extensive contact with an interest that had a large stake in his sympathy. If this were not clear before Justice Fortas resigned from the Supreme Court, it is clear enough now. In this respect, the judiciary's independence may be owed in the final analysis mainly to the mystique of the courts, to the respect that people—even cynical superlawyers and lobbyists—have for a judge.

Indeed, this convention of our political culture is probably more potent than the configuration of political incentives sketched above, and certainly more than the mere legal safeguard of constitutional life tenure. One could, after all, provide the federal maritime administrator with life tenure, but his agency would not cease to be a pipeline through which economically indefensible subsidies flow to the shipping industry and the shipping unions. Or one could give FCC commissioners life tenure, but one suspects that they would still maintain frequent contacts with industry officials and representatives, and that they would still be sensitive to industry opinion. But our expectations of judges are different. In much greater measure than in the case of maritime administrators or FCC commissioners we expect them to live up to the standards prescribed by civics lessons as to how government is supposed to be conducted. In large measure because we have these expectations, they are fulfilled a good part of the time. Respect for the sanctity of the courts affects all of us—the public, the special interests, and the judges themselves.

Courts and the Pageant of Reform

Hence, the national mystique about the judiciary undergirds its political independence. The mystique of the courts also contributes to a second major asset which makes the judiciary a promising instrument of the populist ideal. The courts, unlike regulatory agencies, have not even a pretense of being able to bring the elements of power to bear in support of their objectives. They have, as Alexander Hamilton said in a famous passage of *The Federalist,* "neither FORCE nor WILL, but merely judgment; and must depend on the aid of the executive arm even for the efficacy of [their] judgments." Virtually the only access to influence open to the judiciary, or to those who would use the judiciary to promote their objectives, is persuasion, the weakest of the three elements of democratic influence: wealth, organization, and persuasion. But because of the judicial mystique, because of the status courts enjoy in our civics class mythology, and especially because of the priesthood function we delegate to the federal courts to speak for our basic political values, their judges are unusually gifted in the process of political persuasion. "The Supreme Court is, among other things, an educational body," Eugene V. Rostow wrote twenty years ago, "and the justices are inevitably teachers in a vital national seminar."[14] Putting the same point somewhat more precisely a decade later, in *The Least Dangerous Branch,* the landmark study that has made him the most respected constitutional scholar of his generation, Alexander Bickel wrote:

[The] Court [is] in a Socratic colloquy with the other institutions of government and with society as a whole concerning the necessity for this or that measure. . . . In American society the colloquy goes well beyond the [legal] profession and reaches deeply into the places where public opinion is formed.[15]

Bickel and Rostow write in the tradition of criticism of the work of the courts that traces itself back to Thomas Reed Powell's aphorism that the courts by themselves can only "say something. The effect depends on others."[16]

The relative impotence of the judiciary and the courts' dependence on myth and rhetoric to achieve objectives they choose to endorse have generally been considered reasons why courts should play a passive role vis-à-vis the other branches of government. But if courts are weak, then there is little to fear if they occasionally overstep the proper boundaries of their authority. More important, if they depend on the public and the other branches of government to effect their objectives, then, by hypothesis, the process of implementing (i.e., generating consent for) their aims must necessarily be a democratic one. It is rather more far-fetched to characterize as "undemocratic" the process of deciding national policy about public-school segregation which the courts initiated, than, for example, the process of deciding national policy on airline rate regulation, which Congress and the CAB control. If courts and the law have a self-conscious sense that theirs is what Professor Bickel calls a "deviant" status in a democratic society, the best remedy need not be abstention from participation in the democratic process. On the contrary, what could be a more appropriate— a more democratic—role for the judiciary than to participate actively in the process of public persuasion? This is an especially appropriate prescription when the interests and values that the courts are being asked to further are those of the majority, of the public itself.

The populist ideal of the sovereign public is part of the civics text litany we expect the courts to vindicate. In this respect, it is no different from the principle that all races should have equal access to education, or the principle that every vote should count equally at the polls. All these are public ideals in which we as a nation believe, but which cannot be realized by the elective branches of government left to their own devices. Judicial intervention is a prerequisite to squaring such principles with the reality of our social arrangements. By the same reasoning which has prompted the federal judiciary to protect racial enclaves and political protesters, it should pay special heed to pleas to defend the public interest against organized minorities and unresponsive regulators.

The fact that the courts are limited to persuasion as a means of influence does not render them useless, relative to other institutions, as candidates for promoting the populist ideal of democracy. The fact is that advocates of the populist ideal are essentially confined to persuasion as an element of influence in whatever forum of government they find themselves involved in political combat. The regulatory bureaucracies, once thought to be the most efficient means of vindicating the populist ideal, have in many respects turned out to be the least efficient. Administrative decision making (or decision avoiding, as the case may be) is often structured to downgrade the usefulness of public persuasion. Low-visibility decisional processes are characteristic of bureaucracy (a tendency that is to some extent inherent but that has been seriously exacerbated by the judiciary's inclination over the years to defer to administrative discretion).

To be sure, organization and wealth are not irrelevant to successful use of the courts to vindicate one's interests or values. It takes money to fight and win a lawsuit, often a great deal of money. Usually, one needs a certain amount of organization, at the very least, in order to raise enough money to conduct litigation effectively. No matter how generous standards become for awarding compensation to victorious public-interest litigants, it would be foolish to expect that the need for some small measure of organized support will disappear altogether. (And, to be sure, a minimum of financial and organizational competence is an entirely appropriate thing to require of prospective public-interest advocates in the courts. It makes perfect sense to demand a certain threshold of community support from some concrete group somewhere, before we let would-be private attorneys general take up the precious resources of the judicial system to air their grievances.)

But the amount of money and organization needed to influence social decisions through the litigation process is, in general, slight compared to what it takes to have a systematic effect on the elective branches. And the resources of persuasion that the judiciary can muster on behalf of a protected interest are formidable, in many respects more formidable than any executive agency or congressional committee can command.

Judicial Populism: Prudence and Politics

Even though the judiciary can be an effective combatant for populist values, there remains the prudential question of whether such a stand will end in damaging the judiciary's own overall strength and status in the polity. This prudential argument has often been raised against judicial activism in the more traditional areas of civil rights and civil liberties. Justice Frankfurter warned in a famous aphorism that entry into the apportionment controversy would push the courts into a "political thicket" from which they would inevitably emerge not only unsuccessful but also gravely weakened in their ability to do battle for other social interests.

Of course, the judiciary, like any other institution, must take such prudential concerns into account when weighing the costs and risks of intervention in some broiling social controversy. And in fact, without exception, every one of the Supreme Court's major initiatives of the 1950s and 1960s—race, reapportionment, prayer in the schools, protections for accused criminals—has gravely imperiled the court as an institution. That the judiciary has so far survived each of the serious efforts to cripple it does not mean the problem is not real. But a generalized fear of reprisal makes little sense as an argument against judicial activism on an across-the-board basis. Fear of reprisal may be well-grounded in some instances and not in others. And in the great majority of cases, the prudential argument centers around the question of when and how to intervene, not *whether* to intervene at all. Moreover, it should be remembered that the judiciary, because of its protective mystique, and more importantly because of the great variety of stratagems it can employ to avoid head-on collisions with its foes while acting to promote public support for its objectives, is not without defensive assets or allies when it finds itself under attack.

One would expect that the courts' defensive position would be especially strong where their constituency was the public itself, and where the object of their ire was a minority interest that had winnowed its way to a position of excessive influence over the legislature or the bureaucracy. Vice President Agnew need not be afraid of offending the populace when he vents his antagonism to the Legal Services Program of OEO. But the enemies of public-interest law may experience more difficulties, at least if public-interest lawyers are skillful at keeping visible the efforts of the Agnews to destroy them. No politician would at the moment find much to offer in the suggestion of launching a crusade against Ralph Nader. It is at least equally unlikely that the federal courts, were they to develop a reputation for courageous action in behalf of the values with which Nader is associated, would prove a promising political target. Indeed, it would enhance the courts' general standing with the electorate if they were to propagate and demonstrate the idea that their resources could be mobilized to support otherwise neglected interests of the majority, as well as to protect oppressed and unpopular minorities.

Finally, there is one last consideration that must be noted in assessing the future of public-interest law. At a time when Richard Nixon is appointing conservative judges throughout the federal judiciary, it may seem like folly to expect the courts to look favorably on invitations to stand up for consumers or taxpayers or environmentalists. Obviously, this fear is not without foundation. Still, there remains some basis for hope that, as is the case with public opinion generally, the outlook of the judiciary will move to the left on populist issues even though it has moved to the right on civil-rights and civil-liberties issues. More importantly, the populist ideal will often hold appeal for judges who would be considered die-hard conservatives on other issues. The defense of the public interest, the demand that law be applied to situations where—largely because of the ideological legacy of the radicalism of the 1930s—unbridled discretion was formerly the rule, these are pleas that may attract even the sternest enthusiast of a hard-line approach to criminal justice. In short, the causes furthered by public-interest law largely promote middle- and upper-class interests and they involve values that are fundamentally conservative.

It is not, therefore, an accident that traditionalist Judge Sirica cracked the Watergate scandal, nor that Chief Justice Burger himself made the decision that history will recognize as the foundation of the public-interest law movement, and that he articulated the concept of public-interest law more effectively than any other judge. When he forced the FCC to permit the representatives of Jackson's black community to challenge WLBT's license renewal, he signaled the end of reverence for the myths spawned by the New Deal. "The theory," he said,

> that the Commission can always effectively represent the listener interests in a renewal proceeding without the aid and participation of legitimate listener representatives fulfilling the role of private attorneys general is one of those assumptions we collectively try to work with so long as they are reasonably adequate. When it becomes clear, as it does to us now, that it is no longer a valid assumption which stands up under the realities of actual experience, neither we nor the Commission can continue to rely on it.

The fact of the matter is that the chief justice is as aware of Grant McConnell's "Open Secret," as is, for example, Ralph Nader. It is at least plausible that he and the judiciary that must follow his lead in the next decade or so will not steer the courts off the course they are now on toward ministering to this malady of democracy.

Populism in the Courts: Some Early Returns

Already, of course, many courts have been moving in this direction, with impressive, though still quite preliminary, results. The direct result of Chief Justice Burger's *WLBT* decision was to make television programming in Jackson, Mississippi, more responsive to the needs of its black community; the indirect result has been to make FCC procedures more accommodating to public-interest intervenors and to make its interpretation of substantive law more sensitive to the dictates of the doctrine of broadcast fairness. USDA, a producer-oriented agency that displays little zeal for enforcing the several consumer and environmental protection laws it has been handed in the past two decades, has earned the honor of being the most frequent target of public-interest lawsuits. Courts have, at the invitation of plaintiffs in these cases, ordered USDA to fulfill its statutory obligations to phase DDT out of use as a pesticide, to prohibit meat companies from hawking hot dogs containing 15 percent cereal filler as "100 percent beef," to hold administrative hearings before imposing protectionist restraints against imports of tomatoes, and to permit poverty-stricken counties to take advantage of special food distribution programs that Congress had enacted but that USDA officials did not approve of. Cases still pending against the department seek such objectives as implementation of a five-year-old statutory requirement for informational labeling on meat and poultry products and reinstatement of a poultry inspector demoted in reprisal for his public disclosure of the inadequacy of the agency's inspection procedures.

Environmental litigation is probably the largest field of public-interest legal activity, though the quantitative impact on the federal judiciary's work load has by no means been as great as is sometimes asserted. Environmental suits have produced a number of dramatically innovative decisions. The FPC has been ordered to take environmental considerations into account in deciding power plant siting controversies. The AEC has been ordered to institute a new set of rigorous procedures designed to assure that challengers of nuclear power plant siting decisions will be able to test thoroughly the agency's obligation to screen applicants' safety precautions. The Department of the Interior was forced to delay for two years the construction of the Alaska pipeline, during which period pressures from environmentalists resulted in substantial modifications of the original construction plans.

Michigan Law Professor Joseph Sax has shown effectively how the courts, through these "colloquies" with agencies, legislatures, and the public, have promoted democratic resolution of specific environmental issues. Sax details instances in which courts have "remanded" bills sneaked through legislatures with no public notice or discussion, how courts have created counter-pressures to help bureaucrats fend off the pressures of industry representatives, and in general how they have acted as catalysts for genuine public consideration of environmental questions that would otherwise have remained the private affair of corporate and bureaucratic executives.[17]

None of these early cases has shed much light on whether litigation can upset basic principles and practices cementing agency-industry accommodations such as those in the CAB under assault by Congressman Moss. However, one decision that comes close to granting the sort of far-reaching relief that Moss's lawyers seek was handed down in late August, 1972, by District Judge William Bryant of the District of Columbia. The agency involved is the FDA. The case, brought by a frequent public-interest plaintiff, the American Public Health Association (APHA), alleged in essence that, after Congress in 1962 outlawed prescription and over-the-counter drugs that were *ineffective* (previously, drugs were only illegal if they were positively *harmful*), the FDA had simply refused to enforce the law. James Goddard, a reformist FDA chief appointed in 1966 by Lyndon Johnson, had put the enforcement wheels in motion by contracting with the National Academy of Sciences (NAS) to conduct studies of the effectiveness of the myriad drugs approved as safe by the FDA since the Food, Drug, and Cosmetic Act was originally passed in 1938. NAS began to submit its studies in 1967, but by December, 1970, when the lawsuit was filed, FDA had released only half of NAS's results to the public and had acted on few of them.

In curt language that provoked a page-one story in the *Washington Post,* Judge Bryant condemned the "solicitude" the agency showed the industry. He held that the doctrine of administrative discretion contained no warrant for "interminable delay." Noting that a summary of NAS's findings with respect to over-the-counter drugs, released on July 8, 1972, indicated that only about 25 percent of "the nation's leading cold medications" are effective, Bryant held that the FDA must stop inventing dilatory procedures, release the reports, and enforce the law—even if many of the nation's most familiar over-the-counter cure-alls were to disappear from drugstore shelves in the process. In October Bryant issued a detailed order, putting the FDA on a strict timetable for complying with the statute. The order required FDA to release all of the individual NAS reports which had been suppressed up to that time and to "release all such reports received in the future immediately upon receipt." The agency was ordered to finish its drug effectiveness review promptly, to withdraw approval for all drugs found to be ineffective, and to file regular reports with the court on the status of its compliance program.

A Decadent Union and a Captive Bureaucracy:
Struggle over the United Mine Workers of America (UMWA)

Although it did not involve corporate interests specifically, one other recent court struggle deserves mention as a test—and a promising one at that—of whether litigation can "crack" the combination of a powerful private institution and a captive regulatory bureaucracy. This was the effort, spurred by numerous individual suits, to wrest control of UMWA from Tony Boyle and the rest of the leadership faction that inherited the union from John L. Lewis. The fight began in May, 1969, when Joseph Yablonski announced that he would challenge Boyle for the presidency of the union in the December, 1969, elections. The legal and political side of the campaign was directed by Joseph Rauh, Yablonski's original lawyer, and by Yablonski's sons. Harry Huge, once co-director of the Washington Research Project and more recently an Arnold & Porter partner, initiated a major side lawsuit challenging Boyle's control and corrupt use of the union's pension fund.

From the day Yablonski announced his candidacy, Boyle subjected him to an avalanche of illegal harassment, including one unsuccessful murder attempt—a karate chop in the back of Yablonski's neck. Rauh continuously petitioned and pleaded with Labor Secretary George Shultz to exercise his investigatory powers under the fair elections provisions of the Labor-Management Reporting and Disclosure (Landrum-Griffin) Act of 1959. Rauh showered the Labor Department with evidence of Boyle's illegal electioneering activity and warned that violence would occur unless the department asserted its presence and showed its intention to enforce the law. Shultz refused to act, even after the karate-chop incident and after Rauh had won four court suits invalidating four specific Boyle actions as violations of Landrum-Griffin. Boyle won the election on December 9, 1969, but Yablonski said he would fight on. He and Rauh asked the Labor Department to impound the ballots and bring a court action to upset the election results; their petition urged that Boyle's victory margin was created by his gaining advantages as implausible as 50–1 at those polling places where Yablonski had no observers; wherever Yablonski had observers in place, he had sometimes beaten Boyle and generally held his own.

Within a month, Yablonski, his wife, and daughter were found shotgunned to death in their beds. But still Labor's hierarchy dragged their feet and Rauh got action from the administration only when he went to Attorney General Mitchell in the wake of national outrage over the slayings. Indeed, even then, though the FBI and the Justice Department pressed the murder investigation with admirable persistence and skill, the Labor Department showed signs of an intent to sabotage the effort to set aside the election. Though Labor did institute a Landrum-Griffin proceeding to upset the December 9 election, Rauh was distressed at the department's failure to allege as grounds for the action the most outrageous illegalities committed by the Boyle forces. Fearing a less than 100 percent effort by the department, Rauh asked to intervene in the case as a private prosecutor on behalf of Miners for Democracy, the organization formed by Yablonski's sons and other supporters to carry on the fight for which he was killed. This unusual request was rebuffed by the department and by lower federal courts, but it was granted by a unanimous Supreme Court in a decision that dealt a blow to the old New Deal jurisprudence based on unquestioning trust in government to vindicate the public interest.

The court did not attack the department's integrity in the harsh terms used by Burger against the FCC in the *WLBT* case, but made clear that its decision sprang from the same sentiment underlying the *WLBT* decision. Noting that in an enforcement proceeding to upset a union election, the labor department acts in effect as the lawyer for a union member who has complained to the department about election irregularities, the court said pointedly, "Even if the Secretary is performing his duties, broadly conceived, as well as can be expected, the union member may have a valid complaint about the performance of 'his lawyer.' "[18]

When the case was returned for trial, the district court took its cue from the Supreme Court. After invalidating the election as illegal, District Judge Bryant—the same Judge Bryant who enjoined the nonenforcement of the Food, Drug, and Cosmetic Act—scheduled a new election for December, 1972. His decree imposed a variety of safeguards against union abuses and labor department indifference. Rauh's clients, Miners for Democracy, were given extensive rights to station observers at union locals throughout the course of the campaign, and to use space in the union newspaper in which to present their campaign to the membership. With this court-enforced protection, the insurgents won a spectacular victory in December.

Bryant's tough decree resembled the strong action taken by his colleague on the District Court for the District of Columbia, Gerhard Gesell, in Harry Huge's suit against Boyle and the National Bank of Washington, a bank owned by the union, for extraordinary mismanagement of the union's pension fund. Gesell found the bank, the union, and Boyle guilty of depriving pensioners of tens of millions of dollars, by keeping balances of between $20 and $90 million continually in interest-free checking accounts at the bank. As relief, Gesell awarded three years' damages, or $11 million, to the pension fund, ordered the fund to cease dealing with the bank for as long as UMWA continued to own stock in the bank, and removed trustees from the fund, including Boyle himself.

Without the boldness of these district judges, the principles of union democracy in the Landrum-Griffin Act would never have been respected. Surely Congress would never have enforced its own statute—any more than it would have in the case of the CAB. Rauh had tried to get Congress to take an interest in enforcing the law it had passed twelve years before by persuading liberal Democrat Harrison Williams to have his labor subcommittee investigate Boyle's abuses and hold hearings. But soon after Williams began his inquiry, George Meany let it be known that he preferred that the matter should proceed at a very slow and, especially, a very quiet pace. Williams is not by instinct a determined inquisitor in any event, and he pursued the quest erratically. At times, he seemed to drop it altogether. When confronted by Rauh, AFL-CIO chief lobbyist Andrew Biemiller did not deny that he was pressuring the Labor Department and Senator Williams to keep the lid on the Boyle affair. On the contrary, he excoriated Rauh. Rauh had done something that simply "was not done"—at least not by someone like Rauh who was once counted as a hero of the labor movement. He had aired labor's dirty linen in public.

However parochial Biemiller's line may have seemed, the AFL-CIO stuck to it, and neither the congressional committees nor the administrative agency formally responsible for dealing with the situation seemed inclined to buck big labor's will. Only the judiciary was safely outside the union's domain.

Both Rauh and, eventually, the courts recognized the captivity of Congress and the labor department. Because they did so, and because they were able to exert effective counterpressure, a fair election occurred three years after the original rigged travesty took place.

In short, the struggle of Miners for Democracy to enforce the Landrum-Griffin Act perfectly illustrates the defect in democracy that public-interest law is trying to remedy. It is also an example which demonstrates that, at least in some situations, the judiciary, with the assistance of effective counsel for public-interest litigants, can succeed in making democracy work, despite the pressures of private interests as powerful as Tony Boyle's UMWA and the AFL-CIO.

Judicial Stagecraft: The Example of Reapportionment

The potential of the courts should not be exaggerated, of course. Where the public is indifferent to a particular problem, it may well be impossible to defeat the focused power of a special interest group in Congress or the executive branch, even if the judiciary does stand up for a clear interest of the public. But we do have at least one major example of the courts taking the side of a significant majority interest that had been neglected elsewhere by government, and then of using its prestige and its potential for stagecraft to drive home the program of reform it initiated, over bitter opposition from its opponents. That example is reapportionment. Although many law professors have looked down their noses at the Supreme Court's simplistic and rigid "one-man, one-vote" formula, it was actually a shrewd political tactic on the part of the court. While professors versed in pluralist political theory can readily imagine other bases for allocating voting power, "one-man, one-vote" seems to the ordinary citizen like the very definition of democracy. Populist precepts learned in civics class require each citizen to have an equal say at the polls. And the court's decision not only squared with public instincts about how voting power should be apportioned, but with public expectations about the proper role of the court itself. Here the court was expounding and vindicating basic principles of governmental organization in which the public strongly believed. In the struggle that ensued as to whether reapportionment would be consummated, the court and its allies prevailed precisely because they had focused the issue successfully and, through invocation of approved populist symbols, generated wide public support.

There is much reason to suppose that the judiciary could generate similarly persuasive pressures in support of causes like Congressman Moss's challenge to the CAB. However, the specific strategies available to courts, if they do choose to press such populist battles against special interests, will necessarily differ. Unlike reapportionment, a judicial crusade against corporate and bureaucratic abuse of the public could not be based on the Constitution. Unequal access to the franchise was—quite plausibly—characterized as a denial of equal protection of the laws, and hence a violation of the Fourteenth Amendment. But it does not seem plausible to describe a transfer of wealth from consumers to producers, a tax loophole, or a franchise to run a highway through a mountainside as an offense of constitutional dimensions.

In such instances, the courts can legitimately favor the side of unorganized public interests. They can hold up the process of administrative decision, or, by construing a statute in a manner favorable to the public, reverse, at least temporarily, a congressional, industry-oriented decision. The courts can broaden public debate, and attempt to focus attention on the issue. But ultimately, after a reasonable debate has taken place, if the elective branches still decide to turn the treasury over to an aircraft company or the shipping industry, no version of democratic theory requires a judicial reversal. It would be neither appropriate nor ultimately consistent with the judiciary's own self-interest as an institution for it to insist too stubbornly on its conception of what is right.

Populist Law Enforcement

In the public-interest area, an activist judiciary would be best advised to characterize its task as one of straightforward law enforcement. Rather than appearing to take on Congress by invalidating statutes, the courts should be Congress's agent. They should reprimand public or private bureaucracies for brazenly defying statutory commands to respect the public interest. In principle this approach is very limited and moderate, but in practice it would only infrequently keep the courts from attempting as vigorous a role as political and administrative constraints would permit.

In Chapter 2 we detailed the ideological, psychological, and political incentives which time and again prompt Congress to resolve regulatory issues through broad and platitudinous statutes. Many observers have attacked this resilient congressional habit as a major cause of the malaise of the regulatory establishment. Professor Lowi has even gone so far as to recommend that the Supreme Court commence to invalidate excessively vague regulatory statutes, on the ground that they represent unconstitutional delegations of legislative power to the executive branch. He pictures this exhumation of an old and discredited constitutional doctrine as a "radical" step forward which would help to free regulators from their thralldom to special interests.[19] But the vagueness of regulatory legislation can be of great positive value to public-interest advocates. The proper objective is not to do away with platitudinous mandates, but to seize upon them as an opportunity for construing the law in ways that emphasize the public ends the platitudes purport to serve. Indeed, this is precisely the course that Congressman Moss's lawyers are taking in their case against the CAB. It has been employed by courts in several recent rebuffs to USDA for its inattention to consumer interests.[20]

In most instances, this strategy—of assigning populist interpretations to ambiguous statutes and then enforcing them vigorously—will enable the judiciary to put itself in the best possible position to succeed in its "colloquies" with agencies. By liberally construing, and then enforcing, a statute, the judiciary not only creates time and opinion pressures for an anti-industry swell of sentiment to crystallize, it also puts the burden of persuading Congress to "change the law" on the agency and its industry clients. If the court's decision is laced with strong language spelling out the reasons the public interest requires the construction it has adopted, it may add considerably to the burdens that agency and industry lobbyists will have to face in trying to get their views put back in the statute. A good example is this judicial denunciation of a USDA labeling which the Court of Appeals for the District of Columbia Circuit found to be invalid because it was deceptive to consumers:

> A serious infraction of the faith upon which our citizens live and upon which the Government exists . . . would start . . . on the shelves of the markets where people in the mass come into direct contact with the Government and its operation. . . . We should brook no loose handling in these mundane but delicate matters. If executive officials fail here, or grow autocratic, the judicial branch of government must bring them within the confines of their duty.[21]

By confining its attack to the agency and the industry, and in effect saying that the Congress's beneficent intentions have been subverted by those delegated the task of carrying them out, the court gives Congress the option of letting the matter rest where the court has left it. There will often be a reasonable chance that Congress will decide to do just that.

This strategy is not merely a gimmick. On the contrary, it is perhaps the only posture—compatible both with democratic principle and the practical limits of the ideal of popular sovereignty—that an independent judiciary can assume in these regulatory controversies. It is unrealistic to expect that the mass enthusiasms that induce Congress to pass populist legislation can be sustained permanently. It is equally unrealistic to expect that the objectives reflected in such laws will long be respected by the political branches of government once the original wave of support dies away. Indeed, it is even unrealistic to expect that the public will frequently be in a position to block potentially dangerous regulatory schemes devised by special interests for their own ends, especially if those ends are concealed by grandiloquent gestures promising that the law will promote the public interest. But it is not unreasonable to believe that the judiciary might realistically assess these inherent faults in the political process. And it would be a plausible and wholly "democratic" mission for the courts to interpret these laws in ways that emphasize the populist mood which gave them birth, to lean, in other words, to the side of the impotent public, insofar as the courts' own—admittedly limited—capabilities permit.

This is a mission that the courts can—indeed, must—undertake largely on their own initiative. Congress, under the lash of populist leaders and an aroused public opinion, can spur efforts on the part of the judiciary to recast its relationship to the rest of government and to the public. A variety of proposals have been introduced and several enacted by Congress designed to further this aim—most notably "NEPA" (the National Environmental Policy Act), the ambitious Hart-McGovern Environmental Protection bill drafted by Professor Sax, and several consumer class-action measures. Populist forces in Congress have also provided for parallel mechanisms of private judicial enforcement in some of the new regulatory schemes. But, though congressional initiative is welcome in this area—and indeed, though such legislation deserves more attention from new populist leaders than it has generally received—there is very little in any of these bills that the courts could not do on their own, if they dared to. And even if populist legislators induce Congress to transfer to the federal judiciary some of the statutory responsibilities for regulation that they originally delegated to administrative agencies, doing so can only yield meaningful change if the courts want such change, and if the litigation process is capable of executing their aims. Individual court cases will have to determine the difficult and crucial questions which cannot be solved by statutory generalities—when and whether public-interest lawyers will be compensated, how far a decree for equitable relief should invade the domain of a regulatory agency, how great should be the measure of damages in a consumer class-action case.

By answering such questions, litigants and judges will determine whether the concept of public-interest law will evolve into an effective set of protections for the public or become merely another grand design, another embellishment of the verbal superstructure of government that has no impact on the reality of its operation.

Whatever the outcome of the quest, it would be a tragedy if this promising enterprise were aborted altogether. Not just "the public interest," but the judiciary itself will suffer if the partisans of judicial abstention prevail. There are those who, like Solicitor General Robert Bork, warn judges to avoid the risks of engagement with corporate and bureaucratic interests.[22] These are false friends of the courts. Their dogma, that courts are irrelevant to the democratic process, is simplistic political science and false history. It will not prove valid in the future, except as a self-fulfilling prophecy. The courts have often shaped the terms and even the outcome of political debate. And they have almost never found themselves without resources and allies to protect their own integrity as institutions. For, just as judicial activism breeds enemies, it also fosters loyal constituencies. Only if the courts abdicate, ignoring the flaws of elective government, will they prove that they have no proper democratic role, and no interests to protect. They will surely lose their friends as fast as they confirm their irrelevance.

Prospect

It may seem unrealistic to expect the courts and the law to clamp down on corporate and bureaucratic abuse in the name of the public. For this is a time when lawyers and the law have become targets of suspicion. Singled out for special concern are the "Washington lawyers," who practice before the federal agencies and courts in the District of Columbia, and who would surely bear much of the onus of any reformation of federal regulatory law. From Joseph Goulden's bestseller, *The Superlawyers,* to *Fortune* magazine, to Ralph Nader (who is studying Washington's blue-chip firm Covington & Burling), people are fascinated with the Clark Cliffords and Abe Fortases and Lloyd Cutlers who "make things happen" in Washington. Of course, lawyers and the legal process have always been seen to play an unusually influential role in public affairs in the United States, a phenomenon noted by de Tocqueville as early as 1835. If de Tocqueville admired lawyers as an aristocracy of merit, the current view is less favorable. Lawyers are seen not as wise interpreters of the Constitution, but as sinister manipulators.

267

Despite the public's distrust of lawyers, the remarkable abilities imputed to them still make them an object of admiration and even hope. Nader in particular casts the law as a kind of chosen profession, specially endowed and specially obligated to put its endowments at the service of democracy and the public interest.

The ambivalence of the public image of lawyers is readily understandable. It corresponds to the highly ambivalent nature of the lawyers' role in the governing process. In law school and in their early years after graduation, lawyers undergo a socialization process that provides them with a peculiar, and largely unconscious, understanding both of the pluralist mechanisms by which government mainly functions and of the populist mythology in terms of which government is described in laws, writings, and the conventions that structure ordinary people's images and expectations. On the one hand, lawyers are experts at writing up the grand populist generalities of statutes and court decisions. On the other hand, they know what the hard practical questions are—how those generalities will be applied to specific cases. Lawyers work with the verbal superstructure of the governing process at its closest point to the level of actual operations. They internalize the fierce tension—the schizophrenia, perhaps—between the populist ideal of democracy and the pluralist reality of the process in its routine operation.

Inevitably, this makes lawyers seem like double agents. There is a deceptiveness inherent in their function of moving back and forth across the border between legal rhetoric and operational reality. Sometimes the deception is willful. A lawyer representing corporate clients before Congress deliberately sets out to deceive the public when he drafts a bill ostensibly aimed at subjecting his clients to public control, but which he knows will be innocuous in practice. But from a purely objective standpoint, lawyers on the side of reform end up playing the same role when they draft their reform legislation in terms of populist principles that are inherently incapable of functioning in the pluralist environment in which they will have to be administered. That was the point Gabriel Kolko made in his study of the origins of railroad regulation.

It has even been argued that the virtual hypocrisy built into the lawyers' role serves a vital and useful social function; even if the populist notion that the people should be sovereign is an impossible dream, it may help keep the people happy to go on promising that it can come true or by pretending that it has come true. Richard Hofstadter argued that the lawyers and judges engaged in antitrust enforcement during the Progressive period performed this function of calming the national psyche. More recently Yale Law Professor Jan Deutsch has argued that the Supreme Court's recent reapportionment decisions are similar exercises in national myth making. Political power is not really distributed among the citizens of the republic in accordance with the populist formula of one-man, one-vote, Deutsch observes, but it is good for the nation's morale for the court to come along and say that it is or can be made to be. It would be intolerable, Deutsch says, for the judiciary to examine the real workings of the political system, or to admit that vastly disproportionate power is held by pressure groups and campaign contributors; such facts would be too offensive to the populist mythology that the nation cherishes and that enables the people to respect their government. Pulling the wool over their eyes keeps the people happy, a function the law performs well in instances of the triumph of populist doctrine such as the reapportionment decisions.

Traditionally, lawyers have not acknowledged the ambivalence inherent in the processes of law making and law applying. Rather, they have embraced both aspects of their role without explicitly acknowledging or even perceiving the tension between them. In the exterior part of the system, the lawyers employ the appropriate populist platitudes. In the sub rosa sectors of the system, where a very different idiom is appropriate, the lawyers leave their populist blinders behind. This is rarely, however, a conscious process.

For example, Abe Fortas, the corporate lawyer, was said to know no peer as an analyst of the mechanics of Washington. Abe Fortas's opinions on the Supreme Court were laced with the literalist faith in the populist ideal that underlay the reapportionment decisions. Until his tragic departure from the court, Fortas was the very definition of what the profession—and the public—regards as a great lawyer precisely because he was a virtuoso in both worlds.

The simple complaint of the new populist movement—no different from that once made by the Stimsons and the Brandeises—is that the two roles of the lawyer have fallen out of balance. The law purports to embody the commands of the people. But the resources of the legal system are in fact disproportionately devoted to aiding centers of private power to evade those commands. Hence, the claim that the system serves as an instrument of democracy is at best ambiguous, at worst fraudulent.

Within the legal profession many elements are now sensitive to this new populist critique of the law. Many lawyers wish to redress the imbalance between the aspirations of legal rhetoric and the private ends to which legal resources are mainly deployed. At this stage, of course, skepticism remains entirely warranted as to the capacity for self-regeneration of a profession so comfortable and established as the law. Internal resistance to change is stronger no doubt than present appearances reveal,[1] but the door to reform is still open. The effort to create in the legal system a shelter for heretofore neglected public interests is one social struggle that it still seems possible to win.

Richard Hofstadter once criticized the Progressives for trying to "institutionalize a mood." His point was that this was an absurd and irrational goal. But the problem with past reform generations is not simply that they sought, through new institutions, to carry their objectives forward into the future. After all, every political movement entertains similar hopes and could be dismissed on similar grounds. The problem with populist reformers has been that the particular institutions they designed were ineffective. Their ambitious new agencies could not survive in the political environment they encountered after they were first enacted into law. In this regard, the new populists' turn to the concept of public-interest law is promising.

Public-interest law is no harbinger of revolution. But it may be a hopeful omen nevertheless, an indication that in renewing the populist tradition, contemporary reformers are going further than simply copying the rhetoric of their elders. They may be learning from the mistakes of the past. Rather than dreaming of taking power, they are working on mechanisms to *check* power.

Elites faithful to unorganized social interests may not be able to capture the CPA or the FTC. But they may well be able to generate a body of judicial doctrine that imposes more meaningful obligations on public and private bureaucracies. And with some perseverance they can form enduring nongovernmental mechanisms for applying and enforcing such obligations. There is no mass movement in the cards for the new populists, and if there were, it would prove no more efficient a device for realizing their ideals than did the anti-corporate passion that dominated public opinion during the Progressive era. But constituencies could be organized to support private organizations as resilient, for example, as the American Civil Liberties Union (ACLU). Some of the environmental groups may have the stamina to survive longer than the vogue that supports them now. Common Cause or Public Citizen may also build up an effective permanent staff and a loyal constituency, though this seems less likely. More promising than Common Cause or Public Citizen is the "radicalization" that Consumers Union (CU) has undergone in the past few years. Once staid and studiously nonpolitical, CU has begun to place activities like Ralph Nader, Bess Myerson, and public-interest lawyer John Banzhaff on its board of directors, and to expand the uses to which it is willing to commit the revenues raised through the sale of its magazine, *Consumer Reports*. CU has appeared with increasing frequency as a plaintiff in public-interest lawsuits, and in the autumn of 1972 it established a Washington arm to engage in public-interest law activities.

And apart from the formation of durable private organizations, the new population may plausibly look forward to institutionalizing its aims through the modification of the structure of commercial law practice, as court-awarded legal fees are made available in a broader array of public-interest cases. Already, in 1972, a survey by Jury Verdict Research showed that lawyers were bringing an annual number of 500,000 cases for plaintiffs injured by defective products—up from 100,000 five years before—and that corporate defendants in these cases were losing an average of $70,000 in jury-awarded damages in each case lost—a figure that had jumped over six times since 1965.

In short, the concept of public-interest law reflects a modest strategy of change, and a conservative vision of the structure of society. But it is attuned to the political realities with which any agency of populist reform must cope. It can make efficient use of the particular political resources available to support the populist ideal.

This is not, of course, to dismiss elective politics outright as an instrument of reform. Much less is it to claim that one would see no differences if George McGovern, rather than Richard Nixon, were staffing the Antitrust Division or the new Commission on Product Safety. Nor is it to forecast that populist rhetoric will soon disappear from left-of-center politics. Despite the public's repudiation of Senator McGovern in 1972, the election showed no general trend of distaste for populist aims. Tax reform, consumer protection, the environment—such themes enabled candidates to overcome the Nixon landslide and replace conservative incumbent senators and governors in at least ten statewide races. In one of these states, mid-American Iowa, Republican Jack Miller lost his senate seat mainly because the *Des Moines Register* accused him of writing a loophole into the 1969 Tax Reform Act to help a large corporate client of lobbyist Tommy Corcoran. When the story appeared during the last weeks of the campaign, it was skillfully exploited by new populist challenger Richard Clark; he jumped from a seven-point deficit in the final preelection poll to a resounding 55–45 percent triumph in the election two weeks later. In 1973, outrage over new Watergate disclosures showed that the public had not been apathetic about the official corruption issue the year before; rather, ITT, the milk scandal, and the first revelations about Watergate apparently seemed not insignificant but simply *less* significant than issues such as busing, foreign policy, and "competence," where President Nixon was perceived to be decisively superior.

These developments will be taken as evidence that populist appeals to voters can be effective, as long as a candidate is not hobbled by the personal and ideological drawbacks of the McGovern campaign. Moreover, many reform leaders in the generation of Iowa's new Senator Clark themselves admire the populist ideal as a matter of emphatic personal conviction. Populism will therefore continue as a staple of liberal politics beyond the near term. If a liberal Democrat gains the White House in 1976, the performance of the federal regulatory establishment will, for a time in any event, reach more satisfactory levels than it has under Richard Nixon. And the integrity of the political process itself may be improved—if not to any revolutionary extent, by legislative controls on campaign finance imposed in the wake of Watergate, at least for as long as public concern makes reprisals at the polls a credible threat.

But this achievement, if it comes, is beside the point that bedevils thoughtful adherents of the populist tradition. After all, the challenge reformers face is not how to achieve the temporary appearance of change. Relatively speaking, that is a simple goal to attain; in many areas the new populists have already attained it, even with Nixon in the White House. Their real challenge is how to achieve some measure of enduring, institutionalized support for their goals, support that can last after mass enthusiasms have faded. Left to themselves, the elective branches of a democratic government cannot fulfill that commitment.

Reformers need to focus less attention on what could be called the "promise-making" parts of the democratic process. They need to concern themselves more with improving the promise-keeping—or, as is more often the case—the promise-breaking parts of the system. To meet that challenge, the conservative vision of public-interest law is now the last best hope to vindicate the populist ideal.

Much of the credit for maintaining democratic values through the nation's first two centuries must go to the persistence of populist faith among its established and professional elites. For the future, the health and perhaps the survival of American democracy—currently threatened by unprecedented subversion at the highest levels of government—depends on their continued faith and their continued determination to make that faith effective.

Notes

Chapter 1
1. Arthur M. Schlesinger, Jr., *The Vital Center* (Boston: Houghton Mifflin, rev. ed., 1962), p. xii.
2. Ralph Nader, Introduction to Morton Mintz and Jerry S. Cohen, *America, Inc.* (New York: Dial Press, 1971), p. xi.
3. John Leonard, "Nader's Raiders Ride Again," *The New York Times,* July 24, 1970, p. 29.
4. Joseph Kraft, Review, *The New York Times Book Review,* March 12, 1972, p. 3.
5. Robert A. Dahl, *After the Revolution* (New Haven: Yale University Press, 1970), p. 3.
6. S. Rep. No. 46, 49th Cong., 1st sess., 1886, p. 2.
7. Hans Thorelli, *The Federal Antitrust Policy* (Baltimore: Johns Hopkins University Press, 1955), pp. 371–80.
8. Gabriel Kolko, *The Triumph of Conservatism* (Glencoe: The Free Press of Glencoe, 1963; Quadrangle, 1967), pp. 250–54.
9. Harold Ickes, *The New Democracy* (New York: Norton, 1934), pp. 77, 121.
10. Paul MacAvoy, *The Economic Effects of Regulation: The Trunkline Railroad Cartels and the Interstate Commerce Commission Before 1900* (Cambridge, Mass.: MIT Press, 1965).
11. Kolko, *Railroads and Regulation 1877–1916* (Princeton: Princeton University Press, 1965).
12. Robert Heilbroner, *Between Capitalism and Socialism* (New York: Random House, Vintage ed., 1970), p. 31.
13. Zbigniew Brzezinski, *Between Two Ages* (New York: Viking, 1970), pp. 247–48.

Chapter 2
1. Tom Wicker, "The Checkoff Scheme," *The New York Times,* November 21, 1971, Section 4, p. 13.
2. Kenneth Culp Davis, vol. 1, *Administrative Law Treatise* (St. Paul: West Publishing Co., 1958), p. 82. See Theodore J. Lowi, *The End of Liberalism* (New York: W. W. Norton, 1969), pp. 302–3.
3. Louis L. Jaffe, Review, *Yale Law Journal* 65 (1956): 1068, 1070.
4. Robert Cushman, *The Independent Regulatory Commissions* (New York: Oxford University Press, 1941).
5. Marver H. Bernstein, *Regulating Business by Independent Commission* (Princeton: Princeton University Press, 1955).

6. U. S. Senate, Committee on the Judiciary, James A. Landis, *Report on the Regulatory Agencies to the President-Elect,* 86th Cong., 2d sess., 1960.

7. Philip Elman, "A Modest Proposal for Radical Reform," *American Bar Association Journal* 56 (1971): 1045.

8. Arthur M. Schlesinger, Jr., *The Vital Center* (Boston: Houghton Mifflin, rev. ed., 1962), p. xii.

9. House Committee on Government Operations, *Deficiencies in the Administration of the Federal Insecticide, Fungicide, and Rodenticide Act,* 91st Cong., 1st sess., 1969, p. 13.

10. William F. Buckley, Jr., *Up from Liberalism* (New York: McDowell-Obolensky, 1955).

11. John Kenneth Galbraith, *Who Needs the Democrats?* (New York: Signet, 1970), p. 73.

12. Woodrow Wilson, *The New Freedom* (Englewood Cliffs, N.J.: Prentice-Hall, 1961), p. 165.

13. Jaffe, unpublished manuscript.

14. TRB, *The New Republic* (November 27, 1971): 1.

Chapter 3

1. Mark Pilisuk and Thomas Hayden, "Is There a Military-Industrial Complex Which Prevents Peace? Consensus and Countervailing Power in Pluralistic Systems," in *The Bias of Pluralism,* ed. William E. Connolly (New York: Atherton Press, 1969), pp. 123, 149–50.

2. Richard Goodwin, "Sources of the Public Unhappiness," *The New Yorker* (January 4, 1969): 38, 50.

3. Reprinted in D. Schwartz, "The Public Interest Proxy Contest: Reflections on Campaign GM," *Michigan Law Review* 69 (1971): 419, 534.

4. *Office of Communication of the United Church of Christ* v. *Federal Communications Comm'n,* 359 F. 2d 994 (D.C. Cir. 1966).

5. *The New Yorker* (June 3, 1972): 29.

6. Leonard M. Chazen, "Participation of the Poor: Section 202(a)(3) Organizations Under the Equal Opportunity Act of 1964," *Yale Law Journal* 75 (1966): 599.

7. By way of partial qualification, it should be added that the result may be less inconsistent with majority rule if it is assumed that most voters expect to attain a higher living standard than they actually will; if that is true, then it may also be true that a majority of the electorate believed that they would be worse off under the Democratic plan, even though in fact they would be better off.

8. Michael E. Levine, "Is Air Regulation Necessary?" *Yale Law Journal* 74 (1965): 1416, 1420.

9. Mancur Olson, *The Logic of Collective Action* (Cambridge, Mass.: Harvard University Press, 1965).

Chapter 4

1. John Kenneth Galbraith, *The New Industrial State* (Boston: Houghton Mifflin, 2nd ed., 1971), p. 295.

2. Charles Camp and Walter Mossberg, "Sniffing the Tailpipe," *Wall Street Journal,* June 6, 1972, p. 1.

3. See Paul H. Weaver, "Is Television News Biased?" *The Public Interest* (Winter, 1972): 57.

4. Robert Heilbroner, "The View from the Top," in E. Cheit, ed., *The Business Establishment* (New York: John Wiley & Sons, 1964), p. 2.

5. Richard Hofstadter, *The Age of Reform* (New York: Random House, Vintage ed., 1960), pp. 247–8.

6. Homer Cummings and Carl McFarland, *Federal Justice* (New York: Macmillan, 1937), p. 331.

7. *United States* v. *American Can Company,* 230 F. 859, (D. Md. 1916), pp. 901–2.

8. Woodrow Wilson, *The New Freedom* (Englewood Cliffs, N.J.: Prentice-Hall, 1961), pp. 119, 122.

9. Hofstadter, "What Happened to the Antitrust Movement?" in *The Business Establishment,* ed. Earl F. Cheit (New York: Wiley, 1964), pp. 113, 124 n.11.

10. Hofstadter, *The Age of Reform,* p. 252.

11. *Ibid.,* p. 245.

12. Thurman Arnold, *The Folklore of Capitalism* (New Haven: Yale University Press, 1937), p. 220.

13. Hofstadter, *The Age of Reform,* p. 247.

14. Others on the list are the CAB, the FCC, the Federal Deposit Insurance Corporation, the Federal Home Loan Bank Board, the Federal Maritime Commission, the National Labor Relations Board, the Commodity Credit Corporation, the Rural Electrification Administration, and the Maritime Administration, all of which enjoyed the sponsorship of major organized interests. See W. A. Jordan, *Airline Regulation in America* (Baltimore: Johns Hopkins University Press, 1970); J. R. Meyer, M. J. Beck, J. Stenason, and C. Zwick, *The Economics of Competition in the Transportation Industries* (Cambridge, Mass.: Harvard University Press, 1959); D. F. Turner, "The Scope of Antitrust and Other Economic Regulatory Policies," *Harvard Law Review* 82 (1969): 1207, 1232–41; M. Bernstein, *Regulating Business by Independent Commission* (Princeton: Princeton University Press, 1955).

15. See, in addition to sources cited in note 16, Levine, "Is Air Regulation Necessary?," *Yale Law Journal* 74 (1965): Robert Fellmeth, *The Interstate Commerce Omission* (New York: Grossman, 1970), pp. 311–26; Louis M. Kohlmeier, Jr., *The Regulators* (New York: Harper & Row, 1969); U. S. Task Force on Communications Policy, *Report to President Lyndon B. Johnson* (Washington, D.C.: Government Printing Office, 1969), ch. 5.

16. Grant McConnell, *Private Power and American Democracy* (New York: Random House, Vintage ed., 1966), pp. 281–95, 305; George F. Stigler, "The Theory of Economic Regulation," *Bell Journal of Economic and Management Science* 2 (1971): 3.

17. Arthur M. Schlesinger, Jr., *The Politics of Upheaval* (Boston: Houghton Mifflin, Sentry ed., 1966), pp. 386–87.

18. Ernest W. Hawley, *The New Deal and the Problem of Monopoly* (Princeton: Princeton University Press, 1966), p. 281.

19. Galbraith, *American Capitalism: The Concept of Countervailing Power* (Boston: Houghton Mifflin, 1952), p. 56.

Chapter 5

1. Gabriel Kolko, *The Triumph of Conservatism* (Glencoe: The Free Press of Glencoe, 1963; Quadrangle, 1967), pp. 228–47.

2. Robert H. Wiebe, *Businessmen and Reform: A Study of the Progressive Movement* (Cambridge, Mass.: Harvard University Press, Quadrangle ed., 1968), pp. 138–40.

3. David Broder, "Political Reporters in Presidential Politics," *The Washington Monthly* (February, 1969): 20.

4. Victor S. Navasky, *Kennedy Justice* (New York: Atheneum, 1971), pp. 302–21.

5. *Decision with Respect to Proposed Amendment of Tomato Marketing Agreement and Order,* 37 Fed. Reg. 17, 479 (August 29, 1972).

6. 9 FCC 2d 546.

7. *Office of Communication of United Church of Christ* v. *Federal Communication Commission,* 359 F. 2d 994 (D.C. Cir. 1966).

8. *Ibid.*

9. *Ibid.*

10. *Ibid.*

Chapter 6

1. Woodrow Wilson, *The New Freedom* (Englewood Cliffs, N.J.: Prentice-Hall, 1961), p. 121.

2. Richard Hofstadter, *The Age of Reform* (New York: Random House, Vintage ed., 1960), pp. 143–64.

3. *Ibid.,* p. 238.

4. Hofstadter, *The Age of Reform,* p. 163.

5. Alpheus Thomas Mason, *Brandeis: A Free Man's Life* (New York: Viking, 1946), p. 107.

6. John W. Gardner, "You Are Being Had," *The New York Times,* July 4, 1971, Section 4, p. E 11.

7. Charles A. Reich, *The Greening of America* (New York: Random House, 1970), pp. 87–89. (Originally published in *The New Yorker,* September 26, 1970.)

8. Brief for Appellants, pp. 12–13, in *Walter Holm & Co.* v. *Hardin,* 449 F. 2d 1009 (D.C. Cir. 1971).

9. Quoted in H. B. Thorelli, *The Federal Antitrust Policy* (Baltimore: Johns Hopkins University Press, 1955), p. 346.

10. *Ibid.*, pp. 346–47.

11. Merle Fainsod, Lincoln Gordon, and Joseph A. Palamountain, *Government and the American Economy* (New York: W. W. Norton, 3rd ed., 1959), p. 148.

12. Frederick G. Dutton, *Changing Sources of Power* (New York: McGraw-Hill, 1971), pp. 143–47.

13. A footnote to the episode bears mention here: in amending the campaign finance reform bill, COPE had overlooked an obscure provision in the old law, not involved in the Justice Department's prosecutions, that forbade *any* political giving, whether voluntary or not, by government contractors or their employees or officers. AFL-CIO chief lobbyist Andrew Biemiller and his astute staff had overlooked this potentially far-reaching provision for a simple reason: it had never been enforced by the Justice Department. But Biemiller became concerned when Common Cause won the right to invoke the neglected section of the law in a private civil suit against TRW, Inc., which held about $230 million in federal government contracts, and which had also given $75,000 to members of congressional committees of special interest to the corporation in 1970. If Common Cause won this innovative suit, the unions as well as corporate aficionados of the voluntary fund technique of contributing would be affected; virtually all major unions hold contracts with the government through the Labor Department and other agencies. Common Cause staff attorney Kenneth Guido was informed by COPE officials that they were concerned about the effect of the case— "but if we have to," they said, "we'll change the law." Their confidence turned out to be well-grounded. A bill was soon introduced in Congress by a cooperative Republican congressman to amend the section under which Common Cause's TRW lawsuit had been brought, and the Justice Department supported the bill this time. Just before the end of the 1972 term of Congress, the bill passed and was signed into law by President Nixon.

Chapter 7

1. John Kenneth Galbraith, *The New Industrial State* (Boston: Houghton Mifflin, 2nd ed., 1971), p. 214. These remarks about Professor Galbraith's thesis expand upon a similar analysis contained in my review of *The New Industrial State* in *The New Republic* (October 16, 1971).

2. Galbraith, *The Affluent Society* (Boston: Houghton Mifflin, 1958), p. 156.

3. Galbraith, *American Capitalism: The Concept of Countervailing Power* (Boston: Houghton Mifflin, 1952), p. 102.

4. Grant McConnell, *Private Power and American Democracy* (New York: Random House, Vintage ed., 1966), pp. 10–29.

5. Walter Lippmann, *Public Opinion* (New York: Macmillan, 1922).

6. Elizabeth Drew, Review, *The New York Times Book Review*, May 19, 1972, p. 7.

7. Lippmann, *The Public Philosophy* (New York: Mentor ed., 1956), pp. 123–39.

Chapter 8

1. Theodore J. Lowi, *The End of Liberalism* (New York: W. W. Norton, 1969).

2. Arthur M. Schlesinger, Jr., *Kennedy or Nixon—Does It Make a Difference?* (New York: Macmillan, 1960), p. 43. See Lowi, *The End of Liberalism*, p. 78.

3. Seymour Martin Lipset, *Political Man* (Garden City, L.I.: Doubleday, 1960), p. 439.

4. David Truman, *The Governmental Process* (New York: Knopf, 1951), pp. 53–54.

5. Robert A. Dahl, *A Preface to Democratic Theory* (Chicago: University of Chicago Press, 1956), p. 145.

6. John Kenneth Galbraith, *American Capitalism: The Concept of Countervailing Power* (Boston: Houghton Mifflin, 1952), p. 111.

7. Joseph A. Schumpeter, *Capitalism, Socialism, and Democracy* (New York: Harper & Row, 3rd ed., 1950), p. 106; Adolph A. Berle, *The 20th Century Capitalist Revolution* (New York: Harcourt Brace Jovanovich, Harvest ed., 1954), pp. 41–43; Frederick Lewis Allen, *The Big Change 1900–1950* (New York: Harper & Row, Bantam ed., 1952), p. 212. See Frederick M. Scherer, *Industrial Market Structure and Economic Performance* (New York: Rand McNally, 1970), pp. 346–78.

8. David Riesman and Nathan Glazer, "The Intellectuals and the Discontented Classes," in *The Radical Right*, ed. Daniel Bell (Garden City, L.I.: Doubleday, 1963), pp. 87, 94.

9. Richard Hofstadter, *The Age of Reform* (New York: Knopf, Vintage ed., 1960), pp. 4–5.

10. *Ibid.*

11. *Ibid.*, pp. 11–12.

12. James MacGregor Burns, "The Case for the Smoke-filled Room," *The New York Times Sunday Magazine*, July 13, 1952, p. 9.

13. E. E. Schattschneider, *Party Government* (New York: Holt, Rinehart and Winston, 1942), esp. pp. 65–98; V. O. Key, *Politics, Parties, and Pressure Groups* (New York: Crowell, 3rd ed., 1953), p. 474.

14. Nelson W. Polsby and Aaron B. Wildavsky, *Presidential Elections* (New York: Scribner's, 2nd ed., 1968), p. 239.

15. *Ibid.*, p. 320.

16. Alexander M. Bickel, *Reform and Continuity* (New York: Harper & Row, 1971), p. 22.

17. Frederick Lewis Allen, *The Big Change 1900–1950* (New York: Harper & Row, Bantam ed., 1952), p. 251.

18. *The New York Times,* January 19, 1969, Section 4, p. 23.

19. The most articulate statement for the lay reader is Milton Friedman, *Capitalism and Freedom* (Chicago: University of Chicago Press, 1962), esp, chs. 2 and 9; an impressive summary of the academic literature can be found in Richard A. Posner, "Natural Monopoly and Its Regulation," *Stanford Law Review* 21 (1969): 548.

Chapter 9

1. The argument developed here about the proposed CPA was presented in similar terms in two articles in *The New Republic:* "Defending Consumers" (September 26, 1970), p. 10; and "Advocates for the Consumer" (May 29, 1971), p. 22.

2. Ralph Nader, "The Case for Federal Chartering," in *Corporate Power in America,* eds. Ralph Nader and Mark Green (New York: Grossman, 1973), pp. 79–81.

3. Address to Conference on Corporate Accountability, October 30–31, 1971.

4. Morton Mintz and Jerry S. Cohen, *America, Inc.*

5. *Ibid.*

6. *Ibid.,* pp. 361–63.

7. Gabriel Kolko, *The Triumph of Conservatism* (Glencoe: The Free Press of Glencoe, 1963; Quadrangle, 1967), pp. 132–38, 176–77.

8. Robert W. Bennett, "Media Concentration and the FCC: Focusing with a Section 7 Lens," *Northwestern University Law Review* 66 (1971): 159.

9. See Kolko, *The Triumph of Conservatism,* pp. 176–77; Robert H. Wiebe, *Businessmen and Reform* (Cambridge, Mass.: Harvard University Press, Quadrangle ed., 1962), pp. 45–47, 139, 218.

10. Nader, Introduction to Mintz and Cohen, *America, Inc.,* p. xi.

11. Leonard M. Ross, Review, *The New York Times Book Review,* August 8, 1971, p. 1.

12. Nader, "Making Congress Work," *The New Republic* (August 21, 1971), p. 19.

13. William Greider, "A 'Raider' Rating of Nader: Ineffective," *The Washington Post,* December 6, 1971, p. A–1.

Chapter 10

1. *Moss* v. *Civil Aeronautics Board,* 430 F. 2d 891 (D.C. Cir. 1970).

2. 49 U.S.C. section 1302 (b).

3. Actually, in a separate investigation, some progress has already begun toward developing meaningful substantive standards to implement the statute. This proceeding, called the Domestic Passenger Fare Investigation, began as an offshoot of Moss's appeal, under pressure from the Court of Appeals. After the board granted the airlines a rate

increase over Moss's protest, his lawyers first placed an appeal for immediate injunctive relief before the entire membership of the Court of Appeals for the District of Columbia Circuit. During the oral argument, attorneys for the board claimed that the board was giving "consideration" to undertaking a comprehensive study of the various technical factors which might be taken into account in setting a rational level for air fares. The court seized upon this representation to put pressure on the board. Since it appeared that this study would commence in the immediate future, the court said, it would put off for thirty days its ruling on Moss's request for an injunction against the fare increase. Implicit in this postponement was a threat that the injunction would be granted if the board did not start the investigation it purported to have under consideration before the thirty days were up. Duly impressed, the board instituted the investigation twenty days after the court's decision. In this wide-ranging inquiry still in progress, separate investigations have been made and staff reports filed on a variety of technical issues which had heretofore been left entirely to the airlines' unfettered discretion. These include load factor (the percentage of seats which the airlines are expected to fill on an average flight), percentage rate-of-return, fare structure (the individual fares to be charged to different classes of customers), depreciation guidelines, joint fares, discount fares, and other similar matters. The board has adopted specific standards with respect to these factors designed, in principle, to evaluate future airline requests for fare increases.

4. 14 FCC 2d 431 (1968).

5. Herbert Wechsler, "Toward Neutral Principles of Constitutional Law," *Harvard Law Review* 73 (1960): 1: Alexander M. Bickel, *The Supreme Court and the Idea of Progress* (New York: Harper & Row, 1969), p. 173.

6. See, for example, *National Broadcasting Co.* v. *United States,* 319 U.S. 190, 216 (1943).

7. Quoted in C. Reich, "The Law of the Planned Society," *Yale Law Journal* 75 (1966): 1227, 1235.

8. *Ibid.*

9. *Schwegmann Brothers* v. *Calvert Distillers Corporation,* 341 U.S. 384 (1951); *United States* v. *Philadelphia National Bank,* 374 U.S. 321 (1963); *State of Georgia* v. *Pennsylvania Railroad,* 324 U.S. 439 (1945); but see *Pan American World Airways, Incorporated* v. *United States,* 371 U.S. 296 (1963).

10. Bickel, *The Supreme Court and the Idea of Progress,* p. 37.

11. Indeed, Bickel's argument is based on a construct which misconceives pluralist theory even as it existed in the 1950s. Bickel's point is that the political process, through the pluralistic mechanisms of give and take described by Dahl and his colleagues, provides legitimate access to all groups and points of view; therefore, the (nonpolitical, nondemocratic) judiciary has no business attempting to correct apparently

—but, more or less by hypothesis, only temporary—unjust political outcomes. There is no need for judicial activism, since the democracy is self-regulating. By the time Bickel wrote *The Supreme Court and the Idea of Progress*, this simplistic version of pluralism had been discredited in political science literature. See the essays collected in *The Bias of Pluralism*, ed. William Connolly (New York: Atherton, 1969). See also Robert A. Dahl, *After the Revolution* (New Haven: Yale University Press, 1970). But even Dahl vintage 1956 provides no support for the uses to which Bickel wishes to put pluralist theory. In such works as *A Preface to Democratic Theory*, Dahl did contend that all "groups," including relatively disadvantaged groups such as blacks, had meaningful access to the political system. But to Dahl, the activist federal judiciary that produced *Brown* v. *Board of Education of Topeka* was the saving grace of the system for such minorities. *Only* because blacks and similar groups could air their grievances through the courts, did Dahl portray the system as open to them to any meaningful extent. See *A Preface to Democratic Theory* (Chicago: University of Chicago Press, 1956), p. 138.

12. J. Skelly Wright, "Professor Bickel, the Scholarly Tradition, and the Supreme Court," *Harvard Law Review* 84 (1971): 769, 789.

13. Jaffe's article is reprinted in slightly condensed form in his treatise *Judicial Control of Administrative Action* (Boston: Little, Brown, 1965), pp. 11–27.

14. Eugene V. Rostow, "The Democratic Character of Judicial Review," *Harvard Law Review* 66 (1952): 193, 208.

15. Alexander M. Bickel, *The Least Dangerous Branch: The Supreme Court at the Bar of Politics* (Indianapolis: Bobbs-Merrill, 1962), pp. 70–71.

16. Quoted in *ibid.*, p. 258.

17. Joseph L. Sax, *Defending the Environment* (New York: Knopf, 1970).

18. *Trbovich* v. *United Mine Workers*, 404 U.S. 528 (1972).

19. Theodore J. Lowi, *The End of Liberalism* (New York: W. W. Norton, 1969), pp. 297–99.

20. *Environmental Defense Fund* v. *Hardin*, 428 F. 2d 1093 (D.C. Cir. 1970); *Butz* v. *Federation of Homemakers*, 466 F. 2d 462 (D.C. Cir. 1972). See also *Citizens to Preserve Overton Park* v. *Volpe*, 401 U.S. 402 (1971); *Rockbridge* v. *Lincoln*, 449 F. 2d 567 (9th Cir. 1971).

21. *Armour & Co.* v. *Freeman*, 304 F. 2d 404 (D.C. Cir. 1962).

22. R. H. Bork, "We Suddenly Feel That the Law Is Vulnerable," *Fortune* (December, 1971), p. 115.

Prospect

1. For example, Lewis F. Powell, Jr., just prior to his appointment to the Supreme Court, submitted a memorandum to the U.S. Chamber

of Commerce which described Ralph Nader as the leader of an "assault on the [American] enterprise system . . . broadly based and consistently pursued," and recommended a variety of means to defeat the aims of Nader and his followers, through propaganda, and political and judicial action. The hostility to new populist leaders, objectives, and methods evident throughout this document, whether or not it reveals itself in Mr. Justice Powell's performance on the Court, must find echoes in at least some sectors of the corporate bar, of which Powell was an eminent member before his appointment.

Index

289